THE NEGATIVE TRAIT THESAURUS:

A Writer's Guide to Character Flaws

Angela Ackerman
Becca Puglisi

First print edition, September 2013
ISBN-13: 978-0-9897725-0-1
ISBN-10: 0989772500

Edited by: C. S. Lakin (http://www.livewritethrive.com) and Christine S. Zipps (studio_luna@comcast.net)

Book cover design by: Scarlett Rugers Design 2013
http://www.scarlettrugers.com

Book formatting by: Jason Chatraw
http://greene-books.com

ABOUT THE AUTHORS

Angela Ackerman is a member of The Society of Children's Book Writers and Illustrators (SCBWI) and writes on the darker side of Middle Grade and Young Adult. When she isn't creating new writing tools or plotting mayhem, she's carefully deleting her browser history and pretending to live the life of a normal, quiet Canadian.

Becca Puglisi is a YA fantasy and historical fiction writer who enjoys slurping copious amounts of Mountain Dew and snarfing snacks that have no nutritional value. She has always enjoyed contemplating the *What if?* scenario, which serves her well in south Florida. As a result, during hurricane season, you can find her stalking the local weather forecasters and muttering unkind words toward the Atlantic.

Together, Angela and Becca host *The Bookshelf Muse*, an award-winning blog at the Writers Helping Writers website. This resource offers a number of unique thesauri to aid writers in their descriptive writing efforts. Their best-selling book, *The Emotion Thesaurus: A Writer's Guide to Character Expression,* is the first in their "Writers Helping Writers" series.

MORE WRITERS HELPING WRITERS BOOKS

The Emotion Thesaurus: A Writer's Guide to Character Expression

The Positive Trait Thesaurus: A Writer's Guide to Character Attributes

For more information on how to purchase these books or take advantage of the many articles and free writing tools, please visit us at Writers Helping Writers (http://writershelpingwriters.net/). We also offer free writing tools, unique descriptive thesaurus collections, and hundreds of articles that will help you strengthen your writing.

DEDICATIONS

To my second set of parents. No one could ask for a more supportive, encouraging, loving, accepting, and fun pair of in-laws. Thank you for everything that you've done for your son, for me, and for our children. Love you bunches!
—*Becca Puglisi*

To my family and friends (online and off!) who taught me to believe.
—*Angela Ackerman*

Our deepest gratitude to writers everywhere, who inspire us through their dedication, perseverance, and heart. With this book we particularly honor the memory of Carolyn Kaufman, who was taken far too soon. Her insight and friendship will be greatly missed.
—*A & B*

PRAISE FOR THE EMOTION THESAURUS

"One of the challenges a fiction writer faces, especially when prolific, is coming up with fresh ways to describe emotions. This handy compendium fills that need. It is both a reference and a brainstorming tool, and one of the resources I'll be turning to most often as I write my own books."

- James Scott Bell, best-selling author of *Deceived* and *Plot & Structure*

TABLE OF CONTENTS

FOREWORD

by Carolyn Kaufman, Psy. D.

Personality theory says that all of us have five to ten central traits that define us. It's easy to identify them—just make a quick list of the characteristics that best describe you. If you want some verification, ask a couple of close friends or family members to make their own lists describing your personality and then compare notes. You'll likely find striking similarities.

While you and the people who care about you will probably emphasize your positive qualities, there's more to all of us than positive attributes. As a writer, you'll want to make sure you also explore your characters' more problematic traits, because that's where you'll find both inner and outer conflict. That's where you'll find your story.

When I started doing psychotherapy as a counselor, I was privy to many people's secrets. I quickly learned that no matter what you see on the outside, everyone struggles on the inside. Everyone is damaged, some people more severely than others, and the hurts we've experienced in life leave wounds that change the way we view the world and ourselves. Sometimes flaws develop as we attempt to defend against further hurts.

Other flaws are the dark sides of our positive attributes. For example, if your character is a confident, attractive, high-powered success, there's a good chance that those positives qualities are also casting shadows. For example, taken to extremes, confidence can become swaggering haughtiness, just as attractiveness can lead to vanity and superficiality. And for all of their charisma, successful people don't usually get ahead by being gullible or wishy-washy. Your character may have climbed to fame or fortune by relying on the positive aspects of manipulation, scheming, and cold-hearted decision-making. But those very same flaws may be his downfall.

Sometimes people know their flaws are problems, but other times they live in merry denial. Even when their flaws are pointed out to them, these people say things like "Oh, I've heard that before but I don't believe it." A few people are so blinded by their flaws that they've lost all perspective. For example, the arrogant intellectual might claim that he'd treat others better if they weren't so dumb. Or the self-absorbed television personality might argue that she'd be happy to listen to others if they ever talked about anything interesting.

Each human being exists inside of a subjective sphere created by his own experience. The truth is that you can never truly know just how another person feels or views the world. We must do our best based on our own knowledge of the world and by being open to exploring experiences that are different from our own. *The Flaw Thesaurus* can help you better understand the flaws you have already chosen or discovered in your characters, and it can lead you to consider possibilities you might not otherwise have.

If you, the writer, are a forthright person, you may find it difficult to get inside the head of someone who is timid or withdrawn; if you are cautious and conscientious, you may find it difficult to understand people who are reckless and impulsive. Fortunately, you have in your hands the writer's solution to that dilemma: flip to the entry on *Reckless* and find out what causes people to become reckless, and how they might characteristically act based on that trait. Remember, in real life there is no narrator to announce the flaws of others to us ("she was obviously a hypocrite"); instead, we have to rely on behavior to tell us what we need to know.

Once you have identified or developed the flaw, you will need to force your character to deal with it. *The Flaw Thesaurus* will also help you understand both the negative and the positive aspects of each flaw, since people continue to rely on a flawed approach because it is somehow working for them. The book presents you with possible ways to make your character aware of his flaws, and explains how that new knowledge can force him to confront his issues.

Listen, change is hard. *Hard.* Even Abraham Maslow, the psychologist who created the familiar hierarchy of needs, acknowledged that many people stall before they reach the self-actualization stage. He called this the Jonah complex.

In the Biblical story of Jonah and the whale, God gave Jonah a challenging task. Jonah subsequently did what many if not most people do when confronted with such a situation—he ran the other direction in hopes of avoiding it. In this case, quite literally, as he booked passage on a ship heading away from the city where God told him to go. A violent storm arose and the sailors, believing God was angry with Jonah, threw him overboard, where he was swallowed by a whale.

While most religious interpreters argue that Jonah stayed inside the whale for three days and three nights because God was foreshadowing the time period between Christ's crucifixion and resurrection, I'm wondering if Jonah didn't take a while to come around to God's way of thinking. Ever seen a little kid who doesn't want to do what he's been told? There are refusals, arguments, and tantrums, all part of the power struggle between the child and the adult. As we get older, we get more subtle—and sometimes more passive aggressive—in our refusal to change, but we are enormously stubborn creatures, and we will take extraordinary measures to stay in our old comfort zone. Even when it's not very comfortable.

What that means is that, as Angela and Becca explain in their Building the Characters from the Ground Up section, you have to give your characters real motivation to change their flaws. Change doesn't usually happen because we make a New Year's resolution—it happens when we find ourselves backed up against a wall because our normal responses aren't working. A crisis is an opportunity for change, but you need to provide a whale of a reason to convince your character that he has no choice.

As writers work with characters that can be described with words like obsessive, moody, grandiose, paranoid, and so on, they sometimes get confused about whether a psychological diagnosis is warranted. Because we use diagnoses in our society to indicate problems that are making someone's life (or the lives of others around him) difficult to live, many writers are unsure how to write about character flaws *without* assigning a diagnosis.

A character is impulsive and easily distracted? He must have ADHD. A character is always nervous? She must have generalized anxiety disorder. A character is egocentric? He must have narcissistic personality disorder.

Many people think of human beings' mental health as falling into two mutually exclusive categories: normal and disordered. The reality is that there is a whole range of behaviors in between.

For a real diagnosis to be made, a normal tendency like sadness becomes excessive (as with a depressive disorder) or vanishes altogether (as with the manic phase of bipolar disorder), making normal life nearly impossible.

As an example, many people are tidy, and many people like their homes to stay clean. Some of those people are extreme enough that they annoy others and sometimes even themselves. But for something like obsessive-compulsive disorder to be diagnosed, the cleaning problem must be consuming their lives. Perhaps they're getting to work two and three hours late because they can't walk out the door without washing every last stitch of fabric in the house—sheets, clothes, curtains, maybe even the carpets.

Students in psychology classes often seize upon a couple of diagnostic criteria and assume they have the disorder when the truth is that they're actually perfectly normal...just flawed. So maybe you have a nervous character that struggles with his anxiety but is still able to live a normal life? An anxiety diagnosis may be too extreme, but he is still *flawed*.

Interestingly, flaws can be even more insidious than psychological disorders because characters may not realize just how much of a problem they have. Plus, there are medications and therapies that have been shown to work with particular disorders. While the same therapies can be adapted to help a character deal with his flaws, when no diagnosable disorder is present, insurance probably isn't going to pay for treatment, which leaves your character with fewer options for help.

So while you may end up using *The Diagnostic and Statistical Manual of Mental Disorders* next time you're creating a flawed character, don't start there. Start with *The Flaw Thesaurus*.

FLAWED AND HUMAN: CHARACTERS WHO APPEAL

With so many distractions online and off, finding ways to draw readers into our stories has become more important than ever. Yet how do we create a compelling story? What sets one book apart from the rest? And most importantly, how do we build a strong reader-character connection?

It is widely believed that people read to be entertained and to escape, but those aren't the only reasons. If readers took time to reflect, they would likely come to the conclusion that the best books—the ones that stay with them long after the final page is read—are those that reveal a deeper truth about themselves and the world they live in. And how does this insight come about? Through the point-of-view (POV) character's own self-awareness, inner transformation, and growth.

Well-drawn characters can feel so real that when we read about them, it's like we're sharing their experiences. We ache when they ache. We want what they want. When they're torn and conflicted, so are we. What is it about complex, realistic characters that have such a strong pull? Why does their search for meaning resonate so deeply within us as readers?

It's because we're all on the same search in our own lives. The need to understand who we are is ingrained in each of us. We have desires and needs, fears and hopes. We have questions about our role in this life, and what we should accomplish. In this way, we are on the same journey for answers as that of our characters.

The route we follow on this journey is largely up to our individual personalities. Attitudes, ideas, thoughts, and behaviors are uniquely attuned to one's needs, beliefs, morals, and values. Unlike emotions or moods that come and go, personality traits are consistent and play a big part in determining our actions.

Like real people, each character is a unique fingerprint of flaws and positive attributes that create individual whorls and ridges in the personality. These traits emerge slowly over time, formed by the character's experiences, both good and bad.

When it comes to character creation, it's vital to understand who our characters are and what motivates them, even though not everything we discover will end up in the story. Flaws are especially critical to define, for it is a character's hurts that compel readers to care and the imperfections in their personalities that make them relatable and memorable.

WHAT IS A FLAW?

There are different schools of thought about personality and character traits, many of which are heavily debated. What can be agreed upon is that each person, and therefore each character, is a melting pot of traits that all work together to satisfy basic wants and needs according to one's moral code. For example, a character who dreams of winning an Olympic gold medal may have traits like determination, a strong work ethic, and perseverance. Because he values fairness and hard work, he will most likely avoid steroids and other shortcuts, instead following a routine of strength training, healthy eating, and honing the techniques needed to reach his goal.

Strengths like these undoubtedly help characters achieve their desires. But what role do weaknesses play? How do we know which traits are positives and which are flaws?

A **character trait** is a distinguishing attitude, quality, or behavior—negative, positive, or neutral—that aids in defining someone's personality.

To break it down further, **positive attributes** are traits that produce personal growth or help a character achieve goals through healthy means. They also enhance one's relationships and benefit other characters in some way. *Honorable*, for instance, is easy to place on the positive side of the personality wheel. A truly honorable character is going to use healthy measures to achieve success, and because of his nature, he can't help but aid others and strengthen his relationships along the way.

On the other hand, **flaws** are traits that damage or minimize relationships and do not take into account the well-being of others. They also tend to be self-focused rather than other-focused. By this definition, *jealous* clearly belongs with the flaws. Jealous characters are focused on their own wants and insecurities; their resentment and bitterness make others uncomfortable and hurt relationships rather than build them.

Neutral traits are harder to categorize, containing a mix of positive and negative qualities; because they do not have the limiting or unhealthy aspects of flaws, they do not appear in this volume.

HOW DO YOUR CHARACTER'S FLAWS DEVELOP?

Characters are all about self-discovery, finding meaning, and achieving goals. They're usually seeking to improve themselves in some way—at work, in personal relationships, spiritually, or through self-growth. But time and again, their flaws sabotage them, blocking them from gaining what they want both on a conscious and subconscious level. It's ironic, really; who they are and what they want are often at odds, making it difficult for them to achieve success. So why do they have these flaws? Where do they come from?

It shouldn't be surprising to learn that the past is to blame. Many factors play a part in determining who our characters become, including the way they were raised, their role models, environment, and genetics. If the character's world is anything like ours, it's filled with flawed people, and life isn't the perfect, well-balanced nirvana they'd like it to be. Specific events and long-term exposure to unhealthy ideas, behavioral patterns, and relationships can hamstring a character. An ignorant character, for instance, may be that way due to years of poor teaching, or from being sheltered in a way that limited her ability to connect or get along with others. This history of not being taught the whole truth creates a deficiency in her personality that undermines her ability to reach her full potential.

But the most crippling factor—the one that authors should always strive to unearth from their characters' pasts—is emotional trauma. Old hurts can have a huge impact on our characters, influencing their current behavior. Emotionally painful events like these are called **wounds** and are profoundly powerful. This defining emotional experience from a character's past is so debilitating that she'll do anything to avoid suffering the same kind of pain again. It colors how she views the world and alters what she believes about herself and others. This traumatic experience instills a deep fear that the hurt will happen again if the character doesn't protect herself against it.[1]

Physical defects with a lasting psychological effect, such as a crippling illness or disfigurement, can have the same result. In both cases, the mistaken belief that the character must harden herself in order to be emotionally safe is what allows negative traits to emerge.

THE CHARACTER'S WOUND

Wounds are often kept secret from others because embedded within them is **the lie**—an untruth that the character believes about himself. He may think that he deserved what happened to him, or that he's unworthy of affection, love or happiness, etc. Self-blame and feelings of shame are usually deeply embedded within the lie, generating fears that compel him to change his behavior in order to keep from being hurt again.

For example, if a man believes he is unworthy of love (*the lie*) because he was unable to stop his fiancée from being shot during a robbery (*the wound*), he may adopt attitudes, habits, and negative traits that make him undesirable to other women. If he does grow close to someone, he might sabotage the relationship before it can become too serious. He may also avoid situations in which he is responsible for others, believing that he will only fail them in the end.

To use a less dramatic scenario, consider a daughter growing up with a father whose work was more important than his family (*the wound*). This girl may become a workaholic adult due to her belief that the only way to gain the attention and acceptance of others is through career achievement (*the lie*). Although she wants a family of her own, she may sacrifice that desire so she can dedicate herself to work. Her health declines, friends become marginalized, and her life revolves only around activities that promote her career, leaving her successful at work but unfulfilled at heart.

The lie plaguing your character should center on one of five basic human needs[2]:

BASIC NEED: To secure one's biological and physiological needs
RELATED LIE: *I'm not capable of providing for myself or anyone else.*

BASIC NEED: To keep oneself and one's family safe
RELATED LIE: *I don't deserve to feel safe.*

---

[1] Michael Hauge, author of *Writing Screenplays That Sell.*
[2] Adapted from Abraham Maslow's original Hierarchy of Needs

<u>BASIC NEED</u>: To feel connected to and loved by others
<u>RELATED LIE</u>: *I am not worthy of love or affection.*

<u>BASIC NEED</u>: To gain esteem, both from others and from oneself
<u>RELATED LIE</u>: *I can't do anything right.*

<u>BASIC NEED</u>: To realize one's full potential
<u>RELATED LIE</u>: *I'll never be a good _____ (parent, employee, friend, etc.).*

(For an extensive list of basic needs and associated lies, see Appendix A.)

Many other flaws result organically from one's upbringing or environment rather than birthing violently from a traumatic wound, but a character's **major flaw** should always be traced back to a defining hurtful experience. This flaw will compromise his path to achieving his dreams and prevent him from reaching his full potential. It is this weakness that the character will eventually have to overcome by revisiting the past and coming to terms with his old wound.

PROTECTIVE MEASURES: HIDING ONE'S FLAWS

It's natural for characters to want to hide their weaknesses from others. In social situations, they may wear a mask, or **persona**, putting on an act to hide how they really feel. Imagine a woman who was taken advantage of in the past. Her persona may be to act sour and tough—too strong to be hurt. By acting this way, she keeps others from getting close so they will never know that she's just as vulnerable as she ever was.

The persona also serves to hide the darkness within—the negative, ugly bits of our characters' personalities that they would prefer others didn't see. Prejudices, inappropriate thoughts, unhealthy desires that are selfish or harmful: although these qualities are part of their personalities, our characters hide them to avoid the guilt and shame that occur when their true selves are exposed.

Most importantly, hidden behind the persona is the lie that creates the character's flawed behavior and negative thinking. As mentioned earlier, this lie is different for each character and stems from their emotional wound.

When building characters, uncovering this lie is the key to understanding how certain flaws might develop. Digging deep while in the planning stage and extensively exploring a character's backstory will allow us to better understand his past wounds and what will motivate him in the present.

THE ROLE OF FLAWS WITHIN THE CHARACTER ARC: COMPLICATING THE JOURNEY

Flaws come in different shapes and sizes. Minor ones tend to be common and don't often impact behavior in a life-altering way. The character has learned to live with these weaknesses, which usually show up when he is under high emotional strain. Major flaws, on the other hand, have dramatic results, twisting the character's view of himself and his surroundings.

These major flaws—often referred to as **fatal flaws**—are what cause the hero to be "stuck" in some way at the start of his story. He may be blind to these flaws, or if he does see them, he might misinterpret them as strengths, failing to recognize that they're actually preventing him from achieving his goals. Depending on his perception, the character may seem content at the beginning of the story, although on some level, his life is lacking fulfillment. While there are usually external forces holding him back, there's also that internal flaw that must be overcome for him to feel complete and satisfied with who he is.

The internal change that a character undergoes over the course of a story is called the **character arc**. At the beginning, he views himself and the world one way, but through growth and inner transformation, he comes to view his life on a deeper, more meaningful level.

OUTER MOTIVATION AND OUTER CONFLICT

At its most basic, the character arc consists of four pieces. The **outer motivation** is what the character wants to achieve, and the **outer conflict** is the element that's stopping him from attaining that goal. To use a familiar example, Lieutenant Daniel Kaffee from the movie *A Few Good Men* wants to win his case and absolve his clients of guilt (*outer motivation*), but Colonel Jessup (*outer conflict*), with his ambition and influence, is keeping him from achieving that goal. Pared down, this is the external story of *A Few Good Men*.

INNER MOTIVATION AND INNER CONFLICT

Compelling and multi-dimensional stories also consist of an inner journey that parallels the external one. For every outer motivation, there should be an **inner motivation**; this is the reason the character wants to achieve his goal, and it's almost always an effort, in some way, to gain greater self-worth. This inner motivation should be accompanied by an **inner conflict**: the flaws and/or lies within the character that stand in the way of him achieving his inner motivation.

Kaffee's reason for wanting to win is to distinguish himself (*inner motivation*), to prove that he can successfully argue a court case—as opposed to his usual plea bargain—and live up to his dead father's reputation as an exceptional trial lawyer. This need for validation emerged from growing up in the shadow of his wildly successful father (*wound*). As a result, Kaffee doubts himself and his abilities (*inner conflict*). Though he wants to prove himself, he's afraid that his best efforts will fall short of his father's accomplishments and he will always be second best.

A character arc works best when it mirrors the ups and downs of the outer story. As the character strives to overcome an antagonist or challenge, so must he overcome himself and his greatest fears. Throughout the arc, the damaged character must face himself and his shortcomings. To emerge healed and whole, he must acknowledge his wound and see the lie for what it is. Once he is able to let go of his false belief, the lie that has motivated his actions to this point will no longer control his life.

A character does not have to overcome all his flaws during the journey, but if the story is to end with him becoming a stronger, more balanced version of himself, then the fatal flaw must be vanquished, or at least diminished to the point that it no longer controls his life or holds him back. Unless the story intentionally ends in tragedy with the character being unable to face his fear, then his struggle at the story start should be reversed by the end. If he viewed the future with trepidation, now he faces it with optimism. If he once embraced a life of isolation, he now sees value in building community with others.

For further insight into the character arc and how it fits into story structure, we highly recommend Michael Hauge's *Writing Screenplays That Sell* and *The Hero's 2 Journeys* (CD/DVD) by Michael Hauge and Christopher Vogler.

FLAWS AND INTERNAL CONFLICT

The road to evolution and transformation isn't easy. Flaws act like sharp stones in the path, providing obstacles for the character to overcome. Shadowed by these bumps in the road are life's lessons, waiting to be learned.

Let's take Mickey as an example—fresh out of jail after serving time for a crime he didn't commit. He's alone in the world since his best friends cut him off at the time of his arrest, leaving him hurt by their betrayal. His outer goal is to stay out of jail by playing by the rules and not getting into trouble, but his resentment and anger have created a huge chip on his shoulder, particularly when it comes to the police and the legal system.

We have a beautiful storm of conflict here. Mickey is determined to avoid further jail time, but his resentment and rebellious nature are constantly tripping him up. The powerlessness he experienced during his prison term has given him a thirst for control, yet he has to abide by other people's rules if he's going to maintain his newfound freedom.

This is how a character's flaws can create great inner strife.

Another way to complicate this struggle is to give the character opposing desires or needs, and force him to choose. Let's say that our hero is pursuing his original goal when he discovers that his ex-wife and estranged son have gone missing. Mickey suspects foul play, but the police are apathetic and warn him, an ex-con, to stay out of it. Now he has two goals: keep out of jail by following the rules, and save his ex-wife and son by doing whatever is necessary.

Flaws create contradictions, causing the character to question what's most important. Authentic characters struggle with thorny decisions, and their shortcomings make it hard for them to be objective. This causes tension and conflict, and ensures that their roads will be difficult to navigate.

CAN FLAWS HELP OR ONLY HINDER?

Some people may argue that flaws, on the whole, get a bad rap. After all, many of them initially develop as coping mechanisms to protect our characters from being hurt. And if they aren't harming anyone, then how can they be so bad?

The problem is that flaws are fueled by lies and negative beliefs that stymie the character. These traits can limit learning and growth, hamper judgment, and damage relationships with others. In the majority of situations, flaws keep our characters from reaching personal and professional goals.

For example, a healthy character who has experienced betrayal may find *mistrust* emerging as a personality trait. She doesn't take things at face value, views other people with suspicion until they've proven trustworthy, and investigates before committing to anything.

On the surface, this seems reasonable and smacks of good old-fashioned common sense. But consider that, as a result of this mistrust, she's not as friendly as she used to be. No longer spontaneous, she refuses to take a step without knowing what's coming. She distances herself from others, hides her emotions, and keeps secrets. Committed relationships frighten her, and if one begins to develop, she breaks things off before it gets too serious.

The picture isn't as pretty now, is it?

On the surface, flaws may emerge to protect the character from emotional hurt, but they will always *limit growth* and *create dysfunction* in some way. These negative qualities, minor or major, will bias the character's perceptions and dictate how he or she relates to others.

THE POSITIVE SIDE OF FLAWS

What's important to note is that while flaws themselves are destructive, they can be applied beneficially to help your character within the context of your story. Consider a protagonist who lives in a world of corruption and crime. When people are out to take advantage of everyone else, the ability to lie well could be a valuable asset. Likewise, if an overly competitive character is thrust into a situation where she must compete to the death, this flaw could give her the strength to save herself.

Flaws also have their positive elements, although these aren't as clear because the negatives are so obvious. Gullible characters are easily duped, but they're also trusting, friendly, and generous. Spoiled characters, while over-indulged and selfish, can freely express their wants and desires and have no trouble standing up for themselves. When examining your protagonist's negatives, be sure to explore the positive side of their flaws, since both can be utilized to create a well-rounded and believable character.

THE ROLE OF FLAWS IN RELATIONSHIPS: CREATING FRICTION

Not only do flaws create delicious and powerful internal conflict, they will also cause strife between the hero and his supporting cast. Conflicting traits can bring out your hero's darker qualities, while characters with opposing priorities, desires, and behaviors are sure to produce additional tension.

Imagine this scenario:

> Deana is working hard to prep for her catering event, one that could lead to some high-profile referrals and put her business on the map. A perfectionist, she's stressed out, triple-checking every detail to make sure the appetizers are garnished and at the correct temperature for serving. Meanwhile, her long-time friend and new employee Angie is polishing trays to enhance presentation. She's trying to focus, but her mind keeps slipping away to her recent breakup and her worries that she'll never find the right guy.
>
> When a flirty waiter swings into the hotel's kitchen and invites Angie outside for a smoke, she doesn't think twice. As a result, food is placed on her unpolished silver trays and served to the guests.
>
> Deana discovers the water-spotted trays making their way around the dining hall and becomes furious. This was an important event—how could Angie screw it up? She knows that her friend has a blind spot when it comes to men and that she's been especially fragile since her breakup, but she's hurt that Angie didn't come through when Deana needed her.

Friction is created here on a couple of levels, complicating the plot and putting a strain on this relationship. The situation has become more complex because Deana wants to support her friend through her difficult time, but she also wants to make her business succeed. While she thought she could do both, she's wondering now if she'll have to choose between her two goals.

There's also a clash due to differing personalities. Deana's fussy, hard-working nature is at odds with Angie's impulsiveness. More conflict emerges when Angie's priorities shift from doing her job and helping her friend to flirting with the waiter and fulfilling her own desires.

While some positive attributes can conflict with each other and cause tension in relationships, the biggest blowups happen when flaws are involved. The resulting friction occurs in varying levels of intensity in the form of **sparks**, **fireworks**, and **explosions**.

SPARKS

This low-level friction often manifests as impatience, frustration, irritation, and disappointment—all of which bubble mostly under the surface, affecting a character's mood, judgment, and perception. Outwardly it might cause a verbal exchange that shows a difference of opinions or beliefs. The character may disagree with, doubt the competency of, or pass judgment on another person in the scene. Sparks can strain a friendship, causing one character to question the other's priorities.

Characters on both sides may harbor resentment or request space in the aftermath. Often the point-of-view character will reflect on the confrontation, trying to understand what caused it. When the characters meet again, there will be some awkwardness, but forgiveness can pave the way back to harmony and equilibrium.

In Deana and Angie's scene, the resulting low-level friction might look like this:

> Angie slipped in through the back door, a slight smile on her face. A moment later, the waiter followed, tucking a slip of paper into his jacket. She grabbed the buffing cloth and lifted a tray from her pile of platters, not seeming to notice how it had diminished in her absence.
>
> Deana set down her clipboard. "Lining up a date?" At Angie's goofy grin, Deana had to force her voice to stay even. "Maybe next time you should make sure the platters are done first. Half-a-dozen trays went out covered in watermarks."
>
> Angie's shoulders dipped and her smile melted. "Oh. Well, I had them in two separate piles. You'd think the guys doing the plating would've noticed which ones were clean."

By not accepting responsibility for the dirty platters, Angie hasn't exactly smoothed things over. An apology would have done wonders, but she chose to shrug off Deana's gentle criticism—likely, because she'd expected her friend to be happy that she'd lined up a date instead of rebuking her. Both are feeling less secure in their friendship than they once were, and this unease will likely remain until the air between them is cleared.

FIREWORKS

This intermediate level of friction kicks emotions up a notch. Arguments, tense body language, impulsivity, and reduced empathy may develop. Voices rise as characters speak their minds, often knowingly saying things that will hurt the other person. Fireworks will have a lasting effect on the relationship, making reconciliation more difficult. Healing the rift is possible, but it will take time and effort from both parties to mend their hurt and pride.

Imagine how fireworks might transform the confrontation between Angie and Deana:

> "Lining up a date now, of all nights?" Deana lowered her voice, but each word betrayed her anger. "Come on, Angie! You know how much is riding on this."
>
> Angie froze, mid-swipe. "What's the big deal? It was a five-minute smoke break."
>
> Deana motioned toward the dirty stack. "Yes, and a half-dozen unpolished platters went out because of it." She took a deep breath. "Look, I know you're hurt about Leon leaving and are probably eager to get back into dating, but at work, you've got to put that away. I'm relying on you to do your job."
>
> "I am doing my job." Angie dropped a tray onto the pile, making the whole thing wobble. "Don't blame me that someone wasn't paying enough attention to tell the clean platters from the dirty ones. Besides, the guests won't even notice those tiny spots. Stop being such a perfectionist."

Here, Deana is upset enough that she's careless with her words, getting personal by bringing up Angie's neediness with men and hinting at her unreliability. Angie matches anger with anger by minimizing Deana's frustration over the unpolished platters, and she tops it off with a dig about her perfectionism. Tension crackles between them, and the pride of both characters takes a hit.

EXPLOSIONS

This high-level friction causes the involved parties to feel raw, uncontrolled anger or rage, betrayal, or humiliation. By-products include smugness, pride, and contempt that can lead to feelings of hatred. Characters become volatile, and may yell, scream, turn violent, or walk out. They might break things, literally or figuratively, sabotaging the relationship by hurling insults and revealing secrets. Trust is shattered, and satisfaction blooms when one party is avenged by causing the other emotional pain.

In the aftermath of an explosion, relationships are broken. Long-term resentment sets in and anger flares when the event is mentioned or recalled. If time does eventually bring the parties back together, the relationship is unlikely to return to what it was before. Both parties will be overly sensitive, avoiding certain topics and establishing limits in order to protect themselves. They may find it harder to trust not only the other party but anyone in a similar situation again. Explosions can create new emotional wounds, altering one's perception and behavior in the future.

By continuing the scenario between our two friends, let's see how explosions might develop— this time, viewing the scene from Angie's perspective:

> "Perfectionist?" Deana's voice scaled the walls and shook a rack of champagne flutes. "Is that what they call it in Angie La-La Land? I built this company from nothing because I pay attention to the details—something you might consider doing once in a while."
>
> Angie raised her chin. "What's that supposed to mean?"
>
> "Well, to start with, that guy who just pocketed your number? He's half your age. What do you think he wants from you?"
>
> Angie's face tingled with heat, and she threw down a silver tray. "Oh, suddenly you're the relationship expert? Miss Hasn't-Dated-Since-College, Miss I'd-Rather-Be-Working?" She let out an ugly laugh, not caring that everyone in the kitchen was listening. "I know it must be hard to see other people having real lives, so how about you stay the hell out of mine?"

Here, hurtful words fly, judgments are made, and reputations are damaged. Deana knows she's poking at sensitive areas, but she's angry enough to speak without considering the results. Angie lashes out in return, well aware that others are watching but not caring how this fight might damage Deana's reputation with her employees or the hotel.

When it comes to creating the right amount of conflict, imagine that the tension resulting from clashing traits is a thermostat. Adjust it until you reach the desired heat, then see where the scene goes. For more ideas on how to create fresh body language, thoughts, and visceral sensations that will show your character's volatile emotions, we recommend checking out *The Emotion Thesaurus: A Writer's Guide to Character Expression.*

BUILDING CHARACTERS FROM THE GROUND UP

When creating characters, it's pivotal to understand how flaws are formed and the role they play in the story. The next step is to decide which weaknesses will plague your protagonist. As with any aspect of writing, there are many possible techniques for determining the flaws that will work best.

BE MEAN

To put it another way, figure out what your character wants, then add flaws that will make that desire almost impossible to achieve. If he craves love, a callous or uncommunicative veneer would make it difficult for him to get what he wants. Similarly, someone who desires acceptance would have a hard time gaining it if he was a busybody with a taste for gossip. It sounds heartless, but remember that a good story can't exist without conflict. If tension is what you're going for, use this technique to discover the flaws that will make your characters' lives the most difficult.

SABOTAGE GOAL-FRIENDLY ATTRIBUTES

Unlike the "Be Mean" technique, which uses a character's desires against him, this method exploits the character's positive attributes. Start by identifying the positive traits that would be the most beneficial in helping the character reach his goal. Then give him flaws that do the opposite. For example, let's say that your hero wants to get his GED certification fifteen years after dropping out of school. Attributes that would help him achieve this goal include intelligence, persistence, and industriousness. So to make the journey difficult, pick a flaw that's the opposite of one of these traits. Maybe he's a bit of a flake; he makes decisions but has a tough time sticking to them and gives up at the first sign of trouble. Supporting characters know this about him and doubt his dedication and ability to succeed, adding another roadblock for the hero. By thinking of which traits would work, then choosing the opposite, you're sure to find flaws that will undermine the character and give him even more to overcome.

UTILIZE THE REVERSE BACKSTORY TOOL (APPENDIX B)

This useful tool provides a visual aid that illustrates how a character's goals, flaws, and wounds are interrelated. If you struggle with understanding your character's past, this tool will help you shape it by asking vital questions about his motives and needs. It's also versatile and can be used a number of ways. You can start by determining the character's goal and strengths, and choose his flaws from there, or begin with the character's weaknesses and use those to figure out his goal and the wounding event. It's also possible to begin with the character's needs or the lie he believes about himself and work backward to plot out a suitable and challenging goal. However you choose to use it, this simple but effective resource can be invaluable for filling in the important blanks in your character's backstory.

CHOOSE FLAWS THAT CONTRAST
WITH THE TRAITS OF OTHER CHARACTERS

Conflicting traits, by definition, create conflict. It's the classic *Odd Couple* scenario, and it works well to build tension and complicate matters for the hero. If your character has controlling tendencies, pairing him with a rebellious partner who resists any kind of authority will cause serious problems. Is your hero humorless and overly serious? Then bring on the mischievous sidekick. If you're judicious about choosing flaws for all the players in your story, the characters will create tension just by interacting, making the hero's journey more difficult than it has to be.

PULL FROM YOUR OWN EXPERIENCE

Think about the flaws that limit you and the people in your life. What weaknesses do you wish you didn't have, and why? What flaws do you see in others that drive you crazy? Will any of these work for your character? If so, you now have the opportunity to witness firsthand how a particular flaw manifests itself so you can write it realistically.

TIP: To help you stay organized, try using the **Character Pyramid** (**Appendix C**). This tool will help you figure out your character's flaws and to what degree they will get in the way.

VILLAINS AND THEIR FLAWS: STRIKING A BALANCE

Writing a villain is no easy task. In fact, much of the story's success lies on the writer's ability to craft a credible antagonist to oppose the protagonist. For there to be a hero, there must be a force, usually another character, working against him. A weak villain offers little challenge, yet a strong one forces the hero to step up, demanding more of himself than he even thought possible.

Deeply flawed and driven by morals that may seem unconscionable to the hero, villains must still connect with readers in some way to be realistic. Their presence should command attention, and while their actions cast no doubt that they are a dark force, their intentions or motivations must be logical, and on some level, understandable.

With a troubled past creating fertile ground for flaws to take root, it is easy to go too far and create a character with overblown negative traits. To ensure this doesn't happen, create a balance of traits that allows the villain to showcase his many flaws while still giving the reader a glimpse at a redeeming quality or two.

RESPECT THE ANTAGONIST

The antagonist or villain is a critical part of any story, forcing the hero to find the courage and strength he needs to evolve. From the outside, the writer's job seems as simple as creating a villain so loathsome that readers will cheer the hero on when he smashes him to dust. But the work is actually much more complicated. The villain cannot be a shallow placeholder or cardboard stand-in that conveniently blocks the protagonist's path. To be worthy of challenging the hero, the villain must be as rich and complex as the protagonist himself. Respecting the villain's position within the story means going the distance during character creation.

CHOOSE COMPLEX MOTIVES AND GOALS

Like the protagonist, an antagonist has dreams, needs, and desires. In his eyes, he is the hero of his own story and so strives for higher self-worth just like anyone else. But unlike a protagonist who wishes to become more fulfilled through healthy means, the antagonist embraces undesirable methods. Broken in some deep and defining way, he believes that his goals will bring him closer to feeling complete, not understanding how his flaws and skewed view of the world are the very things holding him back from true happiness.

It's important to delve into the antagonist's personality and possibly show readers his normal world before he clashes with the protagonist. Exploring backstory will help writers understand how the antagonist's experiences, including the wounding event, has contributed to who he is today.

In the novel *Misery*, Annie Wilkes first appears to be a kindly Samaritan who happened to be in the right place at the right time, saving novelist Paul Sheldon from a winter car crash. A retired nurse, cheerful Annie sets his broken leg and manages his pain from her Colorado home. But before long, Paul starts to worry that something might be off. Her fanatical love for his Misery Chastain character, the declarations that she's his number one fan, and her excuses for not transporting him to a real hospital all raise red flags. When she goes into a manic rage after reading his latest manuscript where her beloved heroine Misery is killed off, Paul begins to see the depth of her madness. After stints of neglect and various threats and tortures, Paul sneaks out of his locked room, searching for answers and a way out. He discovers a scrapbook outlining the disappearances of dozens of people, along with a string of infant deaths at the hospital where she once worked. This window into the past confirms his worst fears: Annie Wilkes is a serial killer.

As Stephen King did in *Misery*, sharing some history with readers can provide an understanding glimpse into the psyche of the antagonist, and may help to explain how she became the person she is. Revealing these important tidbits creates a bond between the reader and the villain. And while readers might not agree with what the antagonist wants or condone her methods, they will at least know her well enough to understand why she acts as she does.

DIG AT HIS PAST UNTIL HE BLEEDS

For both protagonist and antagonist, the past shapes the character. Experiences, environment, and influential people within a character's past all contribute to determining who he becomes in the present. Antagonists suffer wounding events just as heroes do, and the outcome of these emotional traumas is what sets them on an altered path. When negative emotions well up from a hurtful event, flaws can distract the villain from his pain or protect him from reliving the same suffering again.

As you would for a protagonist, probe your villain's backstory. Think about how he was raised, and by whom, and how he was treated along the way. Who loved him and who hurt him? What failures and past pain is he determined to avoid, and how do these affect his goals and motivations now? Answering these questions encourages a deeper understanding of who he is and what vulnerabilities can be used to bring out the worst in your villain.

Most of all, think about which events occurred to cause a moral shift. Morality is the biggest difference between an antagonist and protagonist. They can have the very same goals and desires, but their moral barometers will dictate how they go about achieving them. The line in the sand is different for each; the question every writer must answer during the character creation process is *why*.

CHOOSE FLAWS THE ANTAGONIST VIEWS AS STRENGTHS

One main difference between an antagonist and other members of the story's cast is that when he encounters adversity, rather than building up his positive attributes to help him, he hones his flaws. To him, these negative traits don't hold him back; they fuel him with the strength he needs to move forward.

Understanding where your villain came from and what elements shaped him into his current negative state will help you choose flaws that suit his nature. Specifically, seek flaws that he views as powerful—tools he can refine to help him reach his goals. Many negative traits are positive attributes taken too far: confidence can lead to overconfidence; ambition can escalate to greed; supportiveness becomes fanaticism. With the villain's low sense of moral obligation and his warped view of his place in the world, it is easy to see how he may twist positive traits into their darker cousins.

YOUR ANTAGONIST IS THE PROTAGONIST'S MIRROR

When choosing flaws, think about how your antagonist's strengths can be a mirror for the hero's weaknesses. If the hero is timid and uncertain, the villain can be determined and confident. And if the protagonist's attributes are a willingness to trust and a patient nature, make the antagonist untrusting and impatient. By choosing flaws and attributes carefully, you ensure that clashes and conflict erupt whenever the hero and villain meet.

FATAL FLAW AND TRAGIC FLAW

For the protagonist, at least one flaw will stand out as his fatal flaw, emphasizing the deficiency about himself that must be overcome if he is to successfully grow and round out his character arc. Antagonists also have a character arc, and a fatal or tragic flaw which is their undoing. In their case, their inability to minimize or defeat this flaw is what causes them to ultimately fail. The only exception is the rare instance where the villain experiences an emotional awakening, allowing him to recognize his beliefs are false. In this case, a shadow lifts, allowing him to see his world as it really is, and break the hold his fatal flaw has on him. While he emerges changed, it oftentimes comes too late, and the antagonist does not survive it or is forced to pay for the harm he has done.

VILLAIN FAILS: DIAGNOSES AND TREATMENTS

One of the worst things we can do for our story is to include an unworthy villain. Here are a few of the biggest stereotypes writers should avoid.

The "Mua-ha-ha" Villain

This villain is your typical "wants power for the sake of power" antagonist. He takes what he wants, is never satisfied with what he has, and targets the hero only because he has the nerve to stand against him.

DIAGNOSIS: This villain is a sketch, a crayon drawing of the real thing, devoid of real motivations that will make him compelling to readers. He is boring and forgettable.

CURE: Put meat on your antagonist's bones by exploring who he is and why. Delve into his past, understand who he is, and give him compelling reasons for his goals that satisfy a deep psychological need. Build in morals that have been corrupted by wounding events, putting him at odds with the protagonist's own beliefs. Add positive attributes that help readers see him as complex and formidable, capable of succeeding.

The Abysmal Leader

This antagonist has big goals, a minion horde, and a thirst for power. Whatever he wants, he is determined to get it. There's only one problem: his leadership skills are terrible. He mistreats his underlings (who somehow remain loyal), makes strategic errors that lead to calamity, and exhibits poor judgment that results in wasted time, manpower, and resources.

DIAGNOSIS: This is an unrealistic villain, designed to allow the hero to win more easily.

CURE: Antagonists who defy logic are easily beaten, and weaken the story. If the hero is to come out on top, the solution is not to provide an inept adversary, but to create a skilled one who forces the protagonist to evolve and rise to the challenge.

Looks Like a Duck, So It Must Be A Duck

This villain has scars, burns, boils, sports a limps, smells bad, and probably suffers from deformities or handicaps courtesy of altercations with life's ugly bus. Because he looks like a walking, talking horror movie, he's identified as the bad guy before he slaughters a single newborn panda.

DIAGNOSIS: Contrived physical deficits are there to provide neon signs to blast readers with a message: *Warning! Villain Ahead!*

CURE: Ugliness outside doesn't mean ugliness inside, so if your villain carries physiological scars, don't use them as a crutch to avoid having to characterize. Instead show who the antagonist is through action. Utilize the Character Pyramid tool to plan out behaviors, thoughts, observations and deeds that align with a negative personality. Create warped motives and morals to make it clear they are a villainous force, not one of good.

Emotionless and Calculating

This antagonist is cold in good times and bad. He handles disappointments without a flicker of emotion and is able to counter setbacks while carefully pouring expensive brandy from a crystal decanter. He is always in control. Victories might bring a slight smile, and possibly a second glass of amber enjoyed before a roaring fire.

DIAGNOSIS: Fraud alert—the author is flirting with emotional clichés and is ignoring one of the driving force of humanity: passion. No one does things just for the sake of it; if someone is driven to act, emotion is involved and should be expressed, in both good times and bad.

CURE: An in-depth character profile of the villain should be utilized to understand his needs and desires. Pretend that the antagonist is the protagonist, and conduct an interview. What makes him feel joy, sadness, hope? What does he wish for and why? How will his goals make him feel fulfilled and valued? What emotions is he sensitive to or afraid of? If his goals and missions are strong enough to fight for, then passion fuels them. Show him experiencing a range of emotions that drive behavior, affect self-esteem, and impel him to either succeed or make mistakes.

Miles Beyond Redemption

This villain is a cascading nightmare of flaws. Her personality is so negative that no one can stand to be around her, and her every action and choice is vile and depraved. She lacks empathy, delights in pain, and feels no remorse for what she does or who she hurts. She embodies evil in every sense, and exploits everyone she comes across.

DIAGNOSIS: Such a deeply unbalanced personality creates loathing and a reader disconnect. Because the villain is so terrible, readers cannot understand or relate to her needs, desires, or goals. The unwholesome stain of such a character can spoil the book.

CURE: Every antagonist, no matter how unlikable, needs a positive attribute or two. Add qualities that are at odds with her dark side, and you'll create a unique and interesting villain. Don't be afraid to show her sensitivities, passions, or quirky habits. Your point shouldn't be to have readers cheering for the villain, only for them to understand what made her who she is, and to see there is something redeeming within her personality.

Too Self-Absorbed and Careless To Live

Much like the poor leader, this villain makes mistakes to the point of comedy, simply because hard work and taxing decision-making is beneath him. Overly preoccupied with his own comforts and vanities, his attention on his bigger goals is sporadic. Independent wealth usually allows a buffer for costly mistakes, and he is content to source underlings to make sure his missions are successful. This villain will not get his hands dirty and is only concerned with his own prestige.

DIAGNOSIS: Antagonists so prideful that they expect life to be served up to them on a silver platter are a waste of literary ink. These shallow individuals are puppet figures, unworthy opponents, and undeserving of a reader's time and attention.

CURE: No one likes to read about a spoiled brat, so give your antagonist some substance. Privilege and wealth can free a person—or trap them. Show us an antagonist who feels hindered by his circumstances and we have a villain with something to prove. Rather than being content to let others make things happen, he'll become an active participant in his destiny and a worthy force for the hero to defeat.

IMPORTANT ELEMENTS
OF YOUR CHARACTER'S FLAWS

As writers, we must create characters with unique and complex personalities. Traits that work against each other will create a push-pull effect, making it much more difficult for the character to succeed.

As the author, you are the creator, the god of your imagined universe. This means knowing every aspect of your story—including the characters—down to the tiniest details. For your characters to ring true, they must make sense. There are reasons they act the way they do—triggers for their fears, memories that create anxiety, people and places they avoid because of the discomfort they bring. For us to write our characters authentically, we must know why their flaws exist, and how these weaknesses drive their behavior. The following are a few areas to keep in mind during the character creation process.

BEHAVIORS AND ATTITUDES

Once you've identified your character's flaws, it becomes easier to plan how he will react in varying situations—particularly in unexpected circumstances, since these are the moments when responses are more instinctual, revealing true character. For instance, during a city-wide blackout, co-workers in an office high-rise will each react differently. Worrywarts might assume that terrorists are behind the outage and tie up the phone lines trying to reach loved ones. Lazy characters may take a nap. Those who tend toward fussiness will become agitated by lost productivity, causing friction in an already uneasy situation.

The interesting thing about characters is that, like real people, each one will react uniquely in a given situation. Their individual combinations of positive attributes and flaws will work together to create distinctive responses. In the above situation, three characters sharing the same flaw will respond differently because of other traits they possess. The worrywart who is also a nurturer at heart may push her own anxieties aside so she can help others. The whiny worrier will drive everyone nuts with his constant complaining and need for reassurance. A worrywart with impulsive tendencies may rush unprepared into the dark and become injured, creating a new problem for stressed co-workers to deal with.

The options for how characters can respond in any situation are endless. That's why we've provided so many possible behaviors and attitudes for each flaw, to get you thinking about how your individual character may react.

THOUGHTS

While behaviors are visible to others, thoughts remain private, allowing the character to carefully decide what to reveal and how to reveal it. Because his actions and speech are carefully chosen to align with whatever image he wants to portray, it's often his thoughts that show his true beliefs and personality. For this reason, it's important that the author know what the character really thinks about the people, conversations, ideas, and events unfolding around him.

EMOTIONAL SENSITIVITIES

Another important aspect of your character's personality is his sensitivity to specific emotions. We've all known people who respond strongly to certain feelings, like the victim of abuse who visibly and emotionally withdraws when anger is expressed. A confrontational character, on the other hand, is drawn in by the frustration and anger of others. Rather than avoid it, he uses it to fuel his own reactive nature. Some characters become particularly reactive when dealing with people exhibiting the same flaws they themselves struggle with. Identify your character's emotional sensitivities and use them to create challenging scenarios that he must work through to reach his goal.

HOW TO SHOW YOUR CHARACTER'S FLAWS

Unearthing your character's history takes effort, but the familiarity that comes with such research is worth the trouble. Unfortunately, this groundwork does you no good if you're unable to effectively convey your character's personality to readers. As with most areas of writing, when it comes to introducing your hero, it's almost always better to show than tell.

Telling your character's strengths and weaknesses is a sign of lazy writing. This method will lead readers to believe that the author assumes they can't understand anything unless it's spelled out for them, or that the author doubts his own ability to express his character's personality without simply telling it. For ease of explanation, here's an example of what telling a character's flaw looks like:

> No one could deny Joe's good looks, but in Maggie's opinion, his macho attitude made him unattractive.

Okay. So Joe is macho. The reader gets that. But there's more to good writing than simply conveying meaning. To be sucked in, readers need to be touched in some way, to recognize a bit of Joe in themselves or in someone they know. They need to witness Joe's macho tendencies so they can create their own opinions about him instead of being told what he's like. Showing accomplishes all of these things in a way that engages the reader:

> Joe threw an arm over Maggie's shoulders. "What's up, hot stuff?"
>
> Her face flushed and he grinned; they all loved that nickname.
>
> "Paper for English."
>
> He leaned over to read the title, which also gave him a pretty good view down the front of her shirt. "Romeo and Juliet? That's easy. What do you need to know?" Shaking his hair back, he scanned the courtyard for other potential targets.
>
> "Seriously, Captain Lacrosse? You want to school me on Shakespeare?"
>
> His eyes narrowed but he kept his cool. Did she know he'd barely passed that class or was she just being coy?
>
> He let one eyebrow inch upward. "Hey, I can do it all."
>
> Maggie stared back at him for a second, and then sighed. "How about you just win the game tomorrow and leave the sixteenth-century stuff to me?"
>
> She shrugged off his arm. He turned the brush-off into a stretch, making the muscles bulge under his shirt. "Will do, doll."
>
> *Your loss, baby.*
>
> He swaggered his way over to Rhonda Stein. "What's up, hot stuff?"

An exchange like this really shows what Joe is like. He's attractive and athletic, but his macho attitude comes off as a little needy as he desperately tries to maintain a persona that others easily see through. Why is he this way? What is he trying to hide? To add layers to your hero's personality, reveal his true nature by showing his flaws through these vehicles:

BEHAVIORS, QUIRKS, AND THOUGHTS

Joe's behaviors and habits read as macho: his aggressive approach, his swagger, trolling for potential "targets," the gestures that emphasize his physical attributes (flexing his muscles, shaking the hair out of his eyes). His thoughts also show his macho nature. This is why it's so important to know how your character's flaws will affect his actions, thoughts, and overall personality, so you can use these clues to show the reader who your character is at his most basic level.

SENSITIVITIES

We conceal our flaws because we don't want people to know that we struggle in certain areas. Most of us are adept at hiding our weaknesses, but when others poke at our soft spots, we tend to react. In the example above, Joe is clearly sensitive to anyone expressing doubt about his capabilities, as is shown by his evasive response to Maggie's first question. Through the thoughts that follow, one learns even more about Joe—like the fact that his machismo is a cover for insecurity about his intelligence.

Not only can you show your character's flaws through his sensitive areas, you can also reveal a lot through the way he reacts to these threats. Does he panic? Run away? Deflect attention? Resort to violence? In Joe's case, he tries to play it cool because he's very aware of his image, but when Maggie comments a second time on his lack of intellectual prowess, he retreats. A character's sensitivities about his flaws can easily give him away; if the author knows where these soft spots are, they can be prodded, making the character disclose truths about himself that he would never purposely reveal.

FLAWS AS OBSTACLES

One of the reasons flaws are so important is because they get in the way of what the character really wants. What if Macho Joe's intent all along was to convince Maggie to tutor him? Perhaps something important was on the line, like losing his spot on the team if he failed any of his subjects. Had he simply asked Maggie, she might have said yes, but his fear of showing any vulnerability caused him to fall back on his macho ways, turning her off before he could even ask for help.

Along your character's journey, a flaw should repeatedly block him from achieving his goal. Each time he falls short, he's reminded of past failures and wounds, and his flaw will become more pronounced. At the same time, he will see what he most wants slipping out of his grasp, and his desperation for it will increase. Not only does this kind of structure create mounting tension throughout a story, it clearly reveals a character's flaw to the reader, who will realize that this trait must be overcome for him to achieve his goal.

THE CHARACTER'S EVOLUTION

Flaws aren't cured or diminished all at once. It's a gradual process of gaining the upper hand through small victories, then losing control, then trying again, and again, and again. We call it a character "arc," but really it's more like a zigzag as the hero takes three steps forward and two steps backward in pursuit of his goal. Sometimes the flaw will win. Other times, the character will subdue it.

Clearly, Joe's first attempt at improving himself was a failure. But imagine that the stakes increase when he fails an English test. As his GPA nosedives, he decides to try again with Maggie, this time attempting to be more honest and hinting at his need for help. She agrees, and he moves closer to achieving his goal. But his efforts come too late when the grades are posted; he fails English and loses his starting position. To make things worse (which is always a good idea), scouts will be attending the last two games of the season, and Joe needs to be on the field.

Remembering how he gained a measure of success by being honest about his vulnerabilities instead of camouflaging them, he admits to his academic advisor that he's been working with a tutor and asks for a second chance to bring up his grade. His request is granted, and he passes the test just enough to regain his spot on the team. Now the pressure is really on because he has to split his time between the practice field and the library. And when the guy who's after Joe's position hears that he's hired a tutor and starts spreading rumors about Joe's low IQ, the stakes escalate even further.

Showing the character's wins and losses throughout the story will not only keep his flaw firmly in the reader's mind, it will also create empathy and a desire to see Joe succeed.

RELATIONSHIPS

As was evidenced in Joe's example, if your character has people to interact with, there should be no reason to come right out and name his flaw because it will reveal itself naturally. Supporting characters who share your hero's flaw may bring out the worst in him. Conversely, these characters may irritate him, reminding him of what he dislikes most about himself. Like magnets, some traits fit well together while others can't coexist without force. The simple act of bringing other people into your character's life will inevitably create sparks, fireworks, and explosions that will reveal their flaws loud and clear.

AVOIDANCE

What things might a person with your character's flaw likely avoid? Certain situations, kinds of people, emotions, decisions, places, etc., act as triggers, irritating old wounds and current fears. A trigger could be something sprawling, like a city, or as specific as a certain color or object. For Joe, maybe it's the scent of crayons, since that was a prominent smell in the first-grade classroom where he was repeatedly teased for being "stupid." Show your character going out of his way to avoid these triggers, and it will provide a clue to your reader about his flaws.

THE DIFFICULTIES OF CRAFTING FLAWED CHARACTERS

Character creation is a complicated process. It takes a lot of digging and questioning to figure out who your character is, where she wants to go, and how she plans to get there. But knowing these things when you sit down to write helps prevent many common characterization problems. Here are a few of those pitfalls and some advice on how to avoid them.

UNLIKABLE CHARACTERS

For readers to become deeply invested in a story, they have to care in some way about the characters, particularly the hero. When writers create flawed characters, they run the risk of going too far. If readers don't like or respect the character on some level, they're not going to care if the hero achieves his goals or not, and the likelihood of them continuing to read is low.

To create flawed yet likable characters, it's important to have the right balance of negative and positive traits. Especially in the case of an anti-hero, too many flaws will render the character offensive or off-putting. Be sure that your character also has a strong attribute or two—qualities that most people value or respect, such as courage, loyalty, humor, or generosity to balance their flaws. Scarlett O'Hara is a good example of a truly flawed character who captivates readers. Spoiled, manipulative, and utterly selfish, it would make sense for her to be despised. But her determination to save Tara and the resourcefulness that allows her to overcome one obstacle after another are inspiring, causing readers to root for her.

Once you've identified that important positive attribute for your flawed character, it should be revealed as early in the story as possible. Blake Snyder outlines how to do this beautifully in his book *Save the Cat*. To summarize, at the very beginning of your story, include a brief scenario that shows your character utilizing his attribute in an endearing or intriguing way. The screenwriters for *Good Will Hunting* drew on this technique when they opened the movie with a seemingly ordinary janitor exhibiting exceptional intelligence by solving a genius-level math problem. Likewise, Will Freeman from *About a Boy* is self-serving and lazy, but readers are entertained by his sarcastic wit, which is evident the moment Will begins narrating. Show your character's attractive traits early on, in a way that will draw readers to him, and you've taken a big step toward ensuring that your character will be liked.

Another way to endear your character to readers is to show the desperation of his situation. A character who is stuck in a no-win scenario can evoke sympathy in readers who will want him to escape. Melvin Udall (*As Good as It Gets*) is nasty, offensive, and completely isolated from others due to his obsessive-compulsive disorder. As unpleasant as he is, the audience can't help but feel badly for him and hope that his life is somehow going to get better. Villains can play a big part in establishing a hero's desperation; the worse your villain is, the more readers will want the hero to triumph—think the alien from the *Alien* franchise, or Jigsaw from the *Saw* movies. A truly ruthless villain or seemingly no-win situation for your hero will build reader empathy, even for deeply flawed characters.

A word of caution when it comes to flaws and likability: if your character embodies too many flaws, the negative will outweigh the positive, and no amount of cat-saving will endear him to readers. Identify the one weakness that defines your character and emphasize that one over the rest. All other negatives should remain secondary.

UNCLEAR MOTIVATION

What's my motivation? This is a question actors often ask themselves, and it's something every author should know about their characters. The reason a character's inner and outer motivations are so important is because they drive the story. Every decision your character makes is determined by who he is and what he wants to accomplish. Unfortunately, many authors don't clearly know their character's motivations, or they become confused about them as the story unfolds. This leads to character inconsistency and a wandering storyline. If you've ever been reading a book and found yourself wondering things like *Where is this story going?* or *What does the character want?*, unclear motivation is likely the culprit. It leads to reader confusion and a lack of believability, often resulting in the reader tossing the book aside and moving on to something else.

To keep the motivation consistent, first, be clear on what it is. As was explained in the Character Arc section, your character should have an outer and inner motivation for the overall story. The outer motivation can be explained by asking, *What does he/she want?* The inner motivation can be a bit tougher, but with a bit of work you can usually uncover it by asking, *Why does he/she want this, and how will succeeding increase the character's feeling of self-worth?* By keeping the answers to these questions in mind, you'll know how your character should react and what choices he'll make.

Second, ensure that each scene counts. A scene's purpose is to move the story forward; since your story should be about your character achieving his motivation, every scene needs to contribute to that goal in some way. If any of your scenes don't meet this criterion, they need to be reworked or cut. Each scene should also be a mini-story, with its own beginning, middle, and end. Choosing your scenes deliberately and making sure that each one is complete will help keep your story and characters moving smoothly in the right direction.

INCONSISTENT CHARACTER ARC

Another problem authors sometimes encounter is a character with an inconsistent or jerky arc. There are a number of possible causes for this. One could be for the reason stated in the previous section, that the author is unclear on the character's motivation. Another possibility is that the author doesn't know the character well enough. When our knowledge is lacking, our characters end up doing and saying things that don't make sense. The choices they make don't match their motivation and cause their paths to take weird turns that give the story a lost, meandering feel.

A third cause for an inconsistent arc is that there is no inner motivation. For a story to be successful, characters don't necessarily have to have an inner motivation, but it's harder for an outer motivation to carry an entire story alone. Without an inner motivation and conflict, the hero doesn't have a clear direction for internal growth. This can result in a character who reads as flat because his inner journey has stalled, or an arc that jumps around due to author uncertainty. If critique partners complain about your characters being inconsistent, make sure that you clearly understand their inner motivation, and that they are moving toward change in a gradual and steady fashion.

While a complete inner transformation isn't necessary for all characters, each major one should change in some way throughout the course of the story. Important characters shouldn't be the same people at the end of the journey that they were at the beginning. By successful story structure standards, the character should be so altered that he can no longer exist in his world as he did before.

Throughout his character arc, your hero must make decisions that will elicit change—for good or for bad. Whichever way he decides to go is up to him and to you. But for this change to be consistent and realistic, you need to know your character intimately and clearly understand his inner and outer motivations.

FINAL NOTES FROM THE AUTHORS

While we've tried to include a broad range of flaws in this thesaurus, there are simply too many for the list to be complete. We recommend using the index to find the trait that you're looking for since many flaws, by nature, can be grouped together. For example, *unfriendly, crabby, cranky,* and *cross* are practically interchangeable, and are all listed under the parent entry *grumpy.* If you still can't find the trait that you're looking for, consider consulting one that's similar, since the information there may be able to help you.

As well, we chose to focus on flaws that are rooted in the psyche rather than those that are physical in nature (clumsy, messy, delicate, etc.) as the former are the most complex and difficult to write.

It's also important to note that this book is a **brainstorming guide** only. While the entries contain specific information regarding behaviors, emotions, and possible causes for flaws, each character is unique. They will react according to the combination of traits they possess, the intensity of the situation, their emotions at the time, who they're with, and any number of other factors. As such, the entries in this volume should act as a starting point rather than an exhaustive list for determining your character's response to any given situation.

It should also be mentioned that while this thesaurus can be used as a stand-alone reference, we recommend using it with *The Positive Trait Thesaurus: A Writer's Guide to Character Attributes* to ensure the creation of balanced, complex, and unique characters.

Theories and opinions abound regarding the study of character and personality. For the purposes of character creation, we've done our best to stick to common knowledge elements. The root causes of behavior are especially wide-ranging and often are directly related to the individual's past experiences. The causes we've listed in these entries are simply possibilities—ideas to encourage writers to think more about how the past might affect their character's present behavior and help brainstorm ideas for the character's wound.

If there's one thing we've learned from the writing of this resource, it's that there is no limit to the number of unique characters that can be created. By uncovering your characters' wounds, factoring in their genetic makeup, and plugging in other environmental factors, you should be able to birth many never-before-seen characters that readers will find both realistic and intriguing. It is our hope and sincere belief that this resource will help you create a cast of characters so well-drawn that your readers will feel compelled to share in your character's journey from the first page to the last. Best of luck!

THE NEGATIVE TRAIT
THESAURUS

ABRASIVE

DEFINITION: rubbing others the wrong way through lack of thought or care; irritating

SIMILAR FLAWS: annoying, caustic, coarse, galling, irritating

POSSIBLE CAUSES:
Poor social skills
Not caring about what others think
Being issue-oriented rather than people-oriented
Being raised in a verbally harsh environment
Needing to be right
Having a need to prove one's knowledge to others
Mental disorders or learning disabilities
A lack of empathy

ASSOCIATED BEHAVIORS AND ATTITUDES:
Showing impatience with others
Talking or laughing too loudly
Speaking without thought, being overly blunt
Not caring about or picking up on social cues
Not respecting the personal space of others
Deliberately pursuing topics of conversation known to be a source of irritation
Difficulty maintaining friendships
Living in isolation
Lacking emotional constraint
Causing offense or discomfort and being unbothered by it
Saying whatever one thinks or feels at any given moment
Keeping others waiting
Driving offensively; showing little consideration for others on the road
Being conceited (bragging, reminding others of one's strengths, etc.)
Being opinionated and judgmental
Selfishness
Pushing people too far with jokes or teasing
Being inconsiderate (borrowing items without asking, making demands, etc.)
Mistreating others through a lack of respect
Minimizing the accomplishments or contributions of others
Having a lack of mercy (due to the belief that people are to blame for their misfortunes)
Making plans, then backing out with little or no warning
Showing little respect for other people's property (tracking mud into someone's house, etc.)
Playing one's music too loudly
Showing up unannounced and uninvited
Overstaying one's welcome
Valuing certain people over others
Needing to be the center of attention

Living according to double standards: *You can't do this, but I can.*
Not adhering to social norms (picking one's nose, publicly displaying affection, etc.)
Speaking at inappropriate times (during a movie, while someone is talking, etc.)
Excessive criticism
Dressing disrespectfully (wearing a low-cut dress to a parent-teacher meeting, etc.)
Exhibiting poor judgment when it comes to boundaries (going out with a girlfriend's ex, etc.)

ASSOCIATED THOUGHTS:
I know she doesn't want to talk about this, but I do.
Oh, she's going to tailgate me? Let's see how she likes going 25.
What's the big deal? Everybody pees in the pool.
Stupid people like him shouldn't be allowed to breed.

ASSOCIATED EMOTIONS: annoyance, confidence, confusion, contempt, frustration, impatience, loneliness

POSITIVE ASPECTS: Abrasive characters are usually quite focused on their goals without being distracted by other people and their needs. Their lack of concern with what others think makes them transparent; you usually know what abrasive characters think or feel because they don't care enough to hide their thoughts and feelings. Because they will often say things that others won't, an abrasive character is helpful when you need someone to honestly reveal a difficult truth.

NEGATIVE ASPECTS: Abrasive characters are irritating. They hurt people's feelings and either don't realize or don't care that it's happened, which can make them unlikable. Because of this, they may have difficulty connecting with others and become isolated. Due to their lack of social graces, abrasive characters may find it hard to reach academic, professional, or relational goals.

EXAMPLES FROM FILM: Melvin Udall (*As Good As It Gets*) suffers from a form of OCD that is largely the cause of his abrasive nature. He has no verbal filter, is self-serving, and disdains most people in general, making him a very difficult person to befriend. **Other Examples from Film and Literature**: Dr. Gregory House (*House*), Lisbeth Salander (*The Girl with the Dragon Tattoo*), Pat Solitano, Jr. and Tiffany Maxwell (*Silver Linings Playbook*)

OVERCOMING THIS TRAIT AS A MAJOR FLAW: Characters with an abrasive nature often don't realize (or don't care) that they're hurting or annoying others. If the former is the case, this flaw must be brought to their attention and the character must be coached in acceptable ways to communicate and behave around others. If a character is knowingly abrasive, something must happen to show him his lack of connectedness and why he would benefit from developing his relationships. This event should propel him out of his selfishness and compel him to learn how to better relate to others.

TRAITS IN SUPPORTING CHARACTERS THAT MAY CAUSE CONFLICT: affectionate, kind, know-it-all, nurturing, over-sensitive, timid

ADDICTIVE

DEFINITION: a predisposition to becoming unhealthily dependent upon a substance, practice, person, habit, or other intangible

POSSIBLE CAUSES:
Genetics
Drug or alcohol abuse
Low self-esteem and insecurity
A mental disorder
An extreme level of passion
Poor coping skills
An unexpected trauma or devastating loss (losing one's family to a house fire, etc.)
Abuse

ASSOCIATED BEHAVIORS AND ATTITUDES:
Playing video games for long periods of time without breaks
Calling in sick to work or school so one can focus on the object of one's addiction
Abusing substances (drugs, medications, alcohol, etc.)
Exhibiting a lack of common sense
Not knowing one's limitations
Wanting to be with someone all the time (if the source is a person)
Having no willpower or ability to resist one's addiction
Needing to be near the source of addiction
Blowing off important commitments or events in favor of activities featuring one's addiction
Being secretive or untruthful about how much one indulges in the addicting behavior or habit
Obsessively focusing one's attention on the source of desire and need
Exhibiting obsessive tendencies in general
Being impulsive and impatient
Taking foolhardy risks
Needing instant gratification
Resenting family and friends who try to intervene
Living in denial
Injuring oneself for emotional release
Feeling twitchy, distracted, or on edge if too much time has passed without indulging
Having difficulty dealing with stress
Poor appetite or poor nutrition
Experiencing a buzz, rush, or sense of peace when engaging in a habit or behavior
Being overly preoccupied with time when one is not indulging
Feeling alienated from other people or society
Pursuing something to an unhealthy limit (compulsive shopping or hoarding, etc.)
Indulging out of the need to escape or to numb one's emotions
Shutting out friends and family
Desiring privacy
Developing an eating disorder

Changing one's life to accommodate the addiction (moving, changing careers, etc.)
Letting things slide (relationships, personal hygiene, one's finances, etc.)
Disruptive sleep or insomnia
Paranoia
Panicking at the thought of being kept from one's addictions

ASSOCIATED THOUGHTS:
Mark better show up with the stuff. I'm crawling out of my skin here!
I don't care how long it takes—I'm staying up until I knock CrackShot28 out of the top spot.
Why is Mom calling every freaking day? It's my life and she needs to leave me the hell alone.
It's just a little shopping to relieve stress. I can't believe he's asking me to give it up.

ASSOCIATED EMOTIONS: agitation, anticipation, desire, elation, fear, frustration, impatience, overwhelmed, paranoia, relief, shame

POSITIVE ASPECTS: Addictive characters can show great focus, attention, and dedication for a certain activity or desire. Their passion allows them to keep other distractions at bay so they may concentrate on what is important to them.

NEGATIVE ASPECTS: Addictive characters allow their need for gratification or relief from emotional pain to push them into unhealthy dependencies. Unable to set reasonable limits, they also have difficulty dealing with stressors, which can easily send them into a tailspin that furthers their dependence on their source of relief. These characters will often place the source before everything else, including relationships and their own well-being. They tend to hide their addiction from others to avoid interference and judgment, even though in their own mind, they don't believe that they have a problem.

EXAMPLES FROM TV: Dr. Gregory House (*House*) has a long-standing dependency to Vicodin resulting from nerve damage in his leg that causes constant pain. His dependency increases as job and relationship stressors rise, turning him into a full-fledged addict who will do anything for a fix, including stealing drugs and forging prescriptions. **Other Examples from Film and TV**: Joe (*Looper*), Whip Whitaker (*Flight*), Ben Sanderson (*Leaving Las Vegas*)

OVERCOMING THIS TRAIT AS A MAJOR FLAW: To overcome an addiction, the character usually must hit rock bottom. The first steps are for him to admit he has a problem and have the desire to change. Through the support of friends and family, a strong addiction program with mentoring, avoiding triggers, and responding to relapses with grace and forgiveness, the character can learn to cope with and overcome his addictions. Learning healthy strategies to deal with stress and disappointment will be key.

TRAITS IN SUPPORTING CHARACTERS THAT MAY CAUSE CONFLICT: devout, innocent, needy, persistent, proper, pushy, rebellious, responsible, tactless, volatile

ANTISOCIAL

DEFINITION: opposed to social order or the founding principles of society
*Note: **antisocial** shouldn't be confused with **unsociable**, which indicates reserved behavior and a reluctance to engage with others*

SIMILAR FLAWS: misanthropic

POSSIBLE CAUSES:
A genetic predisposition
Distrust of social institutions due to negative experiences in the past
A lack of empathy
Antisocial personality disorder
A dysfunctional family life
Insufficient emotional bonding during infancy and/or childhood
A history of abuse and/or neglect
Repeated rejection by others
Having a weak moral compass

ASSOCIATED BEHAVIORS AND ATTITUDES:
Criminal or gang-related activity
Substance abuse
Rejection of authority figures (parents, police, religious figures, teachers, etc.)
Aggression and violence (toward other people and their property)
Not feeling remorse over one's injurious actions
Narcissism and arrogance
Activities that disregard the well-being of oneself or others
Dishonesty and manipulation
Impulsivity
Instigating or escalating tension in volatile situations
Seeking out unhealthy relationships
Encouraging others to rebel
Difficulty keeping a job
Cruelty to animals and others
Purposely trying to make others uncomfortable (flouting the law openly, etc.)
Preferring to work on one's own rather than with others
Bullying or antagonizing others for entertainment
Volatile mood swings
Reckless behavior with little or no thought for the consequences
Lacking empathy toward people or animals in need
Self-centeredness
Preferring instant gratification over delayed gratification
Difficulty following instructions or rules
Looking forward instead of backward
Blaming others and society rather than taking personal responsibility for one's actions

Disdaining social norms, customs, beliefs, and traditional roles
Refusing to explain one's actions to others
Feeling validated when society or governments struggle
Using kindness or concern to manipulate
Impulsivity
Promiscuity
Parasitic tendencies (taking but not contributing)

ASSOCIATED THOUGHTS:
Who are they to decide what's right and wrong?
I answer to no one but myself.
I didn't make these rules. Why should I have to follow them?
Why are they after me? I haven't done anything wrong.

ASSOCIATED EMOTIONS: anger, contempt, hatred, hurt, indifference, rage, resentment

POSITIVE ASPECTS: Antisocial characters can be charming, though their likability is usually achieved through manipulation and falseness. Because of their lack of guilt, they believe that their choices are reasonable and acceptable and will do things that most other people would never do.

NEGATIVE ASPECTS: Antisocial characters have contempt for social mores and find it difficult to abide by them, making them a danger to themselves and to others. For a variety of reasons, they lack empathy and may feel little or no remorse when they cause harm. Because they see nothing wrong with their choices, it's hard to persuade antisocial characters to seek help. Their behavior is often a continuation of what has been done to them, so unless it's corrected, antisocial individuals are likely to continue the cycle of hurt and abuse.

EXAMPLES FROM FILM: Alex DeLarge (*A Clockwork Orange*) has no regard for the rules of society. He commits heinous and violent crimes with no sign of remorse and even continues his antisocial behavior in prison. **Other Examples from Film**: The Joker (*The Dark Knight*), T-bird and his gang (*The Crow*)

OVERCOMING THIS TRAIT AS A MAJOR FLAW: Studies show that the longer antisocial behavior continues, the more difficult it is to defeat. So if your character is to overcome this flaw, it would be best if he didn't have to battle it for too long. To change this trait, it would be helpful for the individual to experience an event that clarifies the need for social mores and establishes right and wrong.

TRAITS IN SUPPORTING CHARACTERS THAT MAY CAUSE CONFLICT: cowardly, devout, ethical, just, honest, honorable, meticulous, nagging, perfectionist

APATHETIC

DEFINITION: lacking emotion, passion, or interest

SIMILAR FLAWS: impassive, indifferent, unmotivated

POSSIBLE CAUSES:
A past hurt that one wants to avoid in the future
A lack of purpose or desire for achievement
Repeated failures and disappointments
Depression
A terminal diagnosis
Hypothyroidism
Neurological and psychological disorders (Parkinson's, Alzheimer's, schizophrenia, etc.)
Excessive alcohol or drug use
A brain injury
Selfishness; wanting to live one's life without being inconvenienced by others
A sense of powerlessness
A fear of failure
A lack of faith in one's capabilities

ASSOCIATED BEHAVIORS AND ATTITUDES:
Disengaging from others
Dropping out of clubs and activities that one used to enjoy
Decreased concern, interest, or emotion about anything
Being content to coast
Not setting goals
Exhibiting a general lack of respect for others (not listening when others are speaking, etc.)
Being unmotivated
Being late or not showing up at all to meetings, appointments, or events
Underperforming at school or work
Becoming uncommunicative
Passivity, boredom
Depression
A numb response to triggers that should cause excitement, anger, or sadness
Lethargy
Starting projects and not finishing them
Letting one's physical appearance go
Experiencing unexplained weight gain or loss
Responding inappropriately (offering a humorless smile instead of answering a question, etc.)
Going through the daily motions without expressing any real feeling
Knowing that something is wrong but lacking the energy to fix the problem
Showing up to school or work unprepared
Preferring to be alone rather than with others
Avoiding social events or family gatherings
Taking short cuts to finish duties
Not taking care of one's things
Sleeping more as a means of escaping
Rejecting genuine gestures of concern from others
Mental drifting; difficulty focusing
Neglecting one's relationships

ASSOCIATED THOUGHTS:
The house is a disaster, but I don't feel like cleaning.
I'll just write something quick for my sociology paper.
I suppose I should get out and vote, but nothing's going to change, so why bother?

ASSOCIATED EMOTIONS: depression, doubt, indifference, resignation

POSITIVE ASPECTS: As a defense mechanism, apathy makes it possible for victims and survivors to cope with their trauma until treatment can be applied. It can also be useful from a storytelling perspective; since apathetic characters aren't interested in challenge or change, a character's prolonged indifference can be used to allow tension and pressures to build up to a point of crisis, forcing him into action.

NEGATIVE ASPECTS: Apathetic characters are unmotivated and their lack of energy, interest, and emotion makes it difficult for them to do more than the bare minimum, affecting productivity and success at work or school. Withdrawal from others is a common sign of apathy, leading to isolation and loneliness. Without treatment, apathy can easily progress to depression and despair in a short period of time.

EXAMPLES FROM FILM: Will Freeman (*About a Boy*) is a self-professed island—independent and disengaged from others. His days are filled with meaningless activities like watching TV, playing pool, and having his hair cut. When a troubled boy invades his island world, Will resists helping him, knowing that doing so will be inconvenient and render him vulnerable. It's not until he steps out of his isolation and opens himself up to Marcus that Will sees the connectedness he was lacking and recognizes that no man is an island. **Other Examples from Literature and Film:** Mr. Bennet (*Pride and Prejudice*), Phil Wenneck (*The Hangover*)

OVERCOMING THIS TRAIT AS A MAJOR FLAW: There are so many reasons for apathy; knowing the contributing cause(s) is paramount to overcoming it. If there is a medical or psychological basis, proper diagnosis and treatment are necessary. Other characters may only need a sense of purpose—a reason to get out of the house each day. Sometimes, change can be brought about by shifting a character's attention from himself to others. Create a scenario where his apathy will negatively impact his family, neighborhood, or culture, and it may engage his emotions significantly enough to break his apathetic pattern.

TRAITS IN SUPPORTING CHARACTERS THAT MAY CAUSE CONFLICT: enthusiastic, fanatical, flamboyant, melodramatic, nagging, nosy, passionate

CALLOUS

DEFINITION: emotionally hardened

SIMILAR FLAWS: cold, cold-hearted, frigid, icy, unfeeling

POSSIBLE CAUSES:
A history of abuse
Growing up with an emotionally unavailable or distant caregiver
Parents who modeled a lack of compassion or empathy
Bullying that left one scarred
A past trauma that one avoids dealing with by disconnecting all feeling
Repeated exposure to violence or callous behavior
Addiction

ASSOCIATED BEHAVIORS AND ATTITUDES:
A lack of remorse
Disregarding the needs of others
Impersonal interactions (not asking for or offering personal information, etc.)
Manipulation
Dishonesty
A lack of empathy
Refusing to accept emotional responsibility or show mercy
Maintaining relationships that are superficial
Expressing frustration and disdain at the perceived neediness of others
Independence and self-reliance
An aversion to physical touch
A reluctance to express emotion
Distrust
Negativity
Not feeling the need for creativity or self-expression
Being adverse to change or variety (adhering to patterns and routines, etc.)
Avoiding neighbors and withdrawing from the community
A hands-off parenting style
A startling lack of emotion, even in the face of tragedy
Doing only what is required for others and no more
An absence of true joy or happiness
Decisiveness
Being highly logical and systematic
Being unbothered by tasks that others cannot stomach (working in a slaughterhouse, etc.)
Resenting family obligations
Pushing people away to avoid complex emotions that one is not willing to experience
Going without rather than asking for help
Unfriendliness
Shutting down anyone's attempt to engage one in meaningful conversation

Equating "being in need" with "weakness"
Viewing suffering as part of the human experience
Believing that people who complain about mistreatment are whiners
Being task-focused, not people-focused

ASSOCIATED THOUGHTS:
Why are they crying? They're so weak.
Why can't she control herself? It's ridiculous, the way she carries on.
Jeez, she's calling again. She's SO clingy.
He's so stupid. Anyone that dumb deserves to overdose.

ASSOCIATED EMOTIONS: agitation, anger, anxiety, denial, depression, disgust, frustration, hurt, loneliness
*NOTE: Due to the repressive nature of many callous people, some or all of these emotions may be inhibited.

POSITIVE ASPECTS: Because callous characters are emotionally detached, they can easily navigate devastating circumstances that might destroy a well-adjusted person. Also, decisions that others may find difficult due to personal involvement are simple for those without emotional attachments.

NEGATIVE ASPECTS: Callous characters are incapable of connecting on a deeply emotional level so their relationships are usually superficial at best. Because of their detachment, callous individuals lack empathy and may feel nothing in the midst of traumatic events. In extreme cases, callousness can affect one's morality, enabling a character to do things that others would find disturbing, abhorrent, or even unforgivable.

EXAMPLE FROM LITERATURE: In Dickens' *Great Expectations*, Estella's vengeful caretaker has raised her to hate men and break their hearts. When Pip becomes smitten with Estella, she is cruel, insulting him, calling attention to his lower social class, and leading him on. Although at times she seems conflicted, she is unable to overcome her upbringing and defy her caretaker until well into adulthood, when experience becomes the greater teacher. **Other Examples from Film**: Sergeant Barnes (*Platoon*), Colonel Hans Landa (*Inglourious Basterds*)

OVERCOMING THIS TRAIT AS A MAJOR FLAW: As with so many other flaws, if a certain event or thought pattern is the major cause of the callousness, it must be addressed and defeated for emotions to flow freely. If another character refuses to be rebuffed by displaying traits that a callous character holds dear (independence, persistence, resourcefulness, etc.), interactions can eventually lead to curiosity and begrudging admiration. This slow shift may create cracks in the character's emotional armor, allowing the possibility for a meaningful relationship to form.

TRAITS IN SUPPORTING CHARACTERS THAT MAY CAUSE CONFLICT:
affectionate, kind, needy, nurturing, passionate, sensitive, whiny

CATTY

DEFINITION: spiteful, in a sneaky and underhanded way

SIMILAR FLAWS: mean, petty, spiteful

POSSIBLE CAUSES:
A need to control
The desire to exert power while avoiding negative consequences
Low self-esteem
Peer pressure
A desire for social power
Dissatisfaction and envy
Being bullied at home

ASSOCIATED BEHAVIORS AND ATTITUDES:
Manipulation, playing favorites
Passive-aggressiveness
Giving backhanded compliments
Gossiping, exaggerating, and twisting the truth
Talking about people behind their backs
Hypocrisy
Playing mind games
Extreme competitiveness
Creating melodrama at another's expense
Cyber-bullying
Being hypercritical
Trivializing the plights or circumstances of others
Avenging oneself for past slights
Comparing oneself to others
Identifying those who may be a threat in some way
Establishing a pecking order
Spreading lies in an effort to hurt others
Possessiveness (of one's boyfriend, possessions, social power, athletic prowess, etc.)
Paranoia
Enjoying pointing out or picking apart another's flaws
Playing cruel pranks meant to embarrass others
Sucking up to those in authority in an effort to avoid consequences or gain special favors
Belittling others in a public manner
Being obviously secretive in an effort to make someone feel excluded
Negativity
Discrediting or damaging the reputation of those one perceives as threats
Being on the lookout for disloyalty
Encouraging social dependence in friendships to maintain control
Giving ultimatums

Using silence and exclusion to punish those who have fallen out of favor

Being sarcastic and brutally critical of others

Determining to get what one wants without regard for others

Not taking *No* for an answer

Rewarding those who follow one's lead

Taking or moving things so another is inconvenienced

Feeling a rush of power at taking control

ASSOCIATED THOUGHTS:

What is he wearing? The Salvation Army must've had a sale.

Thank God my hair doesn't look like that.

In what universe does she think she has a chance with him?

Does she seriously believe she can hang with us? Someone needs a reality check.

ASSOCIATED EMOTIONS: contempt, excitement, insecurity, pride, satisfaction, smugness

POSITIVE ASPECTS: Cattiness is often a tool used to reach an end goal (acceptance, social ladder-climbing, etc.). Those who participate in this behavior know precisely what they want and are determined to succeed. Catty characters can be very good at reading people, quickly determining who to pick on, who to avoid, and how far to push.

NEGATIVE ASPECTS: Catty behavior is hurtful, and because it often occurs in an underhanded fashion, it can be difficult to catch or prove. Those victimized by it have usually done nothing wrong and are left feeling confused, uncertain, and humiliated. Characters participating in catty behavior are often among the popular set, but in truth, their popularity is fueled by fear, not true respect or affection. These individuals may feel a rush of power or satisfaction at bringing someone else low, but in the long term it only adds to their feelings of inferiority. Over time, cattiness hurts everyone involved.

EXAMPLE FROM FILM: The Plastics (*Mean Girls*) are a group of girls who will do whatever it takes to retain their popularity. Queen bee Regina goes so far as to keep a "Burn Book" filled with rumors, secrets, and gossip about her classmates and teachers. When threatened, the Plastics lie, scheme, verbally abuse others, and betray one another, showing their truly selfish colors. **Other Examples from Literature**: Tinkerbell (*Peter Pan*), the goddess Hera (*Greek Mythology*)

OVERCOMING THIS TRAIT AS A MAJOR FLAW: Cattiness, like any form of bullying, is a power play. One way to overcome it is to have a catty character realize that she can be powerful and strong through non-destructive methods. Another way to defeat cattiness is for the character to recognize the harm that it does; if something horrible were to happen as a result of her catty behavior, she may realize how destructive it is and seek to change herself.

TRAITS IN SUPPORTING CHARACTERS THAT MAY CAUSE CONFLICT: appreciative, confident, devout, easygoing, honest, kindness, vindictive, volatile, witty

CHILDISH

DEFINITION: marked by immaturity or a lack of experience

SIMILAR FLAWS: babyish, immature, infantile, juvenile, puerile

POSSIBLE CAUSES:
A lack of life experience
A sheltered upbringing
Overprotective, smothering caregivers
The desire to be babied or treated like a child
A past trauma that stymied emotional growth
An aversion to growing up or taking on adult responsibility

ASSOCIATED BEHAVIORS AND ATTITUDES:
Preferring babyish activities, immaturity
An indifference to "adult" things (activities, hobbies, interests, clubs, organizations, etc.)
Shallow problem-solving skills
Gullibility
Impropriety; doing or saying inappropriate things
Living life exuberantly
Irresponsibility and impulsiveness
Being forgetful and/or easily distracted
Difficulty prioritizing
Being unreasonably irritable
Shifting responsibilities to others; forcing them to make hard decisions and choices
Wanting to be coddled when in a bad mood
Playing pranks, telling jokes, and enjoying humor that does not align with one's age
Petulance when one doesn't get one's way
Being easily overwhelmed when difficulties come
Poor coping skills
Moodiness
Making demands
Seeking out instant gratification
Deferring action (procrastinating, making excuses to avoid work, etc.)
Overindulging in fancifulness and daydreaming
Being highly imaginative
Naïveté
Not showing interest in worldly topics and events
Hanging around people younger than oneself
Relating more easily to younger people than older
Hanging onto one's youth (through hobbies, fashion, etc.) past the appropriate time to move on
Self-centeredness
Being overly trusting
Choosing the easy option over the hard one

Using slang to express oneself
Being frustrated by structure and rules
Becoming easily bored with routines; needing variety for stimulation
Being spontaneous
Needing praise and positive reinforcement to feel good about oneself

ASSOCIATED THOUGHTS:
This is too hard.
Why does he get all the breaks? It's not fair!
This is so cool!
Oh, I can do that work later.

ASSOCIATED EMOTIONS: amusement, curiosity, eagerness, excitement, happiness

POSITIVE ASPECTS: Childish characters can be innocent and naïve. As such, they're largely oblivious to or unaffected by the bigger problems of the world. Those with a childish outlook see life through a simpler lens; they don't over-complicate matters. Like children, they're teachable and eager to learn and experience new things. They adapt quickly, viewing change as a way of life rather than an inconvenience.

NEGATIVE ASPECTS: Childish characters lack responsibility and often cannot be counted on to complete important tasks with efficiency and care. Their problem-solving skills are weak, making it hard for them to work through conflict. Because of their lack of experience, they may have trouble evaluating complex situations or understanding difficult subject matter. Ultimately, childish characters don't always live up to others' expectations, which can cause frustration and disappointment for everyone involved.

EXAMPLE FROM FILM: Tommy Callahan III (*Tommy Boy*) is just out of college when his father dies, leaving him in charge of the family business. It's a tall order for someone with the attention span of a toddler whose time has been fairly divided between partying with friends and barely graduating. His impulsivity, short attention span, and lack of business sense make it difficult for him to succeed; it's not until he recognizes his strengths and embraces them that he's able to achieve his goals. **Other Examples from Film and TV:** Billy Madison (*Billy Madison*), Pee-Wee Herman (*Pee-Wee's Playhouse*)

OVERCOMING THIS TRAIT AS A MAJOR FLAW: A character can defeat his immaturity by growing up. For some, this will mean encountering trials that force them to mature in a short period of time. Other characters will have to face past demons that are keeping them enslaved in their childish state. Either way, added responsibility, and learning to take it on and succeed, will be key factors.

TRAITS IN SUPPORTING CHARACTERS THAT MAY CAUSE CONFLICT: humorless, impatient, inflexible, judgmental, mature, proper, responsible, unfriendly

COCKY

DEFINITION: brazenly or rudely self-confident

SIMILAR FLAWS: over-confident, swaggering

POSSIBLE CAUSES:
Over-affirming parents
Consistently escaping the consequences for one's actions
Having an overly confident view of oneself
High self-esteem
A history of usually being right
Desiring attention or popularity
Having realized frequent, competitive successes

ASSOCIATED BEHAVIORS AND ATTITUDES:
Peppering comments with sarcasm
Bragging
Vanity
Smirking and sneering
Feeling excessive pride in one's accomplishments
Adapting an air of fearlessness
Playing practical jokes that teeter on the edge of being inappropriate or hurtful
Sparring verbally, mouthing off
Participating in activities that affirm one's prowess (sports, intellectual battles, etc.)
Pointing out the inferiority of others
Dismissing those one views as inferior
Expressing anger when one's ego takes a hit
Showing off or boasting
Extreme competitiveness
Surrounding oneself with people of similar interests who encourage the cocky behavior
Indulging in one-upmanship
Refusing to admit that a competitor is better
Making excuses when things go badly
Becoming mean or defensive when embarrassed
Flouting the rules
Agreeing to challenges without thinking things through
Believing oneself to be better or know more than one's teachers, coaches, or parents
Having difficulty being a team player
Stealing the spotlight from others
Disrespecting those in authority
Saying things that minimize others, whether on purpose or through thoughtlessness
Striving to improve in the area of one's giftedness
Challenging competitors to duels and competitions
Avoiding situations where one's weaknesses might be revealed

Getting in over one's head and being unable to back down
Obsessing over one's image and what others think
Having a tendency toward superficial relationships
Judging others based on their looks or skills
Adrenaline rushes at putting someone in their place by winning
Exhibiting strong focus when one's reputation is at stake

ASSOCIATED THOUGHTS:
I'm the best one here.
This is not even worth my time.
I could get with her if I wanted to.
Coach Smith is a joke. I can't believe someone put him in charge.

ASSOCIATED EMOTIONS: confidence, contempt, determination, impatience, irritation, pride, scorn, smugness

POSITIVE ASPECTS: Cocky characters usually have strengths that others envy: athleticism, artistic ability, intelligence, charisma, etc. People are drawn to them out of admiration for their abilities, which gives cocky people a sphere of influence to work within. Because of their strengths, these characters are usually self-confident and perform well under pressure.

NEGATIVE ASPECTS: Cockiness is confidence taken too far. These characters will often feel disdain or scorn for those who can't measure up to their greatness. When their superiority is challenged, they may turn to intimidation, threats, or bullying tactics to secure their position. While cocky characters can usually back up their bluster with a true talent or skill, they often have an inflated view of themselves and their abilities, which can lead to their downfall.

EXAMPLE FROM FILM: Lightning McQueen (*Cars*) clearly has an aptitude for racing. He's constantly being told by his crew, the media, and adoring fans how awesome he is. The unadulterated praise and frequent wins go to his head, making him believe that he can do anything and doesn't need help or advice from anyone. Overconfidence leads him to snobbish behavior in the form of disdaining his long-time sponsor, insulting his loyal pit crew, and belittling his friends. **Other Examples from Film and Literature**: Maverick (*Top Gun*), Apollo Creed (*Rocky*), Aries (*Percy Jackson and the Olympians*)

OVERCOMING THIS TRAIT AS A MAJOR FLAW: Because cockiness is caused by a hyper focus on oneself, the character needs to change his viewpoint and see things from someone else's vantage point. Empathy is an important factor in turning someone's focus outward; getting a cocky character to feel empathy for others is a first step in bringing about a change of heart. Another possibility is experiencing a deep failure and the dose of humility that comes with asking another for help or advice to succeed.

TRAITS IN SUPPORTING CHARACTERS THAT MAY CAUSE CONFLICT: catty, controlling, fanatical, humble, indecisive, insecure, nervous, unethical, volatile, witty

COMPULSIVE

DEFINITION: subject to irresistible urges

POSSIBLE CAUSES:
Genetics
Chemical imbalances or structural abnormalities in the brain
Growing up in an environment where certain expectations were taken to an extreme
Low self-esteem
A history of abuse
Diseases that alter the brain (Huntington's disease, epilepsy, multiple sclerosis, etc.)
Social pressures (criticism about a child's weight that results in compulsive eating, etc.)

ASSOCIATED BEHAVIORS AND ATTITUDES:
Obsessing over certain thoughts or possibilities
Repeating rituals in an attempt to relieve anxiety (ordering/arranging, grooming, hoarding, etc.)
Other compulsive behaviors (stealing, shopping, sexual compulsions, lying, overeating, etc.)
Difficulty focusing on responsibilities
Highly suggestible
Having time management issues
A shortened attention span
Illogical fears that often compound over time
Hiding one's compulsions from others
Desperately trying to appear normal
Feeling overwhelmed and unable to cope
Anxiety that may escalate to paranoia
Avoiding places, people, or items that may trigger a compulsion
Living in seclusion
Inefficiency
Shame
Being highly stressed out to the point where one's health is affected
An inability to stop one's compulsions, despite seeing them as a problem
Believing in superstitions or irrational ideas
Adhering to patterns and routines
Following schedules to the letter
The need to count, organize or straighten
Needing to do something a certain way, and in a certain order (dressing, bedtime routines, etc.)
Feeling trapped when one is in a place where one's compulsiveness will be noticed
Engaging in one's compulsive behavior when stress or emotions are high
Depression
Rationalizing the behavior to oneself and to others
Denial
Feeling controlled by one's compulsion
Difficulty holding down a job or keeping commitments
Poor sleeping habits or insomnia

An inability to relax without self-medicating
Constantly doubting that one did or didn't do a certain thing
Thinking about the worst case scenario
Feeling weak when one gives in to a compulsive ritual
Worrying about the future

ASSOCIATED THOUGHTS:
I know this doesn't make sense. Why can't I stop?
Ice cream and cake will make me feel better.
I'm pretty sure I turned the light off, but I need to check again.

ASSOCIATED EMOTIONS: agitation, anxiety, depression, fear, frustration, humiliation, overwhelmed, relief, reluctance, shame

POSITIVE ASPECTS: Compulsive behaviors run the gamut from minor to severe. Characters on the minor end can function very well in society. They're organized, meticulous, disciplined, and structured. Sometimes, their compulsions turn to strengths that benefit others, such as the need to finish one's projects or the inability to do a job halfheartedly.

NEGATIVE ASPECTS: Compulsive characters fall victim to their own thoughts—worries that may have merit to begin with (avoiding germs, protecting one's home, etc.) but morph into an all-consuming fear. Their inability to ignore these worries leads them to compulsive behaviors in an effort to alleviate their anxiety. Between their mental battles and ongoing rituals, these characters spend a large portion of the day focused on their compulsions, leaving less time for necessary activities like homework, work projects, and building relationships. Sadly, many compulsive characters know that their fears are illogical but they're psychologically unable to dismiss them, which leads to frustration and shame.

EXAMPLE FROM FILM: Raymond Babbitt (*Rain Man*) is an autistic man who exhibits many compulsive behaviors, such as having to watch certain TV shows at specific times, requiring an exact number of fish sticks for dinner, and only wearing one brand of underwear. Deviating from any of these routines literally sends him into a frenzy that can't be stopped until structure is restored. **Other Examples from TV and Film**: Monica Geller (*Friends*), Roy Waller (*Matchstick Men*), Howard Hughes (*The Aviator*)

OVERCOMING THIS TRAIT AS A MAJOR FLAW: Some behavioral therapies have been successful in treating compulsive disorders, such as gradually exposing a person to his fears without letting him engage in the compulsion, or recognizing one's anxiety as illogical and "reprogramming" one's negative thoughts. Medication or specific nutritional supplements may also help, since a chemical imbalance in the brain is often part of the problem.

TRAITS IN SUPPORTING CHARACTERS THAT MAY CAUSE CONFLICT: catty, controlling, disorganized, helpful, impatient, inflexible, spontaneous, unruly

CONFRONTATIONAL

DEFINITION: eager to challenge, argue, or confront

SIMILAR FLAWS: argumentative, combative, contentious, pugnacious, quarrelsome

POSSIBLE CAUSES:
Believing oneself to be right and everyone else to be wrong
Overconfidence
A history of connecting unhealthily with others through conflict
A pessimistic outlook
Having a compulsive need to stand up to others or defend oneself
Feeling helpless or trapped
Having a subconscious desire to see others brought down to one's level of unhappiness
Depression or a sense of despair
Anger issues

ASSOCIATED BEHAVIORS AND ATTITUDES:
Argumentativeness, verbal sparring
Always taking the opposing viewpoint
Striking up confrontational conversations
Seeking out, rather than avoiding, volatile people and situations
Deliberately making inflammatory statements
Extreme competitiveness
Moodiness
Paranoia
High blood pressure, tension headaches
Intimidation
A critical, negative outlook
Hiding all of one's vulnerabilities so others cannot use them against oneself
Not respecting the personal space of others
Researching topics to prepare for verbal battles
Relishing confrontations with others
Having impossibly high expectations of others
An inability to relate to people in a normal manner
Having strong opinions and wanting to share them
Getting an adrenaline rush after each confrontation
Using low blows or insults to get a reaction
Picking fights to distract or mask one's hurt or vulnerability
Blaming others for one's mistakes
Refusing to see any side other than one's own
Bluntness; delivering truth as one sees it, without mercy
Being hypercritical of others, their work, success, and failures
Talking over others, interrupting
Purposefully taking things out of context to wind someone up or lend weight to an argument

Watching for inconsistencies or sensitivities and then using them as a means to provoke
Taking pleasure when other people are called out for their mistakes
Feeling validated when others give in or give up
Speaking one's mind, unfiltered
Devolving to pettiness, insults and even low blows to win
Seeing someone else's success as a personal challenge to do better
Watchfulness for irregularities or inconsistency so one can point them out
Jumping at chances to confront people on another's behalf
Telling people what they should do
Trust issues
Acting aggressively, a willingness to get physical

ASSOCIATED THOUGHTS:
This guy needs a lesson in manners.
What an idiot. I'm gonna prove that she has no idea what she's talking about.
Everybody else might be afraid of him, but I'm not.
I'll put him in his place.

ASSOCIATED EMOTIONS: agitation, anger, confidence, contempt, desire, determination, eagerness, excitement, smugness, pride

POSITIVE ASPECTS: Confrontational characters are confident in their own rightness, or they wouldn't speak up so loudly. As the frequent sole voice of opposition, they're not afraid to stand alone. Such stubbornness can be an asset.

NEGATIVE ASPECTS: Combative characters irritate or even frighten others. They stir up strife and contention, often deliberately. Their need for conflict makes it difficult for them to connect meaningfully with others, which leads to loneliness and isolation. This constant discord and negativity can also impact the confrontational character's health, leading to physical ailments such as cardiovascular disease and an increased risk of stroke.

EXAMPLE FROM FILM: Will Hunting's (*Good Will Hunting*) horrific childhood of abandonment and abuse have molded him into a person who thrives on confrontation. It is through conflict that he defends himself, defies his shame, and proves his worth. He lives life constantly on the offensive, assaulting others before they have a chance to hurt him and reopen old wounds. **Other Examples from Film**: Tyler Durden (*Fight Club*), Tommy DeVito (*Goodfellas*)

OVERCOMING THIS TRAIT AS A MAJOR FLAW: A confrontational character eventually must come to desire true connection with others. Whether through selfish or altruistic motives, the need for friendship and community can be a driving force in changing his behavior.

TRAITS IN SUPPORTING CHARACTERS THAT MAY CAUSE CONFLICT: cowardly, empathetic, gentle, inflexible, stubborn, timid, vindictive, violent, volatile

CONTROLLING

DEFINITION: inclined to exercise a restraining or directing influence over others

SIMILAR FLAWS: despotic, dictatorial, domineering, tyrannical

POSSIBLE CAUSES:
Growing up in an environment where one had no control
Being raised by a caregiver whose expectations were unrealistic
A thirst for power or the respect of others
Deriving pleasure from the domination of others
Having an intense need to be right
A fear of failure
A need for structure and predictability
Obsessive Compulsive Personality Disorder

ASSOCIATED BEHAVIORS AND ATTITUDES:
Perfectionism and pickiness
A drive to succeed
Difficulty delegating tasks to others
Requiring others to follow one's rules
Hypercriticism; a tendency to micromanage
Involving oneself in every possible decision
Keeping strict control of one's finances
Overriding the suggestions or opinions of others in favor of one's own agenda
Avoiding activities where one must be subservient to another
Intimidation and manipulation
Territoriality and defensiveness
Highly responsible
Feeling anger, frustration, and jealousy when others succeed
Possessiveness (in personal relationships)
Becoming aggressive when one's dominance is questioned
Giving backhanded compliments: *Good game, son. But it would've been better if...*
Being impatient with others
Rewarding loyalty with favoritism
Demanding respect
Surprise visits and "check-ins" to make sure rules are being obeyed
Withholding resources, information, or affection until one's demands are met
Blaming others
Needing to know where one's child or spouse is at all times
Making others feel badly for not measuring up (making comments that demean or hurt)
Noticing flaws rather than assets
Helping someone, then reminding them that they are now in one's debt
Pushing one's interests and hobbies onto others
Making suggestions that are really demands

Separating people from their support systems in order to better control them

Employing double standards (being tardy, yet expressing impatience at being kept waiting)

Requiring things to be in a specific order and place

Rewarding subservience and compliance

Punishing rule infractions or free thinking (withholding affection or help, etc.)

ASSOCIATED THOUGHTS:

This is too important for someone else to handle.

She's inept. How many times do I have to tell her how to do this?

This is my responsibility. How dare he try and tell me how to do it?

ASSOCIATED EMOTIONS: annoyance, confidence, determination, disappointment, frustration, impatience, smugness

POSITIVE ASPECTS: Controlling characters are relentless in their pursuit of perfection. Via this trait, they can push others to be their best. Their fear of failure spurs them on to frequent success, and their competence makes them fruitful project managers in the workplace.

NEGATIVE ASPECTS: Because of their need for perfection, controlling characters can be overly critical of others, undermining their confidence and making them feel unappreciated. This type of character has a hard time delegating work, believing that no one can do it as well as they can. Their constant supervision creates resentment, damaging morale. When their dominance is threatened, controlling characters may employ any method necessary to regain the upper hand, including threats, manipulation, verbal abuse, or physical violence.

EXAMPLE FROM FILM: Among other frightening traits, Hannibal Lecter (*The Silence of the Lambs*) definitely has the need to control, as is evidenced through his interactions with Clarice. He keeps her off-balance by demanding personal information in exchange for his help with her case, yet is personally offended when others treat her disrespectfully. When Miggs, another prisoner, is rude to Clarice, Lecter admonishes him so severely that he commits suicide. It's no surprise that Lecter chose a career in psychology, where he could have immense influence and control over his patients. **Other Examples from Film and Literature**: Don Vito Corleone *(The Godfather)*, Martin Burney (*Sleeping with the Enemy*), General Woundwort (*Watership Down*)

OVERCOMING THIS TRAIT AS A MAJOR FLAW: Understanding the reasoning behind one's need to control and implementing necessary changes to alter the behavior are both important steps to letting go. It can also be helpful to throw the character into a situation where he has no control; in the result of a positive outcome, the character may see that everything can and will work out without his constant micro-managing. Controlling characters can benefit greatly from getting to know the people around them—their strengths and weaknesses, likes and dislikes—and giving them the chance to achieve their own personal best.

TRAITS IN SUPPORTING CHARACTERS THAT MAY CAUSE CONFLICT: compulsive, disorganized, independent, lazy, mischievous, rebellious, uncooperative

COWARDLY

DEFINITION: shamefully fearful or tentative

SIMILAR FLAWS: fainthearted, fearful, pusillanimous

POSSIBLE CAUSES:
Having an overactive imagination that jumps to the worst possible outcome
Having a temperament that is highly fearful or anxious
Being more concerned with one's personal well-being than with the greater good
Being raised by overprotective, fearful, or paranoid caregivers
A history of failing, losing, or being mistreated

ASSOCIATED BEHAVIORS AND ATTITUDES:
Surrendering or giving in at the first sign of a threat
Avoidance rather than confrontation
Choosing actions that further one's interests, regardless of how others are affected
Talking big when friends are around but being easily cowed when challenged
Using underhanded methods instead of facing an enemy head on
Indecisiveness; being reluctant to commit
Having a low pain threshold
Using delaying tactics when a difficult decision needs to be made
Making excuses for avoiding the things that trigger one's fears
Unreliability
Setting safe goals and objectives; avoiding striving for anything too risky
Being noncommittal (leaving oneself a way out)
Timidity
Imagining the worst-case scenario
Watching for shifting emotions that may signal danger
Reliving one's occasional brave moments
Withdrawing from dangerous situations; choosing flight over fight
Showering support and admiration on powerful people in order to earn their protection
Diverting attention to others when threatened
Being wishy-washy or easily swayed
Mumbling
Not meeting other people's eyes
Being keenly aware of one's surroundings
Shifting alliances if it will keep one from peril
Valuing one's life and health, such as it is
Setting others up to take a possible fall
Having a backup plan that will ensure escape from dangerous situations
Playing up one's weaknesses so as not to be perceived as a threat
Downplaying one's importance or skills in order to avoid being given responsibilities
Experiencing shame at one's cowardice
Blowing things out of proportion in one's own mind

A sense of panic when difficult situations arrive
Wanting to be brave and feeling shame when one is not
Choosing what is certain and comfortable over the unknown
Subservience to others
Allowing oneself to be bullied or mistreated, refusing to stand up for oneself
Lying rather than deliver unwelcome news

ASSOCIATED THOUGHTS:
I know it's the right thing to do, but I can't do that.
I'm so scared!
If I avoid him long enough, he'll eventually go away.
Why did I volunteer for this? Now I've got to make up some excuse to get out of it.

ASSOCIATED EMOTIONS: anguish, anxiety, depression, doubt, dread, fear, guilt, regret, reluctance, shame, uncertainty

POSITIVE ASPECTS: Cowards have a strong sense of self-preservation. They are cautious in their decision making and often let common sense rule, ensuring that they rarely do anything rash or dangerous.

NEGATIVE ASPECTS: Cowards are usually controlled by fear—of what others think, of pain or discomfort, of making the wrong decision, etc. They often know the right course of action but are too scared to commit. This dichotomy creates self-doubt, insecurity, and shame. Cowards know that they lack courage and will usually try to hide the fact through deception, hypocrisy, and overcompensation in other areas.

EXAMPLE FROM FILM: No one exemplifies cowardice quite like the Cowardly Lion from the film version of *The Wizard of Oz*. He bullies poor Toto and threatens Dorothy, but when she stands up to him, he bursts into tears. When there is any true danger, he argues against action and hides behind everyone else. As the king of beasts, he is so ashamed by his lack of courage that he agrees to visit the wizard to try and overcome his weakness. **Other Examples from Film**: Donald Gennaro (*Jurassic Park*), Ike Clanton (*Tombstone*), C3PO (*Star Wars*)

OVERCOMING THIS TRAIT AS A MAJOR FLAW: Cowardly characters are usually driven by fear. To overcome cowardice, fearful and negative thoughts need to be acknowledged, banished, and replaced with positive ones. For instance, if one's cowardice revolves around fear of failure, overblown thoughts of failure need to be challenged and replaced with realistic thoughts of capability and possibility. Likewise, feelings of insecurity should be replaced with knowledge of one's accomplishments, which will eventually lead the cowardly character to care more about his own value than the value placed upon him by others.

TRAITS IN SUPPORTING CHARACTERS THAT MAY CAUSE CONFLICT:
adventurous, confrontational, controlling, cruel, courageous, honorable, uninhibited

CRUEL

DEFINITION: intentionally causing suffering by bringing about emotional or physical harm

SIMILAR FLAWS: heartless

POSSIBLE CAUSES:
Growing up in a survival-of-the-fittest environment where everyone was out for themselves
Altered brain chemistry
Role models who taught, by example, that cruelty was a pathway to dominance and power
Childhood neglect or abuse
Personality disorders (borderline personality disorder, sociopathy, psychopathy, etc.)
Prolonged stress
Low self-esteem that propels one to gain power by taking it from others
Racism or prejudice
Fear

ASSOCIATED BEHAVIORS AND ATTITUDES:
Egging others on to explore the depths of their anger or rage
Name-calling with the intent to emotionally wound
Identifying and targeting the weak and vulnerable
Taking the long view; delaying immediate gratification in favor of causing deeper pain
Experiencing an adrenaline rush when others are brought low
Playing pranks meant to embarrass or demean others
Not facing a threat head-on
Physically assaulting animals and/or people with the intent to hurt
Being fascinated with physical, mental, and emotional limitations and how to reach them
Using underhanded methods to get even with others
Intimidating and bullying others
Displaying a lack of emotion
Befriending someone just to betray them later
Witnessing traumatic events and experiencing excitement instead of dread or horror
Victimizing others through arson, vandalism, and other destructive crimes
Applying pressure (squeezing, poking, rubbing, etc.) to a wound or sensitive area to inflict pain
Cyber-bullying
Uncontrolled rage
Vindictiveness
Trust issues
Hurtful pranks that are intended to humiliate others
Spreading rumors and lies
Exploiting innocence, kindness, friendliness, and other dominant positive traits
Liking the smell and sight of another's fear
Playing head games in an effort to keep someone uncertain or confused
Harping on the flaws or weaknesses of others, eroding their confidence
Actively seeking opportunities to exercise power over others

Using secrets and sensitivities to humiliate another
Trying to see how far others will debase themselves out of fear
Thinking about pain and how it feels
Fantasizing about torture
Lying to someone to alleviate their fears, setting them up for certain failure
Allowing someone to achieve something special and then taking it away
Withholding information, help or support in order to cause someone emotional pain
Lacking mercy

ASSOCIATED THOUGHTS:
I can't wait to make him squirm.
How far I can push her before she breaks?
I wonder how long I can do this without getting caught?

ASSOCIATED EMOTIONS: anger, anticipation, contempt, eagerness, elation, excitement, indifference, satisfaction

POSITIVE ASPECTS: With cruelty comes power through intimidation and dread. Cruel individuals are rarely a target for suffering as they are rightly avoided and feared.

NEGATIVE ASPECTS: Cruel characters are takers, not givers, and are often social outcasts. They either become loners who are unable to form wholesome, trusting relationships, or they join forces with others who share the same taste for meanness, forming dysfunctional relationships. Cruel individuals lack empathy, and despite any attempts to hide this deficiency, it's often easily noted by others. Because of the general public's wariness, cruel characters may be blamed for any negative events that occur, even without proof.

EXAMPLE FROM FILM: Percy Wetmore from *The Green Mile* claims to hate his job as a death row prison guard, but he enjoys the power it grants him over the vulnerable inmates. He avoids the aggressive ones, instead targeting those he deems as weak. Biding his time, he waits for opportunities that will provide the maximum anguish for the inmates, then strikes with a satisfied smirk. **Other Examples from Film and Literature**: Chris Hargensen (*Carrie*), Nurse Ratched (*One Flew Over the Cuckoo's Nest*)

OVERCOMING THIS TRAIT AS A MAJOR FLAW: In order to overcome cruelty and succeed at his goals, the character would have to be taught empathy. This might be achieved through the kindness of one who is least likely to offer it—say, a victim of violence. If a terrible tragedy was to befall the heartless character and this unlikely person chose to show mercy instead of cruelty, empathy would be modeled firsthand, giving the main character an opportunity to see its effects and recognize its value.

TRAITS IN SUPPORTING CHARACTERS THAT MAY CAUSE CONFLICT: controlling, intelligent, know-it-all, merciful, suspicious, violent, volatile

CYNICAL

DEFINITION: having a disdainful mistrust of others and their motives

SIMILAR FLAWS: jaded

POSSIBLE CAUSES:
A past betrayal
A history of being shot down despite putting forth one's best efforts
Being surrounded by negative, suspicious people
Growing up in an environment of cynicism and defeat
Being raised by parents or caregivers who frequently broke their promises
Disillusionment
Trust issues
A fear of being hurt or disappointed

ASSOCIATED BEHAVIORS AND ATTITUDES:
Distrusting others
Pessimism; expecting a negative outcome
Hesitating to try anything new; not being spontaneous
Voicing doubts or suspicion
Employing sarcasm
Finding it difficult to support or show enthusiasm when others begin a new endeavor
Experiencing genuine surprise when things work out nicely
A reluctance to join groups or institutions
Complaining or grousing
Disdaining anyone gullible enough to be duped
Assuming that most people and organizations are looking to take advantage of others
Seeking out evidence to prove one's position
Making arguments that don't always make sense or can be backed up by proof
Looking for someone to blame when something goes wrong
Apathy
Grouping with like-minded people
Not showing surprise at the atrocities happening in the world
Not seeing the benefit of striving for something better
Believing that whatever one achieves doesn't matter or will be taken away
Viewing special offers or deals with mistrust
A reluctance to commit without knowing all the details
A decreased interest in solving problems
Expecting people to break their promises
Refusing to be swayed from one's point of view
Fearing that one will be taken advantage of if one is not vigilant
Assuming that anyone in power is corrupt
Being prepared for disappointment; rarely getting one's hopes up
Asking pointed questions in an effort to discover the 'catch'

Being disappointed when good things happen because one can't say, *I told you so.*
Keeping one's feelings to oneself; hiding emotions so others can't take advantage
Not cheering for a local team because they have a pattern of losing
Difficulty with change
Insisting on exact terms to avoid loopholes before making an agreement
Feeling uncomfortable around enthusiastic, optimistic people

ASSOCIATED THOUGHTS:
What a bunch of lemmings. People are so gullible.
Why do they bother trying? Nothing's going to change.
Things are just going from bad to worse.
Free lawn care for a year? Yeah, right. Nothing's ever free.

ASSOCIATED EMOTIONS: anxiety, contempt, doubt, frustration, skepticism, suspicion, wariness

POSITIVE ASPECTS: Because cynical characters are naturally suspicious, they're not gullible and therefore are hard to dupe. They often stick stubbornly to their beliefs and refuse to be swayed. Cynical people don't believe in perfection, nor do they expect anything to work out flawlessly. Because of their low expectations, disappointment rarely catches them off guard.

NEGATIVE ASPECTS: Cynicism, as a form of jaded or even scornful negativity, wears on others and brings them down. A cynic's attitude will impact friends and family, and may cause them to adopt a similar negative outlook. Often, for a cynical character, distrust in one area leads to distrust in others, until he finds himself unable to connect with a range of people, groups, institutions, and belief systems. This makes it difficult for him to learn from others and grow.

EXAMPLE FROM FILM: Han Solo (*Star Wars*) was orphaned at a young age and taken in by a pirate, then treated badly through many years of forced servitude before he made his escape. His heart was broken by a member of the rebel alliance, and he was just beginning to make a name for himself at the Imperial Academy when he saved a Wookiee from an unjust beating and was kicked out. Life taught him that people are fickle, governments are tyrannical, and the only person he can count on is himself. **Other Examples from Film and Literature**: Rick Blaine (*Casablanca*), Benjamin (*Animal Farm*), Etienne Navarre (*Ladyhawke*)

OVERCOMING THIS TRAIT AS A MAJOR FLAW: Cynicism is a difficult cycle to break. There is hope for the cynical character if he can find someone to trust. If a person or group earns his trust through consistency and honesty, then it lends credibility to their ideals and beliefs, even if they differ from the cynic's own. Eventually the character may learn to trust other associates and recognize that his doubt is sometimes misplaced, and not everyone is worthy of suspicion and disdain.

TRAITS IN SUPPORTING CHARACTERS THAT MAY CAUSE CONFLICT: evasive, gullible, hypocritical, idealistic, optimistic, trusting

DEFENSIVE

DEFINITION: marked by the need to defy aggression or attack

POSSIBLE CAUSES:
A history of being falsely accused
A guilty conscience
Bitterness
Having a secret that one wants to hide
Frequently being in the wrong and needing to prove oneself
Abuse or neglect

ASSOCIATED BEHAVIORS AND ATTITUDES:
Jumping to conclusions
Always having a reason to explain one's behavior
Becoming easily angered over little things
Aggression
Indignation: *I would never do something like that! How could you even think it?*
Suspicion
Quitting jobs before one can be fired
Bringing up the past to support one's position or cast doubt on others involved
Dumping one's girlfriend before she can end the relationship
Reacting with anger if one feels threatened
An aversion to admitting wrongdoing; being a right-fighter
Blaming others, refusing to take responsibility for negative outcomes
Highly alert; strong self-preservation skills
Reading into what people say and do
Having thin skin; an inability to take criticism
Becoming fidgety when feeling threatened (shifting, pacing, making an excuse to leave, etc.)
Raising one's voice; talking or shouting over others
Creating distance between oneself and others when conflict arises
Reacting to even a light rebuke with rudeness and sarcasm
Breaking off friendships or refusing to see family if one feels maligned
Becoming offended over the smallest thing
Taking everything personally
Feeling unfairly persecuted when others ask questions about an uncomfortable event
Trying to look innocent or not involved
Feeling panicky at being under the microscope if one is in the wrong
Not taking responsibility for one's actions
Bristling when others make suggestions to improve
Misremembering or giving inaccurate accounts based on one's skewed, defensive viewpoint
Thinking ahead and proactively planning ways to deal with possible fallout
Turning situations around to suggest that one was pressured into acting
Twisting other people's words to avoid blame: *You told me to get the bike back, remember?*
Making a big deal out of nothing to make an accuser feel bad for expressing doubt

Playing the martyr in an effort to shift attention: *Wow. And I thought we were friends.*
Suggesting that the accuser would have done the same thing
Becoming emotional (crying, getting worked up over criticism, verbalizing one's feelings, etc.)
Wanting to be left alone or escape
Widening the eyes as if shocked by the other person's expressed doubt, criticism, or accusation
Displaying disappointment in the accuser (breaking eye contact, shaking one's head, etc.)
Denying one was involved even before being accused
Looking for hidden meaning when none is intended

ASSOCIATED THOUGHTS:
This isn't my fault!
Why doesn't anyone believe me?
Now, watch. Somehow I'll get blamed for this, too.
If he's waiting for me to apologize, he'd better get comfortable, because that's not happening.

ASSOCIATED EMOTIONS: anger, denial, depression, disappointment, frustration, hurt, rage, resentment, suspicion, wariness

POSITIVE ASPECTS: Defensive characters are fiercely dedicated to self-protection. Though they may be mistreated and ill-used, they fight for themselves and don't take abuse lying down.

NEGATIVE ASPECTS: Whether guilty or innocent, these characters tend to defend themselves through ineffective methods, or they wouldn't have to keep employing them. They don't usually address problems head-on; instead, they attack the person behind the problem or focus on secondary issues in order to divert attention from the main concern. After a while, suspicion takes over as the defensive character seeks to ferret out any accusations before they come to light, leading to frustration, anger, and prolonged bitterness.

EXAMPLE FROM FILM: Ever since Red Pollard (*Seabiscuit*) was sent away by his parents at the age of twelve, he's literally been fighting to survive. Finally having achieved some acclaim as a jockey, his livelihood is once again threatened when he loses sight in one eye. Knowing that no one will hire a half-blind jockey, he hides the secret as best he can, making excuses for his losses. Ironically, it is what he fears most—the revealing of his secret—that eventually sets him free.
Other Examples from TV: George Costanza (*Seinfeld*)

OVERCOMING THIS TRAIT AS A MAJOR FLAW: There are basically two forms of defensive behavior: the kind that reflexively appears despite the character's innocence, and the kind that reveals itself when he has something to hide. If innocent, the defensive character should separate himself (as best he can) from the toxic people in his life who seek to bring him down or who caused trust issues to form. By releasing his worry over what others think and accepting himself for who he is, he will encourage others to do the same. If guilty, the defensive character will have to confront his demons and deal with the events of his past before he can find peace.

TRAITS IN SUPPORTING CHARACTERS THAT MAY CAUSE CONFLICT: abrasive, confrontational, cynical, honorable, judgmental, just, nagging, nosy, tactless, worrywart

DEVIOUS

DEFINITION: characterized by subtlety and trickery; not straightforward

SIMILAR FLAWS: calculating, crafty, duplicitous, scheming, shifty, sly, sneaky, wily

POSSIBLE CAUSES:
Growing up in an environment of distrust
Having an overly strict upbringing
Having caregivers who engaged in devious behaviors (criminal activity, etc.)
Substance addiction
Impure motives; having something to hide
Selfishness
A desire to avoid negative consequences

ASSOCIATED BEHAVIORS AND ATTITUDES:
Stealing or cheating
Lying
Sneaking around behind someone's back
Manipulation; pitting people against each other
Maligning others
Using diversionary tactics to draw attention away from oneself
Taking advantage of weaker parties
Working on the fringes to avoid notice
Saying whatever one needs to in order to achieve one's goals
Pretending to believe in a cause or person so one can gain access to connections or power
Saying one thing to one person and something else to another person
Always thinking ahead and maneuvering for one's own benefit
Observing others carefully; watching for weaknesses
Surrounding oneself with other unscrupulous people or those who can be controlled
Playing on others' emotions
Acting with ulterior motives
Being charming in order to disarm others
Choosing relationships and alliances that will benefit oneself
Blaming others for one's sneaky activities
Difficulty trusting others
Making passive-aggressive comments
Looking for hidden opportunities to take advantage of
Going to great lengths to avoid getting caught
Justifying one's behavior; having a "cover story" to avoid repercussions
Sabotaging the work of others
Being goal-focused and highly persistent
Being patient when one needs to be to ensure everything is properly set into motion
Playing the puppet master; letting others think they're in change while subtly controlling them
Constructing elaborate schemes to carry out one's actions and avoid detection

Looking for loopholes and ways to subvert the system
Hypocrisy
Steering conversations to lead people in a specific direction
Using concern and attentiveness to encourage others to let down their guard
Keeping people at a distance to protect one's secrets
Downplaying the importance of something in order to divert attention from its significance
Noting people's sympathies so one can play on them to get what one wants

ASSOCIATED THOUGHTS:
How can I take advantage of this opportunity?
I've got to do this so no one notices.
Stay under the radar.
She's so stupid; she'll never figure it out.

ASSOCIATED EMOTIONS: amusement, contempt, determination, fear, guilt, suspicion

POSITIVE ASPECTS: Devious characters are great at getting things done. When traditional methods fail, they come up with alternate techniques for achieving their goals. They're often very good at reading others and knowing what needs to be done or said. Because they're often saying one thing to one person and something else to another, they're good at thinking in complex patterns and following more than one relational thread at a time.

NEGATIVE ASPECTS: Devious characters are deceptive. They lie, cheat, and manipulate to get what they want and don't often care if their methods hurt others. Because these behaviors are so natural, they aren't only confined to professional or goal-oriented relationships, but tend to bleed into their personal dealings, too. Their ethical lines are much more flexible than the average person's which can cause their morality to shift, creating a slippery slope down a dark road.

EXAMPLE FROM LITERATURE: Since finding the ring, Gollum's (*The Hobbit*) life has become characterized by sneakiness and quiet deception. It starts with the murder of his cousin, and then quickly devolves into a pattern of spying and thieving that eventually sees him banished from his home. Many years later, when his agreement with Bilbo doesn't pan out, Gollum reneges and tries to kill him instead. A ring of invisibility is really the perfect accessory for a devious creature like Gollum, enabling him to act in secret and go undetected wherever he pleases. **Other Examples from Literature and Film**: Grima Wormtongue (*The Lord of the Rings*), Puss in Boots, Philippe the Mouse (*Ladyhawke*)

OVERCOMING THIS TRAIT AS A MAJOR FLAW: The devious character needs to acknowledge the negative effect his behavior has on others. Seeing the hurtful aftermath (especially if ripples reach someone he cares about) may shock the character into recognizing the moral slope he's sliding down, allowing him to hit the brakes and reverse the progression.

TRAITS IN SUPPORTING CHARACTERS THAT MAY CAUSE CONFLICT: alert, honest, honorable, just, lawful, observant, responsible

DISHONEST

DEFINITION: lacking honesty, either overtly or through omission

SIMILAR FLAWS: deceitful, deceptive, disingenuous, false, untruthful

POSSIBLE CAUSES:
Living in an environment of distrust, crime, violence, or abuse
Idolizing role models who embraced trickery or lying
Holding a position of power where dishonesty results in reward
Desiring to keep peace through any means
Substance abuse
Self-centeredness
A lack of empathy
A fear of what the truth will bring
Believing that one's lies will never be discovered

ASSOCIATED BEHAVIORS AND ATTITUDES:
Lying or cheating to avoid consequences
Telling one thing to one person and another to someone else in an effort to maintain friendships
"Misremembering" events in a way that will benefit oneself
Exaggerating to get a bigger response
Saying whatever it takes to get what one wants
Leaving out details that would negatively influence the listener
Not correcting someone's misinterpretation of the facts
Doing and saying things to put up a false front
Using compliments to distract or pump someone up, making them less wary
Claiming someone else's idea as one's own
Using manipulation when one's honesty is questioned
Denial; refusing to admit that one has lied
Compounding lies to maintain one's original untruth
Enlisting others to back up one's stories
Portraying false emotions to achieve a desired effect (fake tears, anger, excitement, etc.)
Lying to spare people's feelings
Lying easily, without any of the usual tells
Thinking before answering or committing to a course of action
An aptitude for reading the body language of others and judging their moods and emotions
Voicing excitement about things that one is not interested in
Giving very few details in order to better remember the lies one has told
Voicing some truth so the lie will go undetected
Checking to see if one's lie has been discovered
Avoiding eye contact, changing the subject, shifting about
Speaking quickly and asking questions in an attempt to change the subject
Downplaying the situation so others don't become concerned when they should be
Making excuses or laughing something off as if it's a joke

Eliciting sympathy in order to exit gracefully: *I should go; my mom's been pretty sick.*
Carefully choosing what personal information one shares with others
Telling people what they want to hear instead of revealing one's true opinions
Having a backup plan or cover story in case one's dishonest actions are discovered
Avoiding pointed questions
Couching one's answers: *I honestly don't remember* or *I can't be sure*

ASSOCIATED THOUGHTS:

I hope no one finds out.
What does she want to hear right now?
How do I get out of this?
What did I say to him last time?

ASSOCIATED EMOTIONS: desperation, guilt, indifference, insecurity, regret, shame, suspicion, unease

POSITIVE ASPECTS: There's a certain reliability with dishonest characters because they can be counted on to act in an untrustworthy manner. They can often be bought and will remain loyal as long as there's something in it for them. Because they can be swayed to do things that honest people wouldn't, a character who embraces dishonesty might do the dirty work on the hero's behalf.

NEGATIVE ASPECTS: An inability to trust others creates barriers, making it difficult for dishonest characters to acquire close friends and have meaningful relationships. They also may become scapegoats because of the mistrust of others. If they are directly involved in a situation with conflicting viewpoints, the person known for dishonesty will always be devalued against anyone else.

EXAMPLE FROM FILM: Fletcher Reede (*Liar Liar*) lies to everyone. He lies to his co-workers, the police, his mother, his secretary, and even to his five-year-old son. It gets so bad that when Fletcher breaks his promise to attend his son's party, the boy makes a birthday wish that his dad would no longer be able to tell lies. The wish comes true, showing Fletcher how far-reaching his dishonesty has become. **Other Examples from Literature and Film**: Pinocchio (*Pinocchio*), Jay Gatsby (*The Great Gatsby*)

OVERCOMING THIS TRAIT AS A MAJOR FLAW: The best way to cure a dishonest character is to have him caught in his lies. The bigger the lie and the more influential/important the person is who discovers the untruth, the stronger the effect will be on the dishonest character. Another angle would be to show a different reaction to the lie than what the character expects (disappointment rather than rage; empathy rather than disgust, etc.). The surprise and relief may create the epiphany that dishonesty is heavier than the freedom of truth.

TRAITS IN SUPPORTING CHARACTERS THAT MAY CAUSE CONFLICT: honest, honorable, generous, gullible, just, responsible, vindictive

DISLOYAL

DEFINITION: being false to one's ideals, allegiances, or duties

SIMILAR FLAWS: double-crossing, faithless, seditious, traitorous

POSSIBLE CAUSES:
Having a self-serving and opportunistic nature
Greed
Being weak-willed or easily swayed
A fear of the consequences for maintaining one's allegiances
A lack of gratitude; not wanting to be beholden to anyone

ASSOCIATED BEHAVIORS AND ATTITUDES:
Cheating on a partner
Siding against one's allies
Secretly working against one's allies, family or friends
Spying; sharing injurious information about another to one's enemies
Breaking an honor code or betraying ties to one's family, an organization, union, religion, etc.
Dishonesty
Claiming to believe one thing and then embracing an opposing belief
Testifying against a family member or organization
Frequently changing friends
Agreeing with whomever one is with at the time
Abandoning a friend to pursue a more advantageous friendship
Rejecting one's allegiance to a team when the team isn't doing well
Being fickle
Breaking the trust of others
Ruining someone's reputation to gain notoriety or power with others
Selling secrets or technology to competitors
Bad-mouthing one's family, friend, or company
Setting a friend up to take the fall for something one has done
Gaining someone's trust with the intention of breaking it when the time is right
Using someone for their money, power, or prestige
Tattling on others to the higher-ups (management, parents, etc.) to improve one's position
Using temptations (bribes, a raise, etc.) to encourage others to be disloyal as well
Quitting a job to work for a competitor
Laughing at jokes made at the expense of one's friends or loved ones
Vacillating between support and disdain for an organization or group
Breaking promises
Committing to following a set procedure, then doing it one's own way instead
Shirking duties or chores and then convincing someone else to do the work to avoid detection
Expressing empathy for someone's problems, then complaining about them to others
Choosing relationships based on what they have to offer

ASSOCIATED THOUGHTS:

We never said this relationship was exclusive.
Mr. Benson will be upset, but I can't pass up an opportunity like this.
I might be a scumbag, but I'm a rich scumbag.
Just because I was friends with Claire yesterday doesn't mean I want to hang out with her today.

ASSOCIATED EMOTIONS: anxiety, conflicted, eagerness, guilt, hopefulness, jealousy, uncertainty

POSITIVE ASPECTS: Disloyal characters are flexible, opportunistic, and open-minded. They see change as a vehicle for improvement rather than something to fear and avoid. They know what they want and will do things that others wouldn't to achieve their goals.

NEGATIVE ASPECTS: Because disloyal characters change allegiances often, they easily break their promises and are difficult to trust. Their unrelenting drive for personal gain leads them to set aside, betray, and hurt those closest to them. While a disloyal character may feel and express true guilt for his choices, actions speak louder than words, revealing that there is one person he will always serve: himself.

EXAMPLE FROM LITERATURE: For three years, Judas Iscariot (the *Bible*) was part of Jesus' inner circle, professing to serve him faithfully and follow his teachings. But all along, he was serving himself by stealing from the disciples' treasury and eventually betraying Jesus for thirty pieces of silver. Though he expressed remorse and returned the payment for his treachery, he couldn't undo the consequences of his actions, which played a part in Jesus' death. **Other Examples from History and Literature**: Benedict Arnold, Edmund Pevensie (*The Lion, the Witch, and the Wardrobe*), the wizard Saruman (*The Lord of the Rings*)

OVERCOMING THIS TRAIT AS A MAJOR FLAW: As with so many self-focused flaws, the key to overcoming disloyalty is to recognize the value of other people. If a seemingly nonchalant act of disloyalty tremendously impacts someone in a negative way, the disloyal character may recognize that his choices have consequences that hurt others. Once he sees that the people in his life have value, it becomes more difficult to run roughshod over them.

TRAITS IN SUPPORTING CHARACTERS THAT MAY CAUSE CONFLICT: gullible, honorable, loyal, needy, oversensitive, passionate, persistent, suspicious, trusting

DISORGANIZED

DEFINITION: lacking coherence, orderliness, or systematic structure

SIMILAR FLAWS: chaotic

POSSIBLE CAUSES:
Growing up in an unstructured environment (one of clutter or lack of planning, etc.)
Being free-spirited; having a desire to live in the moment
Irresponsibility
An inability to prioritize
Laziness
Having a fickle or flaky personality
Experiencing an emotional blow or loss that proves difficult to overcome
Mental instability or learning disabilities
Immaturity
Being overcommitted
Having a poor memory
Being gifted

ASSOCIATED BEHAVIORS AND ATTITUDES:
Being unable to make choices or prioritize
Confusion
Expressing contempt for rules and structure
Feeling overwhelmed
Keeping a messy work or home environment
Not being able to find what one wants when one needs it
Poor time-management skills (missing meetings, appointments or deadlines, etc.)
Misplacing things (keys, files, etc.)
Being easily distracted
Double-booking events and having to reschedule
Shopping for groceries without a list
Willingness to go with the flow
Missing big events (birthdays, anniversaries, weddings, surprise parties, etc.)
Making notes on whatever's handy instead of keeping an organized schedule
Communicating in an unfocused, rambling manner
Thinking incoherently, with one's thoughts jumping from here to there
Difficulty working with others
Financial difficulties due to inept or infrequent bookkeeping
Saying one thing and then forgetting and doing something else
Unintentionally marginalizing others by making them feel that they aren't a priority
Holding jobs that are creative rather than systematic (writing, sculpting, acting, etc.)
Hiring associates to handle the organizational side of things
Making excuses for one's scheduling snafus
Doing things last minute instead of planning in advance

Frequently letting others down
Showing up ill-prepared (not bringing what one signed up to bring to a party, etc.)

ASSOCIATED THOUGHTS:
Where did I put my keys?
Was that today? I thought it was next week!
Is it really 2:45? Shoot, I'm late!
Bob is so stiff. Why can't he just loosen up and enjoy the moment?

ASSOCIATED EMOTIONS: confusion, defensiveness, indifference, overwhelmed, worry

POSITIVE ASPECTS: Disorganized characters don't stress about keeping up appearances or conforming to the expectations of others. They are experts in dismissing the negative and distracting themselves with other things, refocusing on what makes them content. These characters find joy in small pleasures and simple interests. They are not as concerned with the big picture as they are with what's happening right now; this ensures that they don't take themselves or the world too seriously.

NEGATIVE ASPECTS: Disorganized characters frequently suffer the negativity, judgment, and exasperation of others when they fail to meet expectations. A lack of order creates difficulties like forgotten deadlines, lost materials, and missed appointments, which increase their stress levels. These characters often disappoint those around them and make poor leaders. They need help keeping on task and do not inspire confidence in their capabilities.

EXAMPLE FROM FILM: In the classic movie *It's a Wonderful Life*, viewers may wonder what Uncle Billy contributes through his involvement with the Bailey Building and Loan. Files and paperwork clutter his office, his fingers are a tangle of strings meant to help him remember important events, and he becomes so distracted on one trip to the bank that he misplaces a large, important deposit. From a storytelling standpoint, Uncle Billy's disorganization is a great vehicle for conflict, upping the stakes for the hero and testing his character in how he chooses to respond.
Other Examples from TV and Film: Oscar Madison (*The Odd Couple*), Dr. Phillip Brainard (*Flubber*)

OVERCOMING THIS TRAIT AS A MAJOR FLAW: Disorganized characters are most likely to change their ways when they see how this brand of chaos is keeping them from achieving their goals. Even then, a character's tendency toward being organized or disorganized is pretty well ingrained and may not be completely altered. But it's possible to change some of the contributing factors, such as learning to prioritize or keeping an actual schedule. Another option is for the character to recognize his disorganization as a weakness and arrange for someone else to manage that part of his life.

TRAITS IN SUPPORTING CHARACTERS THAT MAY CAUSE CONFLICT: compulsive, fussy, meticulous, organized, proper, pushy, responsible

DISRESPECTFUL

DEFINITION: contemptuous or rude in action or speech

SIMILAR FLAWS: discourteous, impertinent, impolite, insolent, rude

POSSIBLE CAUSES:
A lack of concern for the feelings of others
A general disrespect for authority
Growing up in an environment where respect for others wasn't valued or taught
Having a high opinion of oneself; believing that others are inferior and undeserving of respect
An indulgent upbringing
Desiring to put people in their place

ASSOCIATED BEHAVIORS AND ATTITUDES:
Insulting others
Refusing to comply or cooperate
Defying those in authority
Speaking rudely or using a condescending tone
Ignoring someone on purpose
Talking badly about a person or group of people
Mimicking someone in a hurtful way that highlights their flaws or deficiencies
Belittling others
Sarcasm
Dismissing others
Using rude gestures
Being openly judgmental
Speaking one's mind regardless of how sensitive the topic is
Betraying a loved one or friend
Making fun of someone's age
Breaking promises and lying
Taking people for granted
Ignoring the good someone has done because of one's personal bias
Showing impatience at another's level of grief or pain (telling someone to get over it, etc.)
Criticism that is unprovoked and uncalled for in the situation
Snooping through someone's private area (a desk, a bedroom, etc.)
Making fun of another's accomplishments or status
Minimizing the sacrifice and service of heroes (war veterans, etc.)
Undermining or sabotaging another's hard work because of a personal vendetta
Speaking over others, interrupting, or not letting them finish what they have to say
Abusing someone's property (causing damage out of a lack of care, etc.)
Acting inappropriately (flirting at a funeral, getting drunk at a baby shower, etc.)
Making a scene and causing others embarrassment
Complaining in the face of generosity (grousing about one's meal or accommodations, etc.)
Dishing dirt on people who entrusted one with their secrets

Obnoxious behaviors (shouting, making faces, telling racist jokes, belching, etc.)
Bullying or terrorizing
Using intimidation to show someone's weakness
Ignoring rules, boundaries, or requests to respect another's privacy
Deliberately creating difficulties that hamper another's success
Showing a lack of appreciation for another's hard work when one benefits from it

ASSOCIATED THOUGHTS:
What, she thinks she deserves my respect just because some moron put her in charge?
He bought a Chevy? What a waste of a car.
Time to cut Jim loose. He's a lousy boyfriend, anyway.
Where does Grandpa get off telling me what to do? Mom should put him in a home or something.

ASSOCIATED EMOTIONS: anger, annoyance, confidence, contempt, frustration, impatience, resentment, smugness

POSITIVE ASPECTS: Disrespectful characters are bold and, in some ways, principled. Whatever their flawed reasoning, if they believe that someone is unworthy of their respect they don't hesitate to act on that belief.

NEGATIVE ASPECTS: Disrespect is self-centered, deriving from the belief that other people lack value. When this character type chooses to flout authority in general, he puts himself at risk by dismissing his caretakers and the rules put in place to protect him. Disrespect is also dangerous because it tends to be cumulative; when someone chooses to act rudely to one person, it becomes easy to do so with others. Many societal and global problems stem from a form of disrespect.

EXAMPLE FROM FILM: Erin Brockovich (*Erin Brockovich*) can be as kind and likable as anyone—until someone disrespects her. When her neighbor makes too much noise at night, instead of trying to work things out civilly, she stomps outside and screams at him. Rather than dealing calmly with co-workers, she swears at them, and when her boss politely suggests that she adhere to the office dress code, she refuses and insults him. While she is capable of civility, Erin's tendency to disrespect others in times of high emotion makes it difficult for her to maintain healthy relationships. **Other Examples from TV and Film**: the little league team from *The Bad News Bears*, Walt Kowalski (*Gran Torino*), Bart Simpson (*The Simpsons*)

OVERCOMING THIS TRAIT AS A MAJOR FLAW: One of the reasons disrespectful characters continue to be rude is because there is no true consequence or deterrent. For them to alter their ways, their disrespect needs to keep them from achieving a primary or secondary goal. Then, they will realize that a change is in order.

TRAITS IN SUPPORTING CHARACTERS THAT MAY CAUSE CONFLICT: antisocial, controlling, courteous, diplomatic, haughty, kind, nurturing

EVASIVE

DEFINITION: having an unforthcoming manner; avoiding self-revelation

SIMILAR FLAWS: cagey, elusive, secretive, slippery, vague

POSSIBLE CAUSES:
Trust issues
A fear of failure
A fear of commitment
Shyness
A fear of being hurt or judged
The desire to protect oneself or others from perceived harm
Having something to hide

ASSOCIATED BEHAVIORS AND ATTITUDES:
Keeping opinions to oneself
Maintaining defensive body language (keeping one's distance, crossing the arms, etc.)
Telling half-truths or lies
Shrugging and looking away
Difficulty sharing one's opinion when asked
Avoiding certain topics
Using light manipulation to keep the attention away from oneself
Keeping secrets
Giving vague responses
Holding one's emotions in check
Strong observation and listening skills
Not sharing one's motives out of a fear that others will misunderstand or cast judgment
Maintaining strong personal boundaries
Protecting one's privacy and preferring solitude
Ignoring hints for more information
Being unforthcoming about one's whereabouts
Refusing to explain or give more details
Being hard to get ahold of
Fear of being misunderstood
Being noncommittal (shrugging rather than answering outright, etc.)
Difficulty asking for help or advice
Making excuses in an effort to delay answering
Watchfulness; making sure that one isn't being followed or observed
Nervousness or paranoia
An aversion to change and spontaneity
Appearing uncomfortable (twitchy, nervous) when put on the spot
Self-soothing gestures (stroking the hair, rubbing a sleeve, etc.)
Turning conversations around by asking about someone else: *How's Jane doing, by the way?*
Having unrealistic security concerns (not sharing personal information online, etc.)
Answering questions with a question

ASSOCIATED THOUGHTS:

Why does she have to know everything? Can't I keep anything to myself?
Maybe I don't want the whole world to know my every thought.
I'll ask about Uncle Ethan's divorce and they'll forget about giving me the third degree.
They won't understand, so why even try? Better to just keep quiet.

ASSOCIATED EMOTIONS: agitation, defensiveness, denial, embarrassment, suspicion, worry

POSITIVE ASPECTS: A character with this trait can keep information close to the vest, including potentially hurtful secrets. Because they're not forthcoming, they're often cast in the role of a listener or confidant; relationships like these can be effectively used by the author to impart information to the reader.

NEGATIVE ASPECTS: Evasive characters are guarded and rarely open up, making it hard for others to get close. Friends and family might grow worried and paranoid about an evasive loved one and demand that she share more of herself. If she doesn't, anger and resentment may set in, creating a deeper wedge between them. Devoted lovers may be especially hurt by evasiveness, misconstruing it as selfishness, cruelty, or a lack of trust.

EXAMPLE FROM TV: In the TV show *The Mentalist*, Patrick Jane harbors deep feelings of guilt after his careless words played a part in the death of his wife and child. A fraudulent psychic-turned-consultant, he now works for the police to hunt down criminals, wearing a glib mask of humor and irresponsibility to avoid showing his true feelings. Skilled in the art of perception, he reads people to discern truth, yet avoids revealing any information about himself. **Other Examples from Film**: Elisabeth Burrows (*Don't Say a Word*), Verbal Kint (*The Usual Suspects*), Simon Templar (*The Saint*)

OVERCOMING THIS TRAIT AS A MAJOR FLAW: If a secretive character understood how his loved ones were hurt by his inability to share, it might encourage him to delve into the reasons behind his evasiveness. Realizing that this flaw is undermining his relationships may be the catalyst that can lead to change. "Test sharing" a part of himself with someone he cares about will allow him to see how his trust is met with caring and respect, encouraging more openness moving forward.

TRAITS IN SUPPORTING CHARACTERS THAT MAY CAUSE CONFLICT: curious, controlling, nosy, perceptive, pushy, suspicious

EVIL

Note: While the existence of evil may be a controversial topic in real life, for the sole purpose of character creation, we have chosen to explore it as a character flaw.

DEFINITION: deeply immoral and wicked

SIMILAR FLAWS: depraved, immoral, malevolent, wicked

POSSIBLE CAUSES:
Mental disorders (antisocial personality disorder, psychopathy, sociopathy)
A history of cruelty, abuse, or neglect
Failure to form important relational bonds as an infant or child
Hatred for oneself or others
Altered brain structure and chemistry
Brain injuries
Having role models who used cruelty as a means of gaining power
Indoctrination or brainwashing that convinces the subject that evil is good and vice versa

ASSOCIATED BEHAVIORS AND ATTITUDES:
Seeking out good wherever it exists and destroying it
Consistent sadistic and destructive behaviors toward others without remorse
Playing head games with people to emotionally torture them
Encouraging others to be cruel
Acting out of a lack of empathy and absence of morality
Preying on those who are vulnerable or helpless
Believing oneself to be above the law
Deliberately confusing others and their sense of values
Making people feel or look stupid in an attempt to set them on a self-destructive path
Purposely humiliating others
Playing cruel jokes
Bullying that terrorizes
Worshipping the devil or other negative forces
Getting to know someone for the sole purpose of exploiting their weaknesses
Leaning in closer to watch someone or something suffer
Becoming aroused (sweating, quickened breaths, bright eyes) while watching someone in pain
Committing acts of violence towards animals
Mutilating, raping, and murdering
Hurting living things because one can
Feeling alive through causing death
Overconfidence; having a God complex
Difficulty connecting with others
Complete disrespect and disdain for authority
Spending a disproportionate amount of time thinking up ways to hurt people
Committing mass murder and genocide
Experiencing arousal at the sight of blood

Being preoccupied with religion and how to subvert it
Enjoying the sounds of pain (screaming, crying, pleading, etc.)
Deliberately turning something benign into something monstrous
Taking excessive pride in one's accomplishments; wanting to be exalted and remembered
Being fascinated with weapons, blood, and stories of violence

ASSOCIATED THOUGHTS:
What will it take to break her faith?
People like her make this too easy.
I can get away with anything.
People will always remember my name.

ASSOCIATED EMOTIONS: agitation, anticipation, contempt, eagerness, excitement, hatred, hurt, indifference, smugness

POSITIVE ASPECTS: Many evil characters are quite intelligent and creative. They're good at reading people, and they know just what to say or do to stay out of trouble and win another's trust. While often incapable of empathy, evil characters understand the power of emotion and are able to mimic it well enough to fit in and manipulate others.

NEGATIVE ASPECTS: Evil characters are morally deficient, with little or no guilt or conscience to hold them in check. They do whatever they please, for personal motives or for the sheer pleasure of hurting others. Evil characters make good villains because of their willingness and desire to do terrible things, but it doesn't mean that they have to be all bad. Give your villain a gut-wrenching history, some positive attributes, and a cause he believes to be just, and he will become more complex and interesting.

EXAMPLE FROM FILM: After the violent death of his unborn child, John Kramer (*Saw*) is pushed to the edge of sanity. As Jigsaw, he embraces a dark alter ego, seeking out and capturing those who have done harm during their lives. He forces his victims into painful, unthinkable moral dilemmas where they're forced to answer one question: *How badly do you want to live?*
Other Examples from Literature and Film: Rhoda Penmark (*The Bad Seed*), Randall Flagg (*The Stand*), Voldemort (*Harry Potter* series)

OVERCOMING THIS TRAIT AS A MAJOR FLAW: Some depraved characters can be rehabilitated by identifying and confronting their extreme lack of empathy. While therapy may seem trite and over-applied, it's usually necessary to control a problem of this magnitude. Unfortunately, evil is progressive, and many truly wicked characters can't be saved. It would be difficult and unwise to trust the Jigsaws, Adolf Hitlers, and Jeffrey Dahmers of the world with others; for people like these, death or removal from civilized society may be the only responsible recourse.

TRAITS IN SUPPORTING CHARACTERS THAT MAY CAUSE CONFLICT: devout, honorable, just

EXTRAVAGANT

DEFINITION: exceeding the limits of sensibility or need

SIMILAR FLAWS: excessive, profligate, wasteful

POSSIBLE CAUSES:
Great wealth
Being spoiled
Equating the appearance of wealth with self-worth
Wanting to impress others
Living in a well-to-do society
Envy
Ignorance regarding the value of finite resources
Wanting to make others happy regardless of the cost to oneself; being overly generous
The inability to say *No* to loved ones
Growing up with parents who were "spenders" rather than "savers"
A compulsive spending disorder

ASSOCIATED BEHAVIORS AND ATTITUDES:
Buying things one doesn't really need
Always purchasing the most expensive or highest quality items
Purchasing things on credit
Not keeping or not sticking to a budget
Letting someone else handle the finances
Being in financial debt; spending more money than one takes in
Throwing lavish parties
Spending large amounts of money on others
Not bothering with money-saving methods (coupons, choosing generic brands, etc.)
Not taking care of one's possessions
Impulse buying, or purchasing things and then not using them
Throwing out perfectly good items
Taking expensive trips
Making excuses for one's decisions
Lying to cover one's extravagance
Paying with cash and throwing away receipts
Manipulating spouses, parents, and others to get them to buy what one wants
Flaunting possessions; trying to outdo others with one's purchases
Scorning those whose possessions are considered inferior
Being wasteful with other resources (water, electricity, time, etc.)
Needing to have designer labels, the most coveted brands, and the latest and best of everything
Shallowness
Ignorance about how others live
Paying others to do the jobs that one is capable of doing but doesn't want to do
Preferring to play rather than to work

ASSOCIATED THOUGHTS:
I don't need this but I have to have it.
Money is no object.
I've earned a little spending spree.
Joe will freak out if he finds out how much I paid for this. I'll have to hide it.
People are gonna be talking about my party for years!

ASSOCIATED EMOTIONS: anxiety, conflicted, defensiveness, denial, desire, excitement, guilt, satisfaction, worry

POSITIVE ASPECTS: Many extravagant characters are truly generous at heart, wanting to share what they have to make others happy. Because of their willingness to spend money freely, they're often involved in exciting activities: parties, vacations, shopping sprees, etc. This makes them life-of-the-party characters, and easily likable.

NEGATIVE ASPECTS: Though they might be popular, it is difficult for extravagant characters to tell true friends from scavengers. If there is an ulterior motive behind their wastefulness (insecurity, a desire to maintain appearances, etc.), they can easily fall victim to those willing to manipulate them. Resources are never infinite, and if the extravagant character isn't careful, their waste can lead to financial ruin, affecting not only themselves, but family members as well.

EXAMPLE FROM LITERATURE: As the eccentric owner of Toad Hall, Mr. Toad (*The Wind in the Willows*) has never been held accountable for anything. He buys himself a horse-drawn caravan and decides, willy-nilly, to explore the countryside. When nearly run off the road by a motorcar, he becomes enamored and abandons his caravan to purchase his own motorized vehicle. In a short period of time, he crashes six different cars and has paid a ridiculous amount of money in fines. His extravagance and irresponsibility eventually end up costing him Toad Hall, which he must fight to reacquire. One would think such a loss would have a sobering effect, but the end of the story sees Toad throwing a sumptuous banquet for his friends, once again, the master of "the finest house on the whole river." **Other Examples from Film**: Montgomery Brewster (*Brewster's Millions*), Willy Wonka (*Willy Wonka & the Chocolate Factory*)

OVERCOMING THIS TRAIT AS A MAJOR FLAW: Extravagance is only desirable when one has resources to waste. When the resources run out, so must the wastefulness. But inconveniencing oneself isn't always enough; as in the case of Mr. Toad, characters can run into personal difficulty and still not change their extravagant ways. It's more difficult to see one's wastefulness affect loved ones in a drastic, traumatic way and not come away changed.

TRAITS IN SUPPORTING CHARACTERS THAT MAY CAUSE CONFLICT: cautious, jealous, resourceful, responsible, socially aware, stingy

FANATICAL

DEFINITION: overly enthusiastic and blindly devoted

SIMILAR FLAWS: rabid, radical, zealous

POSSIBLE CAUSES:
Extreme dedication and loyalty to a cause, belief, person, group, or team
A zealous, religious upbringing
Peer pressure
A fear of retribution
The unswerving belief that one's opinion is right and just
Extreme pride (in one's religion, nationality, or heritage)
Brainwashing
A mental imbalance or mania
The need to belong to a group or be a part of something

ASSOCIATED BEHAVIORS AND ATTITUDES:
Gathering with like-minded people
Joining fan clubs, discussion boards, and other official support groups
Seeking to discredit or silence any opposition
Expressing disdain, scorn, or anger when differing opinions are offered
Proselytizing
Wearing clothing that reflects one's loyalty (team jerseys, concert t-shirts, etc.)
Altering one's appearance to look more like the object of one's fanaticism
Strictly adhering to a list of rules or regulations
Not thinking for oneself
Judging people based on their alliances
Offering financial support to one's cause or belief, even when one cannot afford to do so
Blind loyalty; accepting everything coming from the source as truth
Collecting memorabilia (posters, knick-knacks, religious artifacts, etc.)
Making personal sacrifices to show support (boycotting businesses, abstaining from activities)
Dedicating a large amount of time to activities revolving around the object of one's fanaticism
Paranoia and obsession
Becoming violent toward those who disagree
Placing conditions on relationships: *I only go out with other animal rights activists.*
Withdrawing from any portion of society that doesn't share one's beliefs
Using manipulation, brainwashing, fear, and other unsavory techniques to win people over
Expressing high emotion at games, concerts, rallies, etc.
Believing that the ends justify the means (deceit, breaking the law, terrorism, etc.)
Spying on fellow members to make sure they're behaving appropriately
Infiltrating opposing camps, governments, and schools to bring about change in one's favor
Thoughts that revolve constantly around the source of one's devotion
Feeling anxiety when the source of one's devotion experiences setbacks or difficulties
Inciting riots as a way of creating fervor for one's cause

Experiencing rage, despair, or grief when the object of one's fanaticism is brought low
Prejudicial thoughts and actions
Putting one's cause or belief above family and friends

ASSOCIATED THOUGHTS:
One day, they'll see that we were right.
They'll be punished for their disbelief.
Anyone who disagrees doesn't deserve to live.

ASSOCIATED EMOTIONS: adoration, amazement, contempt, determination, excitement, fear

POSITIVE ASPECTS: Fanatics are fiercely loyal, clinging to the subject of their fanaticism even when it's illogical. They are joiners, eagerly jumping into a cause or effort and looking for ways to participate. Because they're not easily swayed, they can be counted on to stay the course. Their loyalty stands firm even in the face of opposition, ridicule, inconvenience, and persecution, making them useful both for the hero (or villain) and the author.

NEGATIVE ASPECTS: Being a fanatic means dedicating a ridiculous amount of time to the object of one's fantasy, often at the expense of other, higher-priority relationships and obligations. Fanatics are so blindly loyal that they often can't be subjective, rendering themselves vulnerable to people who would abuse their allegiance. Hard-core fanatics also can't be reasoned with, making it difficult for loved ones to guide them away from situations and relationships that could be harmful. Fanatics want everyone to partake in the wonder they've experienced, and often ostracize others in their attempts to win them over. In extreme cases, their commitment can be so intense that they see any resistance as opposition that must be stamped out at all costs.

EXAMPLE FROM LITERATURE: Annie Wilkes (*Misery*) is Paul Sheldon's biggest fan. She's read all of his books and even named her pet pig after the main character in his Misery Chastain series. When Paul is in an accident near her home, she nurses him back to health—until she reads his latest manuscript and discovers that it will be the last in her beloved series. Unhinged, she locks him in his room, makes him burn the manuscript and forces him to write a new Misery Chastain story. When he tries to escape, she cuts off his foot. In the end, her fanaticism and inability to see anyone's viewpoint but her own lead to a showdown with Paul that results in her demise. **Other Examples from Film**: Lieutenant Kendrick (*A Few Good Men*), Gil Renard (*The Fan*), Trashcan Man (*The Stand*)

OVERCOMING THIS TRAIT AS A MAJOR FLAW: Being a fan is one thing; it usually only becomes a problem when intolerance is thrown into the mix. For a fanatic to overcome his flaw, he needs to see that people do have the right to their own opinions and viewpoints. Meeting someone from "the other side" who has qualities he values may humanize the opposition in the fanatic's eyes. Another technique would be for a zealot to view deceit within the organization he follows, which could logically lead to a sense of betrayal and disillusionment.

TRAITS IN SUPPORTING CHARACTERS THAT MAY CAUSE CONFLICT:
apathetic, cautious, flaky, indecisive, sensible, tolerant

FLAKY

DEFINITION: inconsistent in thought, opinion, or intention

SIMILAR FLAWS: fickle, flighty, inconsistent, unpredictable

POSSIBLE CAUSES:
Mental deficiency
Living in an environment that encourages free-spiritedness and unconventionality
High intelligence
A true lack of concern for what others think
Self-centeredness; refusing to see how one's choices are affecting others
A disdain for conventionality; not wanting to live by the rules of others
Being highly imaginative or creative

ASSOCIATED BEHAVIORS AND ATTITUDES:
Embracing "out there" philosophies
Indecisiveness
Disorganization and irresponsibility
Incoherent thoughts
Not fitting in with the rest of society
Inconsistency; frequently changing one's opinions
Social awkwardness
Not following through on responsibilities or obligations
Forgetting meetings and appointments
Misremembering things; not remembering past events as they really occurred
Not prioritizing well
Moving from career to career as interests wane
Following a non-traditional schedule
Impulsiveness
Keeping an unconventional appearance (excessive makeup, a strange hairdo, etc.)
Exhibiting unexpected emotional responses (laughing at things that aren't funny, etc.)
Becoming easily overwhelmed or anxious
Disloyalty
Overreacting or knee-jerk reactions
Proposing creative ideas but not being organized enough to make them work
Misinterpreting people's motives
Not speaking in a clear, linear fashion
Forgetting names, even after being reminded
Having a short attention span
Not finishing projects and tasks
Being highly spontaneous
Making reactive-based decisions
Speaking one's mind without a filter for appropriateness or considering who is listening
Jumping to conclusions or making assumptions

Rambling and going off on tangents

Overlooking the obvious (leaving home without keys or with one's makeup only half-finished)

ASSOCIATED THOUGHTS:

I know I agreed to this, but I wouldn't be any help. I'm doing her a favor by backing out.

I thought Ron was right, but Jeff makes sense, too.

Why do they think I'm weird? They're the weird ones.

I'm so sick of the Broncos. Time to root for a winning team.

ASSOCIATED EMOTIONS: conflicted, confusion, curiosity, indifference, irritation, unease

POSITIVE ASPECTS: Due to their unconventionality, flaky characters add interest to a story. Their defining characteristics are usually ones that don't normally go together, making them truly unique. Because they're expected to be unpredictable, flaky characters can usually get away with things that regular people can't.

NEGATIVE ASPECTS: Flaky characters don't live by the same rules as everyone else, making them unpredictable and unreliable. They may be perfectly content with changeability, flitting from interest to interest, but their lack of structure frustrates others and makes cooperation difficult. The flaky character's idea of success may differ from that of her co-workers, causing strife at work. Even simple conversation might be hard, since she may not adhere to the accepted norms for common topics such as politics, entertainment, and current events. Relationships may struggle when the flaky character supports a friend one day but then disagrees the next, or her lack of filter and careless words cause offense.

EXAMPLE FROM FILM: In *Eternal Sunshine of the Spotless Mind*, Clementine Kruczynski exemplifies flakiness from the very start. She's the one who initiates conversation with Joel, talks incessantly about various topics despite his obvious discomfort, then takes offense when he makes a joke. Her flightiness continues throughout their courtship, right to the very end; when things don't work out between them, instead of just ending the relationship, she has all her memories of him erased. **Other Examples from Literature and Film**: Polly Prince (*Along Came Polly*), Phoebe Buffay (*Friends*)

OVERCOMING THIS TRAIT AS A MAJOR FLAW: There's nothing wrong with individuality and free-spiritedness. The problem arises when the character's desire to be different is taken so far that it becomes difficult for her to connect and work with others. In this case, the flaky character must find the balance between being true to herself and adhering just enough to society's norms so as not to annoy and alienate others. As with so many other flaws, other-centeredness is the key—changing the focus from what one wants to what is best for everyone. The flaky character doesn't have to give up her individuality; she just has to adjust in certain circumstances to accommodate others.

TRAITS IN SUPPORTING CHARACTERS THAT MAY CAUSE CONFLICT: analytical, efficient, loyal, meticulous, proper, responsible, sensible

FOOLISH

DEFINITION: lacking good reasoning skills that lead to misjudgments

SIMILAR FLAWS: absurd, asinine, foolhardy, harebrained, moronic

POSSIBLE CAUSES:
Shortsightedness; an inability to see the consequences of one's actions
The desire to do what one wants, regardless of the consequences
Substance abuse
Mental processing deficiencies
Laziness
Ignorance; lacking knowledge in certain areas
Immaturity

ASSOCIATED BEHAVIORS AND ATTITUDES:
Engaging in dangerous activities
Becoming easily confused when decision-making is required
Being easily manipulated or influenced by others
Making off-the-cuff decisions, with very little thought
Overconfidence; not knowing one's limitations
Basing decisions on faulty premises: *If she can do it, then so can I.*
Believing everything one sees
Believing everything one is told
Becoming easily distracted
Repeating the same mistakes without learning from them
Expressing knowledge about topics that one knows very little about
Arguing one's point without logic or reason
Being reluctant to learn from others or take advice
Seeking to lead despite a lack of experience or qualifications
Doing what one wants even when it doesn't make sense
Ignoring the facts in a given situation
Relying on others to provide instead of providing for oneself
Vacillating between different goals and directions; not seeing things through
Not researching important issues when making decisions
Being victimized due to gullibility
Seeking the easy way out
A lack of common sense
Misjudging danger
Being a poor judge of character
Not realizing one is being manipulated or used
Considering only the positive and dismissing any negative possibilities
Obtaining injuries that could have been prevented
Acting silly to get laughs or to avoid consequences
Not considering the consequences

Taking on challenges that are dangerous or foolhardy
Being ill-prepared yet undeterred

ASSOCIATED THOUGHTS:
That looks so fun! I'm totally going to do it.
This is too complicated. I'll just call John and see what he's going to do.
Any idiot could run this office. They should put me in charge.
I can't believe this opportunity fell right into my lap. I'm going to be rich!

ASSOCIATED EMOTIONS: curiosity, determination, frustration, hurt, insecurity, reluctance, sadness, uncertainty

POSITIVE ASPECTS: Foolish characters can be counted on to do silly, irresponsible, or risky things, and as long as they can justify it to themselves, the *why* doesn't have to make sense. They also provide comic relief among their peers and add life to any party by their willingness to try anything. Frequently gullible and easily swayed, fools make convenient fall guys and yes men. This kind of character can be invaluable to both the hero and the author.

NEGATIVE ASPECTS: Fools are constantly getting themselves and others into trouble. They rarely learn from their mistakes, and so end up repeating them. Often, they complain about their difficult circumstances even though they themselves are to blame. Many foolish characters know that their decisions are getting them into trouble, while others don't understand why trouble always seems to find them. These kinds of internal quandaries can lead to a frustrated character battling insecurity, doubt, self-loathing, anxiety, or fear.

EXAMPLE FROM LITERATURE: Of the many fools in literature, Don Quixote (*The Story of Don Quixote*) is possibly the most famous. He spends the majority of the story deluded, both about himself and the world he lives in. His decisions are based on these misperceptions and usually end up bringing harm to himself and the people around him. **Other Examples from Film**: Lloyd Christmas and Harry Dunne (*Dumb and Dumber*)

OVERCOMING THIS TRAIT AS A MAJOR FLAW: Foolishness has many causes and each requires a different solution. If one's foolishness, like Quixote's, stems from deluding oneself and not seeing the world as it truly is, then an important event is required to force the character to see things as they really are. In many cases, foolishness is caused by simple ignorance. Knowledge (whether general or specific) is often the antithesis to foolish behavior. And it often helps for the fool to cross paths with someone wise; this gives the fool an opportunity to see what he could be.

TRAITS IN SUPPORTING CHARACTERS THAT MAY CAUSE CONFLICT: cautious, cruel, evil, mature, manipulative, obedient, proper, responsible, sensible, intelligent

FORGETFUL

DEFINITION: likely to not remember

SIMILAR FLAWS: absent-minded, preoccupied

POSSIBLE CAUSES:
Disorganization
Being overwhelmed or overcommitted
Avoidance (consciously or on a subconscious level)
Being preoccupied with other things
Being a free spirit rather than a planner
An inability to prioritize (forgetting things because they're not considered important)
Traumatic circumstances
Substance abuse
Brain damage

ASSOCIATED BEHAVIORS AND ATTITUDES:
Not writing things down
Missing appointments and meetings
Forgetting birthdays; giving gifts or cards after the fact
Missing important events (a child's recital or game, a spouse's work event, etc.)
Double-booking
Procrastination
Making multiple trips to the store when things are forgotten
Inefficiency
Giving gifts as a way of apologizing for forgetting
Minimizing the forgotten event: *It's just one game. He has one every week.*
Tardiness
Being easily distracted
Misplacing instructions or paperwork
Reading most of a book before realizing one's read it before
Accidentally spilling a secret because one has forgotten it is a secret
Being preoccupied with one's own thoughts
Making excuses for or lying about one's forgetfulness
Putting systems in place to aid memory (leaving reminder notes, setting alarms, etc.)
Worrying about forgetting things
Distracted listening
Missing deadlines
Running out of gas
Accruing interest charges because one has forgotten to pay bills
Burning food, forgetting to add a certain ingredient, leaving the oven on, etc.
Letting others down through lateness or ill-preparedness
Losing items
Getting lost

Worrying over what one is forgetting
Mental fog
Staring blankly or looking dazed
Difficulty recognizing people or remembering names
Making careless mistakes
Making multiple lists in an effort to stay on track
Forgetting passwords and security codes
Always apologizing for one's forgetfulness

ASSOCIATED THOUGHTS:
Oh gosh. That was today?
I'll take care of it later.
I can't believe I missed the recital. I'll send her some flowers to make up for it.
I could've sworn I wrote that down.

ASSOCIATED EMOTIONS: anxiety, confusion, defensiveness, frustration, nervousness, uncertainty

POSITIVE ASPECTS: Although frustrating, these characters are often laid-back and easygoing, not becoming flustered or overwhelmed when forgetfulness causes them trouble. They don't worry about the small stuff, and if they do miss something big now and then, they straighten things out the best they can and keep going. If there is conflict, instead of stewing over something for a long time, they are able to forgive (or at least forget) and move on to other things.

NEGATIVE ASPECTS: Forgetful characters are unreliable. Their absent-mindedness can make it difficult for them to progress professionally and puts a strain on personal relationships. Friends may feel undervalued and loved ones could harbor resentment at never being made a priority. Forgetful characters are also inefficient, wasting time, energy, and resources due to their lack of planning.

EXAMPLE FROM FILM: In *Finding Nemo*, Dory's forgetfulness leaves her isolated, as is evidenced when she tells Marlon that no one has ever stuck with her for so long. Though unintentional, her forgetfulness negatively affects those around her and most likely contributes to her being alone. **Other Examples from Film and Literature**: Leonard Shelby (*Memento*), Lennie Small (*Of Mice and Men*), Lucy Whitmore (*50 First Dates*)

OVERCOMING THIS TRAIT AS A MAJOR FLAW: Some people know they're forgetful and wish that they weren't, while others accept it as part of their personality. In order to change, a forgetful character needs to recognize that this flaw will eventually hurt her relationally and limit her success. When she becomes motivated, change can occur by simply becoming more organized: writing things down, frequently consulting the calendar, and keeping the scheduling area neat and orderly.

TRAITS IN SUPPORTING CHARACTERS THAT MAY CAUSE CONFLICT: efficient, meticulous, organized, responsible

FRIVOLOUS

DEFINITION: lacking seriousness

SIMILAR FLAWS: flippant, shallow, silly, superficial

POSSIBLE CAUSES:
Immaturity
A desire to have fun
Insecurity; the fear that one is incapable of undertaking anything serious or important
Desiring the attention one gains from being silly or superficial
A fear of responsibility

ASSOCIATED BEHAVIORS AND ATTITUDES:
Avoiding heavy topics of conversation
Frequent laughter
Shirking work, chores, and responsibilities
Being undisciplined
Being content to live in the present and not plan for the future
Adopting an easygoing, carefree attitude
Avoiding confrontation
Not being interested in important issues (politics, religion, world issues, etc.)
Declaring oneself inept in an effort to avoid work: *You know I can't cook. Let's go out.*
A lack of ambition or drive
Wasting time, money, and resources
Making decisions based on what one wants right now
Living for the moment
Selfish decision-making that negatively impacts others
Partying
Being the class clown or jokester
Speaking without a filter
Spending rather than saving
Engaging in risky behaviors
Being influenced by peer pressure and what others think
Dismissing advice or concern from others
Ignoring the rules
Laziness
Leaving friends behind to pursue a better entertainment opportunity
Being the one to say *Relax!* during times of stress or worry
Believing that things will somehow work out
Feeling content to let others make the tough decisions or be responsible
Growing bored when the mood grows serious
Getting over things quickly; not holding a grudge
Requiring change and stimulation to be happy
Being highly spontaneous

Having difficulty sticking to schedules or routines
Finding humor in everything
Avoiding venues that one finds boring (the opera, church, lectures, etc.)

ASSOCIATED THOUGHTS:
These people need to lighten up.
I wonder what they do for fun around here?
Why do they have to interrupt my shows with these stupid news reports?
Is it Friday yet?

ASSOCIATED EMOTIONS: amusement, excitement, enthusiasm, insecurity, satisfaction

POSITIVE ASPECTS: Frivolous characters are fun—the life of the party. They're usually easy-going and eager to avoid trouble or confrontation. Since fun is best had with others, frivolous characters are often friendly, outgoing, and open-minded. They can be quite resourceful, especially when it comes to getting out of work or creating new forms of entertainment. These characters also make good peacemakers, using humor to defuse tension and helping conflicting personalities get along.

NEGATIVE ASPECTS: Because of their love of fun and aversion to hard work, frivolous characters are often lazy and undisciplined. They shirk their duties, leaving the people around them to pick up the slack. Loyalty isn't a strength of theirs; since entertainment is their true love, they will drop what they're doing to pursue it, even if it means leaving friends or loved ones behind. Their irresponsibility makes it almost impossible to depend upon a frivolous character for anything important.

EXAMPLE FROM LITERATURE: Elizabeth Bennet's mother (*Pride and Prejudice*) is primarily interested in social climbing, dinner parties, gossip, and making a good match for her daughters. When her equally frivolous daughter Lydia runs away with a soldier, Ms. Bennet is mortified and takes to her bed. She is devastated, not out of grief for the loss of her child or worry for her safety, but because of the shame Lydia has brought upon the Bennet name. **Other Examples from Literature, TV, and Film**: Rachel Green (*Friends*), Daisy Buchanan (*The Great Gatsby*), Prince Naveen (*The Princess and the Frog*)

OVERCOMING THIS TRAIT AS A MAJOR FLAW: Most frivolous characters are intellectually capable of understanding serious matters, but getting involved is just too much of an inconvenience. To change, the character should encounter someone whose need brings the matter closer to home: a wayward teen requiring a role model or a single dad in danger of losing his job due to corporate greed. Empathy is necessary to trigger the desire to mature and insert oneself into a heavy situation.

TRAITS IN SUPPORTING CHARACTERS THAT MAY CAUSE CONFLICT: ambitious, antisocial, disciplined, fussy, grumpy, needy, persistent, proper

FUSSY

DEFINITION: needing or applying too much attention to detail

SIMILAR FLAWS: fastidious, finicky, nit-picking, persnickety

POSSIBLE CAUSES:
Obsessive-compulsive tendencies
Being raised by fussy parents or caregivers
Growing up in an environment that lacked order
Perfectionism
Control issues
A strict military or religious background

ASSOCIATED BEHAVIORS AND ATTITUDES:
Being organized and making lists
Expressing disdain for the free-spirited and those who fly by the seat of their pants
Seeing disorder as a flaw
Not allowing people to eat in the car or in certain rooms
Requiring that people remove their shoes before entering the house
Heightened stress when things are out of order
Choosing a career where meticulousness is an asset (accounting, housecleaning, etc.)
Keeping a neat appearance
Replacing items when they show the first signs of wear and tear
Thriftiness
Having fastidious manners
Pickiness
Criticizing others; "helping" them to improve by pointing out their flaws
Thinking about what to say in advance; researching and preparing for conversations
Obsessive cleaning; keeping things starkly neat and tidy
Examining one's possessions for flaws
An inability to relax when one is in charge
Pressuring others to behave ideally
Noticing when something is crooked or not in its place
Berating children for dirtying their clothes or making messes
Needing to get one's way or be in control
Requiring housemates or co-workers to adhere to one's standard of order
Avoiding disorderly places (kids' bedrooms, storage closets, a co-worker's office, etc.)
Having a results-oriented focus
Strictly adhering to schedules and routines
Hovering and being overly attentive to make sure everyone's needs are met
Washing clothes after one wearing
Researching merchandise before purchasing, so as to buy the best quality product
Scrupulously planning vacations and events
Obsessing over every decision; thinking of all possible repercussions before committing

Nosiness and suspicion
Expressing disappointment when others don't get the details right
Having a strong sense of self-respect and self-worth
Being excessively proactive (hiring roofers to replace shingles before a warrantee is up, etc.)

ASSOCIATED THOUGHTS:
This place is a pigsty—how do people live like this?
I don't like it here. The music is too loud.
Yellow plates? I don't think so. Any fool can see how they clash with the napkins!
Who moved my notepad?

ASSOCIATED EMOTIONS: agitation, anxiety, contempt, determination, frustration, satisfaction

POSITIVE ASPECTS: Fussy characters are neat, organized, and efficient. They can be depended upon to do exactly what they say they'll do and are usually very good at their jobs. Because of their high standards, attention to detail, and drive for efficiency, they can often be the catalyst for positive change in others.

NEGATIVE ASPECTS: Unfortunately, fussy people aren't usually content to control only their own habits and surroundings. They often require the same level of fastidiousness from the people around them, which causes friction and feelings of frustration or insecurity. This need for order often overrides their concern for others, making it difficult for them to deeply connect with people. Some characters' fussiness can become so consuming that it interferes with their enjoyment of life itself. They miss out on experiences and the opportunity to make happy memories because they are so distracted by the imperfections around them.

EXAMPLE FROM FILM: Felix Ungar (*The Odd Couple*) is possibly one of the most famous fussy characters of all. Obsessively neat and pristine in appearance, his need for order is his defining characteristic and is made more obvious and comical by his slovenly roommate. Throwing the two of them together is a great example of the strife and emotion that can be evoked by pairing a hero with someone who has conflicting characteristics. **Other Examples from Film**: Harold Crick (*Stranger than Fiction*), Detective Scott Turner (*Turner and Hooch*)

OVERCOMING THIS TRAIT AS A MAJOR FLAW: Fussiness is a tough flaw to overcome because it's so closely tied to one's personality. It's important to keep in mind that this trait is only a flaw when taken to an extreme. A person can be fussy without imposing it on others or making life more difficult for them. But when this line is crossed, it would help if the nit-picky character is forced to see that there are other things one should strive for above neatness and order, such as love, intimacy, serving others, and overcoming injustice.

TRAITS IN SUPPORTING CHARACTERS THAT MAY CAUSE CONFLICT: childish, disorganized, extravagant, foolish, lazy, playful, scatterbrained, vindictive

GOSSIPY

DEFINITION: reveling in the sharing of sensational news about others

SIMILAR FLAWS: blabby

POSSIBLE CAUSES:
Growing up in an environment where everything was everyone's business
Having a dramatic personality
Nosiness
A desire to elevate oneself by bringing others low
A desire for attention
Envy
Self-esteem issues
Vindictiveness; the desire to slander or harm others
A skewed sense of responsibility when it comes to the sharing of information
Feeling unfulfilled; needing a reprieve from boredom

ASSOCIATED BEHAVIORS AND ATTITUDES:
Having a high sense of self-importance
Needing to be in the know
Feeling an adrenaline rush at obtaining power via information and secrets
Giddiness
Being determined to ferret out secrets
Manipulation
Stretching the truth to make stories more interesting
Adding observations to tie events together (often incorrectly) in order to create drama
Spreading rumors
Exhibiting strong listening skills
Being two-faced
Speculating about people's motives
Questioning someone's character
Reading gossip magazines
Steering conversations away from serious topics toward ones that are superficial
Gathering with others who like to gossip
Sharing scandalous information under the guise of concern: *I thought you'd want to know.*
Eavesdropping and snooping
Being highly observant
Stopping to watch a spectacle (traffic accidents, arguments, etc.)
Taking interest in the entertainment world and the lives of famous people
Name-dropping
Claiming to be closer to someone (the subject of the gossip) than one really is
Mentally comparing oneself to the source of the gossip: *I would never have done that.*
Reporting gossip as fact
Giving disclaimers, to absolve oneself of responsibility: *Now, I can't confirm this, but...*

Sharing bad news with a sense of satisfaction or elation
Wanting to be the first to break a story
Calling or visiting those who are at the center of the gossip
Reading into everything
Being extremely aware of one's own words; carefully planning what to say

ASSOCIATED THOUGHTS:
Sarah isn't going to believe this.
Oh, how awful! I need to tell someone.
This is huge! Who should I call first?
Shameful. MY son would never have done anything like that.

ASSOCIATED EMOTIONS: amusement, anticipation, curiosity, eagerness, impatience, insecurity, satisfaction, surprise

POSITIVE ASPECTS: Gossipy characters always know what's going on. They're observant and resourceful—the perfect vehicles for gleaning and conveying information that the hero or other characters most want to remain hidden.

NEGATIVE ASPECTS: Gossips are hurtful. Regardless of the private nature of the information that is overheard, they share it out of a desire to shock others, gain attention, or be seen as knowledgeable. They don't usually make efforts to confirm their stories, nor are they concerned with the effect their prattle will have on the subject. Many a reputation and future have been irrevocably scarred by a gossip's careless tongue.

EXAMPLE FROM LITERATURE: Anne Shirley's neighbor, Mrs. Rachel Lynde (*Anne of Green Gables*), is such a nosey parker that she had her home built at just the right angle so she could keep an eye on the road that passes by her house. She knows every little thing about each person in Avonlea and sees it as her duty to pass the information on to others. **Other Examples from Literature and Film**: Lydia Bennet (*Pride and Prejudice*), the elephants in *Dumbo*

OVERCOMING THIS TRAIT AS A MAJOR FLAW: The best way to overcome a habit of gossip is to see someone destroyed by it. Gossips tend to think that the passing along of information is harmless. But when a busybody sees someone's life ruined by her thoughtless words, she may be less inclined to participate in it. Alternatively, allowing the gossip to be bit by the tiger she rides has nice symmetry as well.

TRAITS IN SUPPORTING CHARACTERS THAT MAY CAUSE CONFLICT: confrontational, controlling, courteous, defensive, discreet, loyal, private, violent, wholesome

GREEDY

DEFINITION: selfishly desiring money or possessions

SIMILAR FLAWS: avaricious, grasping, rapacious

POSSIBLE CAUSES:
The belief that if one is capable of taking something, one deserves to have it
A desire for power
Being overly competitive
Having experienced poverty and wanting to avoid it in the future
Extreme ambition
Envy; wanting what others have
Self-centeredness
Skewed values; choosing desire over need

ASSOCIATED BEHAVIORS AND ATTITUDES:
Obsessive goal-setting; always knowing what one wants and making plans to succeed
Wanting things that may or may not be good for oneself
Rationalizing one's actions: *If he's dumb enough to think it's a Rolex, I'll charge him for a Rolex.*
Having a bloated sense of pride in one's accomplishments and possessions
Watching for opportunities and taking advantage of them
Educating oneself in an effort to maximize one's chances to amass wealth or power
Discrediting the opposition (spreading rumors, sharing inside information, etc.)
Compromising one's morals or values to get what one wants
Always buying the best
Refusing to trust people, hedging one's bets
Needing to control all aspects of one's life
Rubbing one's success in others' faces
Stealing, if necessary
Envy
Skewed morals and ethics
Highly motivated and persistent
Giving expensive gifts as a means of showing off one's possessions
Comparing oneself to others and aiming to match their level of success
Strategically aligning with people who can help with achieving one's goals
Never being satisfied with what one has; always wanting more
Participating in activities one isn't interested in if they improve one's chances at success
Measuring success by wealth, status, or the quality of one's possessions
Working hard to meet one's goals
Persistence
Difficulty prioritizing; putting goals above people, even above family and friends
Being willing to make personal sacrifices in order to go after more
Having a sense of entitlement
Manipulation

Paranoia; worrying that one's success will be taken away
Investing in safety measures to protect one's assets (security systems, collecting blackmail, etc.)
Satisfaction that is short-lived
Resetting goals once the original has been achieved

ASSOCIATED THOUGHTS:

I want that.
If I can take it from him, he doesn't deserve to have it.
I'll do whatever it takes.
Oh wow—a first edition! Jan will turn positively GREEN when she sees me with this!

ASSOCIATED EMOTIONS: desire, determination, eagerness, envy, impatience, pride, smugness

POSITIVE ASPECTS: Greedy characters are persistent and motivated. Circumstances that might deter others won't faze someone who is so highly determined to reach his goals. The greedy character often has a healthy work ethic, working harder and longer than the average person to get what he wants.

NEGATIVE ASPECTS: Greedy characters are so focused on achieving their goals that people and relationships become expendable. Their desire can become all-consuming, causing them to sacrifice the values they once held dear. They may use people they care about or even actively plot to take what they have. Though a greedy character's focus may seem to be outward, it really is turned inward, toward the self and what one wants, making everyone and everything else secondary.

EXAMPLE FROM FILM: "Greed is good." This is the motto of Gordon Gekko (*Wall Street*), one of cinema's most notorious villains. Though extremely wealthy and powerful, he always wants more and will step on any and everyone to get it. **Other Examples from Film and Literature**: Hans Gruber (*Die Hard*), Tony Montana (*Scarface*), Daniel Plainview (*There Will Be Blood*), the Sheriff of Nottingham (the *Robin Hood* legend)

OVERCOMING THIS TRAIT AS A MAJOR FLAW: The problem with greed is that it robs characters of the ability to be content with what they have. To overcome it, they have to lose everything, or lose what it is they were trying to achieve all along, and see that life is worth living without it.

TRAITS IN SUPPORTING CHARACTERS THAT MAY CAUSE CONFLICT:

generous, greedy, gullible, nurturing, selfish, stingy

GRUMPY

DEFINITION: negative in nature; inclined to surliness

SIMILAR FLAWS: crabby, cranky, cross, curmudgeonly, dour, grouchy, ill-tempered, ornery, sulky, surly, unfriendly

POSSIBLE CAUSES:
Chronic illness or pain
Dissatisfaction with what one has or what one has achieved
Pessimism
An aversion to frivolity or silliness
Wanting to maintain a "tough guy" persona
Dementia
Substance abuse
Guilt

ASSOCIATED BEHAVIORS AND ATTITUDES:
Believing that one is misunderstood
Smiling or laughing infrequently
Having a downcast expression with obvious frown lines
Taking a pessimistic view of things
Irritability
Snapping at people
Expressing contempt for those with a rosy outlook
Arguing for the sake of arguing, without any real passion
Lethargy
Not wanting to participate in activities
Having a slumped body posture
Giving dark looks
Being reclusive
Lack of charity
Not taking joy in the usual things (food, entertainment, etc.)
Talking about unpleasant topics
Feeling or being sick more frequently than is normal
Speaking in a low, monotone, dispassionate voice
Bringing others down
Not showing excitement over anything
Expressing a range of negative emotions (frustration, anger, irritation, etc.)
Moping
Giving one-word responses or answering with heavy silences
Refusing to be social or interact with others
Ungratefulness; difficulty saying *Thank you*
Closing oneself off from others (hiding in one's room, eating lunch alone, etc.)
Choosing solitary activities (gaming, tuning out with headphones, etc.)

Poor communication; uttering grunts or *hmms* rather than words

Being unaffected by happiness or kindness

Criticism and sarcasm

Unfriendly observations and thoughts

Having a poor sense of community or unity

Being unable to feel enthusiasm for someone's good fortune or circumstances

Choosing to say nothing rather than what one really thinks in order to avoid conflict

ASSOCIATED THOUGHTS:

No use getting excited about the pool party when it's just going to rain later.

I can't believe I have to ferry Dan's friends around all week. Like I don't have better things to do.

I wish they'd just be quiet and leave me alone.

Fine, I'll go to Grandma's. But I hope they don't expect me to be happy about it.

ASSOCIATED EMOTIONS: annoyance, depression, indifference, loneliness, resentment, somberness

POSITIVE ASPECTS: Grumpy characters often have insight or experience in areas that have soured their view on life; this knowledge can benefit others—if the grouchy character can be convinced to share it. They can be opinionated; when a subject is important to them, they're unafraid to speak their minds, even when no one else shares their point of view.

NEGATIVE ASPECTS: Grumpy characters are pessimistic, and their tendency to focus on undesirable topics makes people uncomfortable. But despite their fixation on negative issues, they have no real desire to implement change; they just like to complain. They are rarely happy or content with anything, making it difficult for others to be around them.

EXAMPLE FROM FILM: Grumpy (*Snow White and the Seven Dwarves*) lives up to his name with his frequent frowns and pessimistic outlook. When the dwarves discover that someone is in their home, he assumes the worst. And when Snow White tells them her story, he wants to give her the boot out of fear of retribution from the Queen. In the end, he learns to love Snow White and shows true grief when she falls victim to the Queen's poisoned apple. **Other Examples from Literature, TV, and Film**: Eeyore (*Winnie-the-Pooh*), Oscar the Grouch (*Sesame Street*), Mickey Goldmill (*Rocky* series)

OVERCOMING THIS TRAIT AS A MAJOR FLAW: One might think that a character is grumpy because he wants to be, but for the most part, he's simply discontent and unhappy. He often mistakenly believes that no one will understand him or what he's been through, and so he doesn't bother to try to connect with people. If a surly character can find joy in a person or event, or feel valued and understood in some way, he can experience happiness and hopefully strive to achieve it more often.

TRAITS IN SUPPORTING CHARACTERS THAT MAY CAUSE CONFLICT: extravagant, foolish, friendly, frivolous, happy, irresponsible, nosy, nurturing, playful, uninhibited

GULLIBLE

DEFINITION: easily misled or duped

SIMILAR FLAWS: naïve

POSSIBLE CAUSES:
Believing that people are basically good and trustworthy
A lack of worldly experience
Living in denial; an unwillingness to see corruption and falsehood
Low intelligence
Immaturity

ASSOCIATED BEHAVIORS AND ATTITUDES:
Believing whatever anyone says
Not checking people's facts
Unwittingly passing on erroneous information out of a desire to help others
Giving money to strangers who claim to be in need
Being taken in by swindlers and cheats
Showing a lack of discernment; not being able to read people
Honesty
Empathy
Being generous with one's time and resources
Trusting others to do what they say they'll do
Believing a liar even when he has proven himself untrustworthy
Being easily swayed
Wanting to see the best in people
Believing in second (and third, fourth, etc.) chances
Having a strong faith; easily trusting in something without proof
Hearing what one wants to hear
Insecurity over what one knows or what one can accomplish independently
Refusing to believe that someone's intentions were less than pure
Making excuses for those who have proven untrustworthy
Allowing others to make decisions and trusting that they will make the right ones
Being satisfied with the information one is given and rarely requesting more
Viewing people who speak with conviction as experts
Blindly showing respect for authority
Complying without question, regardless of the task
Assuming that others are more intelligent or worldly than oneself
Voicing appreciation at being trusted and brought into another's confidence
Easily forgiving others
Believing someone's excuses, no matter how illogical
Viewing inconsistencies in another's behavior as harmless or unintentional
Being overly accepting of the faults of others
Having a helpful, cheerful, or optimistic attitude
Letting go of stress or worry if others indicate that things will be all right

ASSOCIATED THOUGHTS:
Why would she lie?
This email is so informative; I should share it with others.
Laura swore she heard Amy say she wanted me to ask her to prom, so I'll go do it right now.
Oh, look at that girl begging for money. I'm sure I have some spare change for her.
I'm lucky that man called about the virus on my computer. The software he sold me will sure help.

ASSOCIATED EMOTIONS: amazement, confusion, eagerness, happiness, hopefulness, satisfaction

POSITIVE ASPECTS: By and large, gullible characters are kind and generous with a great deal of empathy. What they expect of others, they often practice themselves, which makes them honest and reliable. While their naïveté is frustrating at times, their hearts are almost always in the right place.

NEGATIVE ASPECTS: While gullible characters are often reasonable, their blind belief in people can override common sense, making them easy marks for those who would take advantage. Although their generosity is commendable, gullible characters are often seen by others as weak and foolish because they are so easily manipulated.

EXAMPLE FROM LITERATURE: During Lemuel Gulliver's (*Gulliver's Travels*) many adventures, he accepts everything anyone says at face value. Even his name hints at suggestibility: *Gulliver* sounding so much like *gullible*, and *Lemuel* as a reference to the lemmings that blindly follow each other in mass migration, many of them to their deaths. **Other Examples from Film**: Clark Griswold (*Vacation* movies), Buddy the Elf (*Elf*)

OVERCOMING THIS TRAIT AS A MAJOR FLAW: Trust and generosity are positive, enviable traits, but they become negative when they're carried too far and turn into gullibility. To change, the gullible character usually must be cured of her illusions through an unfortunate encounter with a liar or shyster. Through this experience, she can overcome gullibility by realizing the importance of other values, such as common sense and discernment. When embracing such values and combining them with her inherent trust and generosity, the gullible character can still help others, but in a way that doesn't put herself at risk.

TRAITS IN SUPPORTING CHARACTERS THAT MAY CAUSE CONFLICT: cruel, cynical, dishonest, greedy, sleazy, unethical

HAUGHTY

DEFINITION: contemptuously proud in a way that disdains others

SIMILAR FLAWS: arrogant, contemptuous, disdainful, imperious, scornful

POSSIBLE CAUSES:
Prejudice
The belief that one's attributes make one more valuable than others (wealth, IQ, beauty, etc.)
Growing up in a family that expressed disdain for others
Being taught that certain people groups aren't deserving of respect
A religious, political, or nationalistic heritage that teaches superiority
Insecurity being masked by overcompensation

ASSOCIATED BEHAVIORS AND ATTITUDES:
Flaunting one's possessions, power, or status
Using one's status to intimidate
Manipulating others to get what one wants
Verbally disdaining the flaws of those outside of one's class
Treating those one considers lower-class as objects
Taking excessive pride in one's family, lineage, or accomplishments
Hiding scandals in an effort to protect one's reputation
Pretending to feel sorry for others because of the "misfortune" of their station in life
Dismissing certain groups of people as if they're not worth the effort
Seeking ways to improve one's status
Wanting to impress those above one's station
Refusing to acknowledge those one deems to be "less fortunate" or "inferior"
Believing that others are less intelligent than oneself
Having a good understanding of social politics
Generosity for show (making large donations to charities to improve one's status, etc.)
A desire to learn about or excel at interests one's class finds worthy (Cricket, horse-racing, etc.)
Viewing the world as *us* and *them* and the *haves* and *have nots*
Controlling others without guilt or remorse
Seeking to discredit others who get in one's way
Obsessing over one's lineage or social class
Making snide jokes and comments about others
Being hyper aware of one's image (being well-dressed, choosing friends carefully, etc.)
Close-mindedness
Creating or joining groups or clubs that are exclusive and discriminatory
Becoming hostile when one's status or authority is questioned
Using one's influence to ensure those deemed inferior do not gain esteem in others' eyes
Insulting others in an effort to put them in their place
Gathering with other "superior" people
Smirking at comments or actions against those considered lower-class
Bragging

Ignoring respectful rituals that others adhere to (shaking hands, smiling, etc.)
Condescending to or patronizing others
Smugness (standing tall, narrowing the eyes, looking down the nose, etc.)
Sharing one's "superior" knowledge and opinions in an effort to instruct others

ASSOCIATED THOUGHTS:
Who does he think he is, questioning me?
Clearly, she has no idea who she's dealing with.
What are THEY doing here?
What a hack. How did he get into this league?

ASSOCIATED EMOTIONS: anger, annoyance, confidence, contempt, disgust, hatred, pride, rage, scorn, smugness

POSITIVE ASPECTS: Haughty characters are overconfident and truly believe themselves to be in the right. These characters are often the first to step up in a difficult situation, eager to prove themselves or assert their superiority. They are bold in speaking their opinions and are unafraid to take action to further their beliefs and values. They can be counted on to put forward ideas and opinions when leadership or decision making is needed.

NEGATIVE ASPECTS: It's fine to be proud of one's achievements, but haughtiness goes a step further, requiring that someone be repressed for another to be elevated. For characters like these, there is no tolerance or open-mindedness, no true exchange of ideas or knowledge because they believe in their superiority. Although their ideas are often just opinions, haughty characters relay them as facts, and it's difficult to sway them, despite the flimsy or erroneous nature of their arguments.

EXAMPLE FROM FILM: As a decorated officer in the U.S. Marine Corps, Colonel Nathan Jessup (*A Few Good Men*) believes he's earned the right to a little disdain. As a marine, he feels superior to anyone in the other armed forces; his success at commanding troops at a dangerous outpost should therefore automatically garner him respect and admiration. And, as he says at one point to his nemesis, he doesn't want money or medals for all the work he's done. He just wants courtesy—respect, from those deemed his underlings. In short, he wants recognition for being better and more deserving than others. **Other Examples from Film**: Louis Winthorpe III (*Trading Places*), Otto West (*A Fish Called Wanda*)

OVERCOMING THIS TRAIT AS A MAJOR FLAW: The haughty character's flaw is really an excess of pride. Since pride often does precede a fall, the best cure for haughtiness is a de-throning—preferably by someone deemed inferior. If the arrogant one's cronies are able to witness the fall and validate the underling's victory, it will go a long way toward humbling the proud and starting him down the path toward admitting he was wrong.

TRAITS IN SUPPORTING CHARACTERS THAT MAY CAUSE CONFLICT: abrasive, cowardly, cynical, flaky, humble, ignorant, intelligent, judgmental, quirky, talented, uncouth

HOSTILE

DEFINITION: marked by open resistance or opposition

SIMILAR FLAWS: antagonistic, bellicose, militant, threatening

POSSIBLE CAUSES:
Imbalances in the brain
Being caught in an undesirable situation with no foreseeable way out
A history of violence or abuse
Chronic pain or insomnia
A history of being treated unfairly through no fault of one's own
Extended periods of stress, anxiety, or frustration
Trust issues

ASSOCIATED BEHAVIORS AND ATTITUDES:
Snapping at people
Verbally abusing others
Becoming enraged with little or no provocation
Looking for a fight; being confrontational
Resorting to physical violence
Issuing challenges
Using foul language
Committing acts of vengeance
Criminal activity (assault, vandalism, theft, etc.)
Having a dark, foreboding demeanor
Abrupt mood shifts
Violence against objects (pillows, doors, walls, etc.) in an effort to keep from hurting others
Prejudice
Having a closed-off stance
Keeping to oneself
Knowing that one's reactions are illogical but being unable or unwilling to change
Self-medicating
Experiencing frustration from the desire to fit in but being unable to do so
Listening to "angry" music and watching violent movies
Exercising as a way to burn off steam
Avoiding intimacy with others; pushing people away
Experiencing associated health problems (high blood pressure, heart problems, etc.)
Having a persecution complex
Expressing one's violent feelings through art or other creative outlets
Sleeping too little or too much
Depression
Thoughts of violence toward a certain person or group of people
Having a quick temper; lashing out without thinking
Road rage

Stubbornness
Being overly sensitive to anger triggers (the sound of someone chewing, etc.)
Converting hurt to rage and seeking violence to release it
Vindictiveness
Difficulty keeping a job or working with others
Viewing other people as inferior or stupid in some way

ASSOCIATED THOUGHTS:

I just want to hit someone.
If one more customer complains about the food, I'm shoving their head into the fryer.
I wish everyone would leave me alone!
They want a piece of me? I'll take 'em all on!

ASSOCIATED EMOTIONS: agitation, anger, anguish, depression, frustration, hatred, paranoia, rage

POSITIVE ASPECTS: Hostile characters are uninhibited. They do and say what they're thinking without fear. They're also able to focus their thoughts on one topic for long periods of time without distraction.

NEGATIVE ASPECTS: Hostile characters are damaged or wounded in some way. Whether mental, emotional, or physical, their pain causes them to lash out at others, furthering the cycle of abuse and inflicting more pain. Their inability to let things go creates a negative thinking pattern that becomes difficult to break. Such an unhealthy focus on the negative can also lead to health problems such as hypertension and stroke and psychological issues like panic attacks and paranoia.

EXAMPLE FROM LITERATURE: *The Taming of the Shrew*'s Katherine Minola is caught in a no-win situation. The only acceptable occupation for her is playing the role of the subservient wife and daughter. The idea abhors her so much that she rails against it, verbally and sometimes physically fighting every man she meets. Ironically, it is her hostility that makes it virtually impossible for her to find peace in the only available position for a woman in Padua in Shakespeare's time. **Other Examples from Film**: John Bender (*The Breakfast Club*), Clubber Lang (*Rocky III*)

OVERCOMING THIS TRAIT AS A MAJOR FLAW: Almost exclusively, hostility is caused by some kind of hurt. These angry characters tend to think the best way to deal with the hurt is through vengeance and withholding forgiveness, but these responses only prolong the pain. Hostility is best laid to rest by dealing appropriately with the root cause or event before it grows into a volatile situation. By working through small upsets, larger explosions can be prevented, allowing the character to build esteem by controlling his anger rather than letting it control him.

TRAITS IN SUPPORTING CHARACTERS THAT MAY CAUSE CONFLICT: controlling, cooperative, friendly, gentle, happy, timid, volatile

HUMORLESS

DEFINITION: having no sense of humor

SIMILAR FLAWS: boring, dull

POSSIBLE CAUSES:
The belief that frivolity is wrong
Snobbishness
High intelligence
Being overcommitted or overworked
A history categorized by sadness, making one afraid to embrace joy
A serious or somber personality
Growing up in a serious-minded family where fun and laughter weren't emphasized
Mental disorders (schizophrenia, Asperger's, obsessive compulsive personality disorder, etc.)

ASSOCIATED BEHAVIORS AND ATTITUDES:
Missing the humor behind jokes
Laughing only when prompted by others' laughter
Refraining from activities that make one feel silly (dancing, karaoke, etc.)
Taking things too seriously
Not understanding sarcasm, teasing, or double meanings
An inability to laugh at oneself
Acting properly and in control at all times
Difficulty relaxing
Being confused by flirting
Struggling with small talk
Rambling instead of getting to the point
Making no effort to fill awkward silences
Having niche hobbies that others don't understand or appreciate
Being unable to connect with people other than on a serious level
Examining a joke or comment to figure out why people think it's funny
Claiming to have gotten the joke, but not laughing because it wasn't funny
Misconstruing what others say
Smiling infrequently
Taking things literally
Being preoccupied with work or other stressors
Having a deadpan expression
Introversion; preferring to be alone
Awkwardness in social situations
Not joining a conversation unless being invited to participate
Being interested in serious topics (religion, politics, etc.)
Becoming irritated when humor is injected into a serious discussion
Stereotyping humorous people as silly, needy, flaky, or insubstantial
Attempting to make jokes that aren't funny
Growing agitated when people suggest that one lighten up

ASSOCIATED THOUGHTS:
Why does he think burp sounds are funny? They're disgusting.
If I stand in the corner and keep eating, maybe no one will try and talk to me.
Was that a joke?
They're so childish. Why won't they just do their work?

ASSOCIATED EMOTIONS: confusion, contempt, doubt, dread, embarrassment, frustration, indifference, insecurity, irritation, loneliness, nervousness, reluctance, unease

POSITIVE ASPECTS: Humorless characters can be very intense about topics, hobbies, or responsibilities that appeal to them. They often work well alone and can be trusted to follow through on their responsibilities.

NEGATIVE ASPECTS: Humorless characters don't know how to reply to jokes, sarcasm, or flirtatious banter. Their awkward responses make others uncomfortable, spurring people to either avoid them or label them as weird, strange, boring, or stiff. If people took the time, they might get to know them and see their many other beneficial and admirable qualities. But a humorless person's inability to connect, even on a superficial level, often keeps them from developing deep and meaningful relationships with others.

EXAMPLES FROM LITERATURE: Darry Curtis (*The Outsiders*) doesn't have time for a sense of humor. Since his parents' deaths, he is responsible for raising his two younger brothers in a rough neighborhood where trouble abounds. He doesn't like movies, doesn't read books, is very reliable, and almost always does the right thing. While these qualities make him successful as a caregiver, they make it difficult for him to connect with his youngest brother, putting a strain on their relationship. **Other Examples from Film:** HAL 9000 (*2001: A Space Odyssey*), Richard Cameron (*Dead Poets Society*), Spock (*Star Trek* series)

OVERCOMING THIS TRAIT AS A MAJOR FLAW: One of the problems with flaws is that they tend to drive people apart, making it difficult for them to connect with others. Humorless characters may never understand the concept of humor, and therefore may never be able to fully overcome this flaw. But if they focus on their positive attributes, letting them shine through, then this is what other characters will see, and their lack of humor will cease to define and limit them.

TRAITS IN SUPPORTING CHARACTERS THAT MAY CAUSE CONFLICT: frivolous, funny, mischievous, playful, rowdy, witty

HYPOCRITICAL

DEFINITION: pretending to be what one isn't; claiming to believe what one doesn't

SIMILAR FLAWS: artificial, dissembling, phony, two-faced

POSSIBLE CAUSES:
A fear of retribution
Wanting to please others
Being uncertain about exactly what one believes
Unreasonable expectations
Growing up in an overly strict, judgmental environment
Having a secret to hide
Having poor willpower and self-control

ASSOCIATED BEHAVIORS AND ATTITUDES:
Saying one thing but doing another
Embracing double standards: *It's okay for me but it's not okay for you.*
Expressing support for a cause but participating in activities that are in opposition
Lying and dishonesty
Judging others
Privately running down someone to whom one expresses loyalty to in public
Switching beliefs or loyalties when it is in one's best interest to do so
Playing the experience card: *I'm the parent*, or *I know more about this kind of thing.*
Making creative excuses or acting haughty when caught
Preaching forgiveness while holding grudges
Shifting attention by citing another's shortcomings: *Well, you're not sticking to your diet either!*
Lacking conviction in one's beliefs but being too afraid to admit it
Allowing peer pressure to overpower one's beliefs
Desiring opposing things and being unable to choose
Pretending that one's job, health, life, etc., is perfect when it's not
Taking extreme care to not be caught doing what one shouldn't
Having an excuse ready just in case: *Oh, this beer isn't mine. I'm bringing it to Uncle Steve.*
Greed
Arrogance and self-centeredness
Being opportunistic
Going to great lengths to hide what one is doing
Rebuking others for infractions that one is guilty of committing
Exhibiting signs of lying (fast talking, jittery movements, lack of eye contact, etc.)
Behaving immorally and then going to church to even the scales
Saying that one is a Christian yet acting rude, unkind, and judgmental of others
Engaging in affairs
Having difficulty accepting responsibility for one's mistakes
Feeling validated by the hypocritical behavior of others
Putting oneself first
Being highly observant

ASSOCIATED THOUGHTS:
I hope no one finds out.
Why can't I do what's right?
How can I spin this so everybody believes me?

ASSOCIATED EMOTIONS: confusion, desire, determination, fear, guilt, shame, smugness, uncertainty, worry

POSITIVE ASPECTS: Hypocrites are often discerning and able to read people. They are also attuned to opportunities that allow them to further their own interests. Because they're accustomed to living a double life, they're adept liars and are able to deceive others if required.

NEGATIVE ASPECTS: A hypocritical character abuses the trust of others and often will play upon that trust to get what he wants. He is comfortable with deception—so much so that the lie and the truth may become confused in his own mind. On the other hand, the unintentional hypocrite may truly want to behave a certain way but struggle to do so consistently. This lack of discipline can lead to insecurity, guilt, and more hypocrisy as he determines to hide his weakness from the world.

EXAMPLE FROM LITERATURE: The Pardoner (*Canterbury Tales*) is a self-proclaimed shyster—a preacher who sermonizes about greed and covetousness, the very sins that enslave him. When his sermons are done, he sells fake relics of healing and salvation. His only goal is to line his pockets, and if he can do it through lying and taking advantage of those who trust him, then so be it. **Other Examples from Film and Literature:** the Bishop of Aquila (*Ladyhawke*), Warden Samuel Norton (*Rita Hayworth and Shawshank Redemption*)

OVERCOMING THIS TRAIT AS A MAJOR FLAW: Hypocrisy can either be overt or covert; some people knowingly deceive others into thinking they're a certain way when they're not, while others truly want to be a certain way but struggle with weakness in that area. Both kinds of people need to do two things: 1) see themselves realistically and accept that reality, and 2) allow others to see who they really are. If there is a weakness to be overcome, it should be faced and dealt with head-on, without trying to deceive others.

TRAITS IN SUPPORTING CHARACTERS THAT MAY CAUSE CONFLICT: disciplined, gossipy, honest, loyal, nosy, perceptive, uninhibited

IGNORANT

DEFINITION: lacking knowledge or education

SIMILAR FLAWS: misinformed, primitive, uneducated

POSSIBLE CAUSES:
Growing up in a secluded society where knowledge of the wider world is limited
Being taught that one way of thinking is the only right way
Receiving an education that didn't address certain topics
Laziness
Immaturity
A lack of empathy
Insecurity

ASSOCIATED BEHAVIORS AND ATTITUDES:
Spouting nonsense as truth
Believing what people say without doing any fact-checking
Being innocent (due to a lack of experience) regarding how society or the world works
Sharing erroneous information without verifying the facts
Repeating what one has been taught without questioning whether it's right or wrong
Close-mindedness
Willfully disregarding the truth about certain issues
Arguing one's point with incorrect or biased information
Sticking to one's opinion regardless of the opposition
Speaking without thought for the feelings of others
Being unwelcoming to strangers
Strong sense of pride
Making (wrong) assumptions based on incorrect teachings
Knowing something is wrong but not caring because everyone does it
Holding onto antiquated beliefs because of pride in one's lineage
Being passionate about one's beliefs, even when they're wrong or hurtful
Hurling insults and attempting to cause emotional pain when one is challenged
Using outdated methods or practices to try to achieve one's goals
Prejudice
Applying stereotypes to a person or group without personally knowing them
Choosing what's easiest
Reluctance to embrace new strategies or methods
Racism
Making jokes about a person's looks or beliefs and expecting them to be okay with it
Being suspicious of anything new (people, ideas, technology, etc.)
Excluding people who are different from oneself (shunning those of another faith, etc.)
Making assumptions about people or places: *Just a bunch of do-gooders living it up in Canada.*
Being swayed by superstitions that have no root in logic or fact
Being loyal to, and depending on, authority figures who seem to be more "in the know"

Online trolling; airing inflammatory opinions while avoiding personal repercussions
Going to great lengths to avoid certain people groups
Being heavily influenced by one's peers
Having difficulty understanding the ripples of one's actions
Reacting with anger if one's obvious lack of knowledge is revealed
Condemning others for being different or strange

ASSOCIATED THOUGHTS:
The world would be better without those people in it.
I can't believe they let people like that out in public.
It's a free country. I can say what I want.
A car broke down on Old Creek Road? I'm surprised any of those hillbillies have a license.

ASSOCIATED EMOTIONS: anger, annoyance, denial, disgust, hatred, satisfaction, suspicion, unease

POSITIVE ASPECTS: Ignorant characters aren't easily swayed and are able to stubbornly cling to their beliefs. They also hold a deep loyalty to family or like-minded groups, protecting and defending them from any threat. Despite often being wrong, they're passionate about their opinions and are eager to share them with others.

NEGATIVE ASPECTS: Though misinformed, ignorant characters claim to be knowledgeable. They stick to their erroneous beliefs despite logical and well-presented arguments by people with firsthand experience of the subject in question. Often defensive and prideful, they say and do things that hurt others and damage their own reputation, killing their credibility and labeling them as idiots to the rest of the world.

EXAMPLE FROM TV: Archie Bunker (*All in the Family*) is a World War II veteran who's having trouble adjusting to the social changes in America in the seventies. He rails against anyone who isn't just like him—a Caucasian, working class, Protestant, heterosexual, conservative male—and often waxes nostalgic for the days when his kind of people were in charge. He clashes incessantly with his hippie son-in-law and African-American neighbor, using arguments riddled with illogical thinking. **Other Examples from Film and Literature**: The Ewells (*To Kill a Mockingbird*), The Clampetts (*The Beverly Hillbillies*)

OVERCOMING THIS TRAIT AS A MAJOR FLAW: Ignorant characters are oblivious due to a lack of knowledge. The best way to transform a character like this is for him to be confronted (and then educated) by someone representing the people group or issue about which he is so misinformed. Believing one thing to be true, then seeing the reality for himself, may change the character's mind and even lead him to become an advocate for change.

TRAITS IN SUPPORTING CHARACTERS THAT MAY CAUSE CONFLICT: cruel, generous, haughty, honorable, idealistic, innocent, intelligent, introverted, just, studious

IMPATIENT

DEFINITION: restless or short-tempered when facing delay or opposition

SIMILAR FLAWS: antsy, restless

POSSIBLE CAUSES:
Immaturity
A history of getting what one wants very quickly
Being prone to excitability
Needing instant gratification
Having great wealth or connections that easily enable one to get what one wants
An egocentric attitude and sense of entitlement

ASSOCIATED BEHAVIORS AND ATTITUDES:
Demanding that things be done right now
Scouting out the fastest way to achieve one's goal (picking the quickest check-out line, etc.)
Competitiveness
Becoming frustrated with laid-back, easygoing people
Being short-tempered
Snapping at people
Irritability
Moving at a fast pace; rushing
Nagging
Micro-managing
Making a nuisance of oneself (calling every day to check the status of a project, etc.)
Complaining when things don't happen as quickly as one would like
Taking over someone else's job so as to make things happen faster
Restless movements (pacing, drumming one's fingers, constantly checking the time, etc.)
Being ungrateful for what one has
Being intolerant of inefficiency
Rushing through chores and duties in a slapdash manner
Employing manipulation and coercion to make things happen quickly
Using a sharp or demanding tone of voice
Ordering rather than asking
Making snap decisions that end up causing more work
Constantly looking forward to the next big event or accomplishment
Invading other people's personal space in an effort to emphasize one's urgency
Helping whether it's wanted or not
Exhibiting a lack of charity toward others
Offering unsolicited advice on how to do things
Lowering one's standards or expectations in favor of expediency
Hurtfully pointing out another's shortcomings: *You're always late. What are you, part sloth?*
Honking the horn, cutting people off, speeding, road rage
Criticizing others for their inefficiency

Sacrificing quality; cutting corners
Reacting in a knee-jerk fashion that only complicates the situation
Acting judgmentally and having unkind thoughts
Single-minded focus on one's needs and wants
A "me first" mentality

ASSOCIATED THOUGHTS:
Lady, can't you freaking read? The sign says, "Ten Items Only."
Get out of the way!
What's taking so long?
I sent the email ten minutes ago. Why hasn't Kim responded?

ASSOCIATED EMOTIONS: agitation, anger, annoyance, frustration

POSITIVE ASPECTS: Because impatient characters want things to happen quickly, they often work quickly themselves. They are forward-looking, keeping their sights on what's coming down the pike, and are generally well prepared.

NEGATIVE ASPECTS: The impatient character's need for instant gratification makes it difficult for him to enjoy what he has. Things rarely happen fast enough to please him, so his thoughts quickly become negative as people and processes move too slowly for his liking. He has no problem complaining, whining, or kicking up a fuss in an effort to move things along. His impatience can also affect the people around him, as his constant griping and restless energy weigh them down. Ironically, a character like this may be slow at certain tasks when he's unmotivated, and will never see this as a double standard.

EXAMPLE FROM LITERATURE: While many may consider ambition to be Macbeth's tragic flaw, impatience also plays a large part in his ruin. When he hears the prophecy that he will one day be king, he is reluctant to let things happen naturally; with the nagging encouragement of his wife, he murders the present king and a slew of other people who could stand in his way. If he had allowed events to transpire organically, he may have had time to attain the strength of character that would have allowed him to succeed as king. But because of his impatience, things happen too quickly and in a fashion that plague his conscience, bringing about his destruction.
Other Examples from Film and TV: Dr. Lawrence Myrick (*Extreme Measures*), Biff Tannen (*Back to the Future* series), Dr. Sheldon Cooper (*The Big Bang Theory*)

OVERCOMING THIS TRAIT AS A MAJOR FLAW: The antithesis of impatience is contentment. For the impatient character to overcome his flaw, he must learn to be content with what he has. Gratitude is key—recognizing that what he has right now is worthy of thankfulness and enough to make him happy.

TRAITS IN SUPPORTING CHARACTERS THAT MAY CAUSE CONFLICT: cautious, easygoing, flamboyant, impulsive, indecisive, meticulous, nosy, organized, relaxed

IMPULSIVE

DEFINITION: acting on desires, whims, or inclination without forethought

SIMILAR FLAWS: hasty, impetuous, precipitate, rash

POSSIBLE CAUSES:
Living in an environment that encourages taking risks
A desire to live in the moment and without boundaries
Growing up in a home with rigid rules and expectations
Selfishness
ADD or ADHD
Having a near-death experience that emphasizes one's mortality
Irresponsibility

ASSOCIATED BEHAVIORS AND ATTITUDES:
Acting in response to one's emotions
Acting without thought for the consequences
An inability to see more than one or two steps ahead
Being legitimately shocked at the undesirable result of one's thoughtless actions
Seeing something that one wants and immediately going after it
Spontaneity; not planning
Chafing under too many rules or restrictions
Acting first, then expressing regret or remorse in the aftermath
Excitability
Impatience
Saying the first thing that comes to mind
Being easily distracted
Transparency; not filtering one's words or acting a certain way to project a desired image
Unwittingly endangering oneself and others by not thinking things through
Inconveniencing others when impulsivity takes over
Unpredictability
Curiosity
Jumping from one passion or hobby to another
Not following through on projects
Making mistakes and causing damage
Having a hard time staying still or focusing on quiet tasks
Exhibiting frustration and hurt feelings if one's actions are met with anger
Creating instability and trust issues in relationships
Not preparing for the future (not saving money, not creating a will, etc.)
Overspending
Being easily bored
Fearlessness
Acting on intuition
Trusting people too quickly
Unpredictability and irresponsibility

A lack of focus that requires twice as much time to complete a task properly

ASSOCIATED THOUGHTS:
That looks fun. I'm in!
We're wasting time. Let's just do this!
Forget it, I'm not waiting. I'll figure it out as I go.
Hurry up with the rules already, so we can get started!

ASSOCIATED EMOTIONS: curiosity, desire, eagerness, elation, excitement, impatience, frustration, regret

POSITIVE ASPECTS: Impulsive characters make life interesting and are often catalysts for change and conflict. Their ability to easily do and say what they please can be viewed by others as the ultimate freedom. If the impulsive character is also loyal to a friend, family member, or cause, there is no limit to what they would do in a time of need.

NEGATIVE ASPECTS: Impulsive characters create problems for those who value forethought and careful planning, causing friction in friendships. Because they're reactive, they don't always think about the big picture or how their actions could affect those around them. These characters can take a situation from bad to worse and lose the trust of others, who may come to view them as self-centered or foolish. They're often volatile, ruled by emotion, and prone to addiction because of their inability to apply the brakes to their own behavior.

EXAMPLE FROM LITERATURE: Anne Shirley (*Anne of Green Gables*) is perhaps the poster child for impulsivity. She's highly emotional and reacts primarily to what she's feeling at the time, whether that means breaking a slate over a classmate's head, dyeing her hair green, or accepting life-threatening dares. The fallout from her escapades usually comes as a complete surprise, and she ends up regretful for having gotten her friends and loved ones into trouble. **Other Examples from TV and Literature**: Lucy Ricardo (*I Love Lucy*), Romeo (*Romeo and Juliet*), Sonny Corleone (*The Godfather*)

OVERCOMING THIS TRAIT AS A MAJOR FLAW: The impulsive character needs to recognize that immediately acting on impulse will often lead to unpleasant consequences—for her and for others. She must learn to slow down, hold her tongue, analyze her options, and base decisions on thought rather than emotion.

TRAITS IN SUPPORTING CHARACTERS THAT MAY CAUSE CONFLICT: analytical, cautious, disciplined, mature, patient, responsible, unselfish, violent

INATTENTIVE

DEFINITION: habitually not paying attention

SIMILAR FLAWS: distracted, negligent, oblivious, unobservant

POSSIBLE CAUSES:
Being overworked
A deliberate desire to avoid or neglect
Having a scatterbrained personality
Being intensely focused on other things (a relationship, a work problem, etc.)
Apathy
A short attention span
Past hurts that distract a person from being able to focus on other things
Learning disabilities or ADHD

ASSOCIATED BEHAVIORS AND ATTITUDES:
Frequent multi-tasking
Neglecting one's duties
Thinking of other things while someone is talking
Leaving others to fend for themselves
Showing care for one person while neglecting another
Being unobservant; not noticing things
Assuming that whoever is in one's charge is doing just fine
Being easily managed or manipulated because one is unobservant
Wandering attention
Not engaging with people
Not participating in the current activity (watching TV instead of playing one's turn at cards)
Losing track of the conversation; missing a question that was asked
Letting silences drag out because one isn't invested in the conversation
Frequent absences due to forgetfulness
Being self-focused; neglecting or abandoning others
Not noticing the condition of something until it's too late (running out of gas, etc.)
Clumsiness due to a lack of focus
Completing projects with a poor quality of work
Losing things
Making other people feel unimportant through a lack of attention
Unintentionally creating distance in relationships
Being late or ill-prepared
Feeling trapped by responsibility or routine
Focusing so intently on meeting important needs that lesser needs are forgotten
Employing others to watch those in one's care
Always having appointments or engagements elsewhere
Being in the same house with someone without engaging with them
Selfishness; doing what one wants to do rather than what should be done for others

Feeling and expressing guilt when one is called out for being inattentive
Missing social cues that end up causing tension or awkwardness

ASSOCIATED THOUGHTS:
Why did Marcy give me that look—did I miss something?
I wish I could be everything to everyone, but I'm only one person.
I've got a message? I've had my phone all morning. When did I miss a call?
I just can't deal with this right now.

ASSOCIATED EMOTIONS: anxiety, conflicted, confusion, desperation, indifference, overwhelmed

POSITIVE ASPECTS: Inattentive characters—particularly parents—are often useful tools in children's and young adult books, when the hero of the story needs to be able to solve her problem on her own. Inattentiveness is also a good way to get a supporting character out of the way so things can happen to the hero.

NEGATIVE ASPECTS: For a variety of reasons, inattentive characters aren't able to focus on what needs attention. Their motives may be good or bad, but the truth is that communications falter, relationships suffer, and people are hurt when someone who should be paying attention is absent. The inattentive character is chronically unobservant, incapable of seeing what's going on right under her nose. Her lack of mental involvement makes it easy for people to manipulate her, either by taking advantage of her absentmindedness or controlling her through the guilt she may feel at not being able to do everything she needs to do.

EXAMPLE FROM FILM: The well-loved storyline of *E.T. the Extra-Terrestrial* is virtually impossible without an inattentive parent figure. Elliott's mom, struggling as a single parent and coming to grips with her recent divorce, is largely absent, enabling Elliott to stay out late, feign sickness to skip school, and hide an alien in his bedroom. At one point, she and E.T. inhabit the same kitchen, and she's so distracted that she has no idea. Inattentiveness is clearly a flaw, but in this case (and many others), it can be used to further the story. **Other Examples from Literature and TV:** the parents in *Mary Poppins*, Homer Simpson (*The Simpsons*)

OVERCOMING THIS TRAIT AS A MAJOR FLAW: In some cases, inattentiveness is unavoidable; a parent having to choose between meeting a child's emotional and physical needs will choose the latter. But in cases where inattentiveness occurs through selfishness or lack of prioritization, it can be overcome by recognizing the hurt one is causing or other consequences of neglecting one's duties. Once the inattentive character's focus shifts from herself to the object of her neglect, she can re-prioritize and use creative planning to better manage her time.

TRAITS IN SUPPORTING CHARACTERS THAT MAY CAUSE CONFLICT: affectionate, demanding, impulsive, needy, oversensitive, rebellious, rowdy, self-destructive

INDECISIVE

DEFINITION: prone to wavering between courses of action

SIMILAR FLAWS: changeable, hesitant, tentative, uncertain, wishy-washy

POSSIBLE CAUSES:
A need to please everyone
Perfectionism
A fear of making a mistake
Being uncertain in one's own mind
Insecurity
Having poor analytical skills
Growing up in a controlling atmosphere where one wasn't allowed to make decisions
Being responsible for past mistakes and being afraid of repeating them

ASSOCIATED BEHAVIORS AND ATTITUDES:
Taking a long time to come to a decision
Being as indecisive on frivolous decisions as important ones
Making a choice, then changing one's mind
Seeking the advice of many people
Over-analyzing and over-researching options
Nervousness
Watching others anxiously to see how they react to one's decisions
Immediately feeling doubt or regret upon making a decision
Allowing the arguments of others to sway one's decision making
Letting others choose
Letting chance decide (flipping a coin, picking a random number, etc.)
Feigning indifference: *Oh, I don't care*, or *I don't have a preference*.
Becoming truly indifferent, so as not to have to make any decisions
Freezing up when a decision is required
Frantically weighing possible options
Stalling for time
Relying on the advice of trustworthy people
Feeling selfish when one chooses an option that benefits oneself
Worrying about how one's choices will affect others
Worrying that the decision one makes will be the wrong one
Acting on the belief that there's only one right choice
Believing what anyone says on the subject in question
Choosing multiple options instead of just one
Becoming overly cautious
Wanting to please everyone; being a peacekeeper
Rambling when asked for one's opinion
Being obsessively careful to not hurt the feelings of anyone involved
Sweating, feeling a tightness in the chest, becoming flustered

Reliving past decisions where one was wrong and held accountable

Making excuses in order to avoid decisions: *Norman, it's your turn to pick the movie.*

ASSOCIATED THOUGHTS:

I wish someone would tell me what to do.

I can see the logic of both sides.

If I stall long enough, maybe someone else will just choose.

Oh gosh, what should I say?

ASSOCIATED EMOTIONS: anxiety, conflicted, confusion, doubt, embarrassment, fear, frustration, insecurity, regret, uncertainty, worry

POSITIVE ASPECTS: The indecisive character does truly care, or he wouldn't agonize over every little decision. Most people plagued with this flaw recognize it as a weakness and would change it if they knew how. Indecisiveness can also make a character more cautious and cause him to do his research before making a decision. From a story standpoint, the indecisive character can be a good source of conflict, making small problems worse and creating tension with others through their inability to commit.

NEGATIVE ASPECTS: Indecisive characters are flustered by decisions. Their fear of making a mistake or experiencing regret can even paralyze them, rendering them incapable of deciding anything. Once a decision is made, the second-guessing begins, sometimes leading characters to retract their choices and begin the agony all over again. This kind of wishy-washiness can be frustrating to others, particularly analytical types who are able to act decisively.

EXAMPLE FROM LITERATURE: Poor Hamlet is plagued with indecision. Should he trust his father's ghost or not? Should he kill Claudius or let him live? Should he avenge himself or take his own life? Though much debate continues over Hamlet's defining characteristic, indecisiveness is definitely a front runner. **Other Examples from Literature and Film**: Ashley Wilkes (*Gone with the Wind*), President Skroob (*Spaceballs*)

OVERCOMING THIS TRAIT AS A MAJOR FLAW: Success is often the outcome to being comfortable with one's decision-making skills. If a character is successful in arriving at the right decision, he'll feel more confidence and less stress when going through the process in the future. It also helps to realize that not every decision is life-or-death. Once faced with a truly tragic choice, the character may come to realize how foolish it is to agonize over simple decisions like what to eat for dinner.

TRAITS IN SUPPORTING CHARACTERS THAT MAY CAUSE CONFLICT: analytical, confident, controlling, cruel, domineering, efficient, excitable, greedy, impatient

INFLEXIBLE

DEFINITION: immovable in will or purpose

SIMILAR FLAWS: close-minded, implacable, intolerant, uncompromising

POSSIBLE CAUSES:
A need for structure
Having a rigid fundamentalist or military background
Firmly believing in right and wrong, black and white
Needing to control
A fear of being perceived as weak or easily influenced
Believing that one should be obeyed or respected without question
Being set in one's ways
Insecurity

ASSOCIATED BEHAVIORS AND ATTITUDES:
Seeing things as right or wrong, with no gray area
Close-mindedness
An inability to see things from a viewpoint that conflicts with one's own
Passionately arguing in favor of one's beliefs
Seeking to bring others around to one's way of thinking
Taking personal offense when one's beliefs are questioned
Refusing to entertain even the idea that the opposing viewpoint might be valid
Defensiveness
Stubbornness
Continuing on despite difficulties or setbacks
Beliefs that are resolute
Determination and commitment to one's path and beliefs
Speaking rudely or brusquely to the opposition
Allowing an argument to turn personal (using insults, questioning someone's integrity, etc.)
Dismissing dissenters as crackpots or flakes
Following a strict routine to reach one's goal
Resistance to change
Being dogmatic
Being willing to suffer hardship to prove one's convictions
Frequenting the same restaurants, stores, parks, etc.
Viewing those who would disrupt one's routine as a threat
Becoming agitated at interruptions
Resistance to new methods, strategies, or technologies
Self-centeredness
Using illogical arguments and outdated references
Living in the past
Employing bullying behaviors to silence the opposition
Stereotyping others based on one's beliefs: *If you ask me, all teenagers are delinquents.*

Dominating conversations
Being easily irritated or overwhelmed
Showing disdain for those who have lesser or opposing convictions
Taking on seemingly impossible challenges
Being undeterred by failure or setbacks
Clinging to one's beliefs despite obvious risk: *Tornadoes never hit us. I'm not evacuating.*

ASSOCIATED THOUGHTS:
I don't care what intellectual argument she comes up with; I'm not changing my mind.
Things were perfectly fine before those people came along.
She's entitled to her opinion—even if it's wrong.
What a bunch of idiots.

ASSOCIATED EMOTIONS: agitation, anger, annoyance, anxiety, defensiveness, desperation, frustration, impatience, reluctance

POSITIVE ASPECTS: Inflexible characters are intensely loyal to people, places, organizations, or beliefs. Their ability to stand firm in the face of opposition and logical argument is really quite remarkable. Their viewpoint is fixed, making it easy to act in accordance with their beliefs.

NEGATIVE ASPECTS: The inflexible character clings to his own way of thinking or acting without considering that there might be a different or better way. He isn't interested in improving himself or making things better; his only concern is with preserving his way of life. His stubbornness is rooted in selfishness, with no regard for the feelings or well-being of others. His resistance to change makes it difficult for him to adapt or evolve.

EXAMPLE FROM LITERATURE: Javert (*Les Misérables*) has dedicated his life to the law and persecuting those who defile it. He never considers the possible innocence of the accused or even the fairness of the law itself. Instead, he sees things in black and white: the law is right, and those who break it are wrong and must be punished. He's so inflexible that when he's faced with the criminal Jean Valjean's mercy and uprightness, he is unable to adjust his thinking to a new paradigm and chooses instead to end his life. **Other Examples from Film and Literature**: George Banks (*Mary Poppins*), Zeus (*Greek Mythology*)

OVERCOMING THIS TRAIT AS A MAJOR FLAW: Inflexible characters want to believe that their ideals and way of life can go on, undisturbed, for the rest of time. But without change or growth, they begin to stagnate or even unwittingly digress. In order to move forward, the inflexible character must recognize that his stubbornness is actually stifling, hindering, or even destroying him. Only then can he see that change is necessary and beneficial.

TRAITS IN SUPPORTING CHARACTERS THAT MAY CAUSE CONFLICT: adaptable, controlling, determined, flaky, indecisive, irresponsible, philosophical, tolerant, weak-willed

INHIBITED

DEFINITION: suppressing desires, impulses, and feelings

SIMILAR FLAWS: constrained, restrained, repressed

POSSIBLE CAUSES:
A mental disorder
A difficult or painful past
Being punished as a child for expressing certain desires or emotions
Sexual abuse
Passive-aggressive parents who toyed with their child's emotions
Growing up with repressed, emotionless parents
Feeling unsafe
Feeling imperfect or unworthy
Caregivers who showed preferential treatment of one sibling over another
Fear

ASSOCIATED BEHAVIORS AND ATTITUDES:
Trying to force a state of emotional numbness
Self-loathing
Apathy and indifference
Frustration at feeling something but being unable to show or act on it
Pulling away from people
Isolation
Paranoid thoughts that keep one from behaving in a certain way
Difficulty becoming intimate with others
Being unable to show vulnerability to others
Explosive reactions when emotions can no longer be contained
Avoiding crowds and events
Refusing to do anything spontaneously
Being unable to cry even when one wants to
Memory problems, forgetting things
Acting overly "proper," in an effort to control one's emotions
Wearing drab clothing in an effort to avoid attention
Adhering to habits and rituals (food choices, unchanging likes and dislikes, etc.)
Risk-averse behaviors
Resisting change
Worrying about losing control, and that it will lead to humiliation and shame
Refusing to defend oneself from attack or hurt
Thoughts of suicide
Wanting to speak up but being unable
Cutting or other self-harming methods
Depression
Nightmares and vivid dreams

Recklessness
A disregard for one's safety

ASSOCIATED THOUGHTS:
John makes me so mad! I wish I could just tell him how I feel.
Don't cry, don't cry, don't cry.
If one more person does me wrong, I swear, I'm going to go off.
Shouldn't I be upset about the cat dying?

ASSOCIATED EMOTIONS: anger, depression, dread, frustration

POSITIVE ASPECTS: Characters who are inhibited have a built-in defense mechanism against any event or person who might cause them psychological damage. Any emotions that they're unable to handle are muted by this coping strategy.

NEGATIVE ASPECTS: Repressed feelings, desires, and needs don't go away. Rather, they simmer beneath the surface, growing in intensity until the character explodes in an overreactive or irrational manner. This inability to express one's feelings in a healthy way can naturally lead to frustration, rage, and self-loathing. While the repressed character may want to feel and express his emotions, his fear of doing so can cause an emotional stalemate that leaves him devoid of all feeling. Because of their inability to open up, these characters find it very hard to extract enjoyment from life or create and maintain healthy relationships.

EXAMPLE FROM LITERATURE: To grow into his role of Dragon Reborn, Rand al'Thor (*The Wheel Of Time* series) is forced to make many large-scale life-and-death decisions. To effectively perform the job he was prophesied to do, he represses his feelings—especially those having to do with guilt and responsibility. As he attempts to mend the Pattern and defeat the Dark One, he internalizes much of the pain from the suffering he causes. His only sense of relief comes from his hope that, once the world is saved, he himself will perish. **Other Examples from Literature and Film**: Brick (*Cat on a Hot Tin Roof*), Nina Sayers (*Black Swan*), Beth Jarrett (*Ordinary People*), Neil Perry (*Dead Poets Society*)

OVERCOMING THIS TRAIT AS A MAJOR FLAW: If a character can acknowledge and accept the presence of good and bad emotions, then with practice and therapy, he may become comfortable expressing them. Probing the past to understand why one fears expressing emotion may be cathartic. Over time, the character may become able to release these pent-up feelings and desires in small amounts, and gradually become more comfortable doing so.

TRAITS IN SUPPORTING CHARACTERS THAT MAY CAUSE CONFLICT: callous, flamboyant, flirtatious, melodramatic, needy, nosy, possessive, promiscuous, pushy, uninhibited

INSECURE

DEFINITION: lacking confidence and surety

SIMILAR FLAWS: diffident, unconfident, unsure

POSSIBLE CAUSES:
Growing up with overly critical parents or guardians
Being surrounded by people who excel in areas where one is lacking
Believing that one is not accepted or liked by others
Abuse, neglect, or abandonment
A tragic, life-altering event
Guilt
Failure
A fear of rejection
Having an unrealistically perfect ideal of oneself
Having a dysfunctional relationship with one or both parents

ASSOCIATED BEHAVIORS AND ATTITUDES:
Exhibiting nervous behaviors when interacting with others
Keeping to oneself
Feeling like one has no gifts, skills, or talents
Being overly critical of one's body image
Avoiding uncomfortable situations (refusing to swim to avoid wearing a bathing suit, etc.)
Overcompensating for insecurities by focusing on other areas
Comparing oneself to others and feeling inferior
Sticking close to the people one feels comfortable with
Having unrealistic personal expectations (believing that one should excel at everything, etc.)
Obsessing over one's negatives and ignoring the positives
Blaming oneself when bad things happen
Having a low self-esteem
Worrying about what other people think
Desiring to fit in and be more confident
Negative self-talk: *I'm so stupid. Everyone must think I'm a total freak.*
Asking for advice before making decisions; needing reassurances
Looking up to those who are vibrant, spontaneous, and confident
Choosing to be alone rather than feeling inadequate around others
Entering into unhealthy relationships
Repeating the same relational mistakes
Driving others away through neediness and clinginess
Seeking acceptance through unhealthy measures
Giving in to peer pressure
Befriending anyone who offers attention
Self-destructive behaviors (drug use, promiscuous sex, developing an eating disorder, etc.)
Emulating those whose acceptance one seeks

Changing one's opinions and views depending upon who one is with
Being easily influenced or manipulated out of the desire to please and be accepted
Worrying about offending or letting others down
Losing one's sense of self
Over-relying on others to supply one's sense of worth

ASSOCIATED THOUGHTS:
Everyone likes Amanda. I need to be more like her.
I hate the cafeteria. Wherever I sit, people go quiet. Why can't I just be normal?
I bet they talk about me when I leave the room.
This project was much harder than I expected. I hope Beth isn't disappointed in my work.

ASSOCIATED EMOTIONS: anguish, anxiety, depression, doubt, fear, jealousy, loneliness, shame, uncertainty, worry

POSITIVE ASPECTS: From a story standpoint, insecure characters can easily be manipulated to act where others might hesitate. Their desperation can drive them to do things that others would not.

NEGATIVE ASPECTS: Everyone is insecure to a certain degree, but the character for whom insecurity is a defining trait will have many struggles. Insecurity causes constant doubt—of one-self, of the motives of others, of one's place and purpose in life. The need for affirmation and acceptance goes beyond that of simple goal-setting; it's a basic need that must be met, and if the acceptable methods don't achieve results, then the insecure character will use whatever means are available. When love is denied him, the insecure character will often blame himself, adding shame to the toxic mix of self-doubt and fear.

EXAMPLE FROM LITERATURE: Witty, brave, and romantic, Cyrano de Bergerac is also an accomplished fighter, poet, and musician. He has so much going for him, but his own hang-ups about his appearance keep him from achieving the one thing he truly desires. **Other Examples from TV and Film**: George Costanza (*Seinfeld*), Robert Barone (*Everybody Loves Raymond*), Todd Anderson (*Dead Poets Society*)

OVERCOMING THIS TRAIT AS A MAJOR FLAW: While human nature makes us wonder if insecurity can ever truly be conquered, it can, at least, be diminished to the point where it doesn't control one's life. To regain control, the insecure character needs to relinquish any unrealistic expectations he has for himself and replace them with achievable goals. He also needs to accept his flaws for what they are: part and parcel of who he is and what makes him unique.

TRAITS IN SUPPORTING CHARACTERS THAT MAY CAUSE CONFLICT: bold, cocky, confident, cruel, manipulative, pushy, timid

IRRATIONAL

DEFINITION: unable to reason or think logically

SIMILAR FLAWS: illogical, nonsensical

POSSIBLE CAUSES:
A lack of education
Growing up with few opportunities to solve problems or think critically
Mental disorders (personality or anxiety disorders, schizophrenia, etc.)
A prolonged lack of sleep
Living with chronic fear, anxiety, or stress
Drug or alcohol use
A dysfunctional upbringing (family feuding, members who tear one another down, etc.)
Suffering from delusions

ASSOCIATED BEHAVIORS AND ATTITUDES:
Worrying about things that may or may not happen
Paranoia
Envisioning the worst-case scenario
Panic attacks
Isolating oneself to escape perceived threats
Extreme emotional responses
Tying together ideas that don't go together or make sense
Being controlled by fears and phobias
Perfectionism; behaving judgmentally
Acting unreasonably while believing that one is being completely reasonable
Taking offense when one is accused of being irrational
Having unrealistic expectations
Not being able to think more than a few steps ahead
Repeating the same mistakes
Arguing a point with flawed reasoning
Contradicting oneself
Giving excuses for one's behavior that make no sense
Unexplained mood shifts
Self-destructive behaviors
Striving for unattainable goals
Personalizing events and situations; making them about oneself in some way
Lashing out at others for seemingly no reason
Aggression
Unwarranted suspicion; jumping to conclusions
Flying into a rage over something small
Refusing to believe things that have been proven to be factual
Becoming easily flustered
Allowing superstitions or omens to dictate one's actions

Blowing things out of proportion

Ignoring or not being able to read the social cues of others (signs of frustration or fear, etc.)

OCD-like behaviors meant to comfort (repeatedly washing one's hands to rid them of germs, etc.)

ASSOCIATED THOUGHTS:

Why is he working so much lately? I bet he's having an affair.

I needed to leave five minutes ago. I've got time for a quick shower.

Did she just ding my car? I'll kill her!

How dare he call me irrational!

ASSOCIATED EMOTIONS: agitation, annoyance, anxiety, confusion, dread, envy, fear, overwhelmed, rage, suspicion, terror, wariness

POSITIVE ASPECTS: The irrational character is a great vehicle for adding tension to a story since he's always saying, doing, and feeling things that don't make sense. Irrationality can be an effective catalyst in setting people off, testing a character, and adding conflict.

NEGATIVE ASPECTS: Irrational characters frustrate the people around them. They say things that don't make sense, respond to stress and stimuli in an abnormal fashion, and act in ways that create more problems. Irrational characters have unrealistic goals for themselves and expectations for others. They often can't see the logical results of their choices and have trouble putting together a reasonable plan of action. In extreme cases, irrational characters suffer from paranoia, panic attacks, phobias, and other debilitating disorders, making it difficult for them to connect with others or function normally within society.

EXAMPLE FROM LITERATURE: In Arthur Miller's *Death of a Salesman*, Willy Loman wanders back and forth between reality and memory, which he often recreates in order to view himself as the man he wishes to be rather than the man he has become. As the play progresses, Willy has more and more difficulty differentiating the past from the present. Eventually, he commits suicide as an irrational means of gaining the success he so desperately craves. **Other Examples from Literature and Film**: Othello (*The Tragedy of Othello, The Moor of Venice*), Marvin Boggs (*Red*)

OVERCOMING THIS TRAIT AS A MAJOR FLAW: Many cases of irrationality are caused by mental disorders and require counseling, medication, or behavioral or talk therapy to overcome them. Other characters might be irrational due to deficient cognitive abilities, which can be altered by compensating for the deficiency (making lists, talking things through with a trusted friend, engaging in logic exercises) and through retraining the brain to think in logical terms. Still others are irrational simply through their own stubbornness. These characters have the simplest cure: recognizing the wisdom in others, realizing that everyone can learn and grow, and beginning to identify and guard against irrational thinking.

TRAITS IN SUPPORTING CHARACTERS THAT MAY CAUSE CONFLICT:

analytical, decisive, efficient, paranoid, reckless, sensible

IRRESPONSIBLE

DEFINITION: refusing to be held accountable for one's actions or obligations

SIMILAR FLAWS: undependable, unreliable, untrustworthy

POSSIBLE CAUSES:
Desiring fun over work
A live-for-today-for-tomorrow-we-die mentality
A history of failures and disappointments
Low self esteem; believing oneself to be incapable, which leads to self-fulfilling prophecy
Growing up in a home where a strong work ethic and keeping one's word weren't emphasized
Selfishness
A history of acting irresponsibly with no consequences

ASSOCIATED BEHAVIORS AND ATTITUDES:
Not completing assigned tasks
Completing tasks in a slapdash manner
Growing bored with routine and needing stimulation
Encouraging others to shirk responsibility and have fun
Giving in to temptation and self-gratification
Following through on the tasks that one is passionate about and ignoring others
Finishing tasks only when a reward is offered
Leaving others in the lurch when a better opportunity comes along
Using charm, manners, and flattery to manipulate others and avoid responsibility
Hopping from job to job
Tardiness
Committing to so many projects that none get done satisfactorily
Believing that one is entitled in some way
Exaggerating to gain sympathy: *The baby has colic; I haven't slept in days.*
Placating others by agreeing to their requests without any intention of following through
Signing on for jobs while lacking the necessary skills, knowledge, or ability to achieve success
Quitting without giving notice
Frequently calling in sick to work
Waiting until the last minute to get things done
Letting partners or co-workers do the lion's share of the work
Signing up for the easiest or quickest tasks
Acting in a reckless fashion
Drawing other people into dangerous or irresponsible activities
Not properly caring for the people in one's charge
Slipping away without telling anyone
Lying to cover one's tracks
Criticizing responsible people for being too rigid, structured, or uptight
Never striving to improve; being satisfied with "good enough"
Fabricating other responsibilities or social engagements to avoid work

Making excuses when the work doesn't get done

Playing on people's guilt, sympathy, or weaknesses to get out of working

Laziness; looking for the easy way out

Not taking care of one's possessions

Forgetfulness and disorganization

Resenting the people in charge (teachers, bosses, parents, etc.)

ASSOCIATED THOUGHTS:

I hate mowing the lawn. If I wait maybe it will rain and I'll get out of doing it this week.

If I let it go long enough, someone else will do it.

We have a week to hand it in? I can be done with this in half-an-hour.

If it's a team project, I want to be with Brett, since he doesn't mind doing most of the work.

ASSOCIATED EMOTIONS: annoyance, desire, impatience, indifference, insecurity, reluctance

POSITIVE ASPECTS: Irresponsible characters are very good at avoiding the consequences for their actions, whether through manipulation, deception, diversionary tactics, or simple charm. Many of them are adept at reading people, which enables them to hook up with capable characters who are easily led. These qualities can be useful to one's hero.

NEGATIVE ASPECTS: The self-centered actions of irresponsible characters inconvenience those around them. Each time a project isn't finished or the work is completed in slipshod fashion, other people have to step in and shoulder the load. Their repeated attempts to buck the system are an affront to those who live by the rules. The laziness and indifference of irresponsible characters make it difficult for them to achieve their goals or rise above mediocrity.

EXAMPLE FROM FILM: Ferris Bueller (*Ferris Bueller's Day Off*) has made an art form out of escaping his responsibilities. His elaborate plans for skipping school include deceiving his parents, avoiding the dean of students, enlisting his peers, and manipulating his best friend into borrowing his dad's Ferrari. As with many irresponsible characters, if Ferris had dedicated as much time, energy, and enthusiasm to completing his duties as he did to avoiding them, there's no telling what he could have accomplished. **Other Examples from Film**: Jeff Spicoli (*Fast Times at Ridgemont High*), Maggie Feller (*In Her Shoes*)

OVERCOMING THIS TRAIT AS A MAJOR FLAW: Many irresponsible characters don't think that their actions are hurting anyone and so they believe that they're not doing anything wrong. Put them in a situation where their unreliability has drastic effects on either an innocent bystander or someone they care about, and they may see the need to change.

TRAITS IN SUPPORTING CHARACTERS THAT MAY CAUSE CONFLICT: ambitious, courteous, honorable, mature, pushy, responsible, workaholic

JEALOUS

DEFINITION: characterized by suspicion and envy

SIMILAR FLAWS: begrudging, covetous, envious

POSSIBLE CAUSES:
Experiencing painful betrayals in one's past
Insecurity
A fear of losing what one has (a material item, person, job, position, prestige, etc.)
Codependence
Dominance or competitiveness (needing to be or have the best)

ASSOCIATED BEHAVIORS AND ATTITUDES:
Comparing oneself to others
Sabotaging a rival
Negativity
Following, stalking, or gathering information about a rival
Being obsessed to the point of it interfering with one's other relationships or job
Striving harder to maintain one's advantage
Dissatisfaction with what one has
Good moods that wane quickly
Difficulty resting, relaxing, or turning one's thoughts to other things
Planning a rival's defeat
Discrediting one's rivals
Believing that one's rival enjoys unfair luck or advantages
Trying to persuade others of the suspected rival's lack of competency
Garnering favor with others
Being mean and petty
Putting others down to build oneself up
Refusing to acknowledge a rival's positive qualities or skills
Physically attacking a possible competitor
Being plagued by doubts that a friend or loved one is loyal
Accusing others of betrayal
Spying on people
Turning the conversation to one's obsession
Constantly checking to see if one is still on top
Becoming clingy or controlling
Possessively guarding one's things
Irrational thoughts, arguments, and actions
Becoming obsessed with the rival
Trying to outdo the rival in other areas in an effort to even the score
An inability to fully enjoy one's accomplishments in other areas
Telling others about the rival's faults and flaws

ASSOCIATED THOUGHTS:
Is he putting the moves on my girlfriend?
Who does she think she's fooling? Those are totally fake.
Is that another new outfit? How many dresses does one woman need?
This job is mine. I'll do whatever I have to in order to keep it.

ASSOCIATED EMOTIONS: adoration, anger, anxiety, defensiveness, desire, determination, hatred, insecurity, jealousy, paranoia, resentment, suspicion

POSITIVE ASPECTS: Jealous characters are driven and highly motivated. They'll do whatever it takes to keep what they have, even if it means going past the accepted norms. They're also persistent and goal-oriented, not giving up until they've defeated any real or perceived rivals and securing their control over the object, person, or intangible thing that was in danger of being lost.

NEGATIVE ASPECTS: Jealous characters are fearful of losing what they have and are suspicious of anyone with the potential to take it from them. Their dependence upon the object or person they wish to keep is unhealthy, bordering on obsession as their thoughts become focused on both it and potential rivals. Their determination to stamp out any competition may drive them to extremes that are illogical, illegal, and dangerous.

EXAMPLE FROM FILM: In *Snow White and the Huntsman*, the evil Queen is obsessed with maintaining her position as the most beautiful woman in the land. While regularly consulting her magic mirror to ensure her dominance in the beauty arena, she steals the youth of women to retain everlasting youth herself. Once it's determined that Snow White is indeed a rival who could bring about her downfall, the queen does her best to capture or kill her to remove the competition.
Other Examples from Film and Literature: Tom Ripley (*The Talented Mr. Ripley*), Baron Danglars (*The Count of Monte Cristo*)

OVERCOMING THIS TRAIT AS A MAJOR FLAW: One of the biggest contributors to a jealous personality is the unhealthy dependence upon whatever it is the character wants to keep. Be it another person, a position, or some other intangible, it is the character's desperate need to attain it and hold onto it that causes her to throw caution, values, and everything else to the wind. Losing the relationship or object and realizing that life goes on can be a catalyst for recognizing one's obsessive nature and working to overcome it.

TRAITS IN SUPPORTING CHARACTERS THAT MAY CAUSE CONFLICT: cruel, extravagant, flirtatious, intelligent, materialistic, sophisticated, talented, vain, vindictive

JUDGMENTAL

DEFINITION: inclined to judge harshly and unfavorably

SIMILAR FLAWS: critical, faultfinding, severe

POSSIBLE CAUSES:
Growing up with a strict moral code
Firmly believing in black and white, wrong and right
A lack of empathy
Needing to be right
Guilt or shame (needing to divert the focus from oneself to others)
Mental disorders (narcissism, obsessive-compulsive disorder, etc.)
The need to control
Envy
Fear
Insecurity; judging someone who has the same weaknesses as oneself

ASSOCIATED BEHAVIORS AND ATTITUDES:
Categorizing people into "types" or "boxes"
Making snap judgments about others
Arrogance
Assuming that one's beliefs are always right and anyone in opposition is wrong
Attempting to push one's belief onto others
Focusing on people's flaws rather than on their attributes
Believing that tough love will make people stronger
Being unwilling to put oneself in another's shoes
Vehemently arguing one's point of view
Avoiding or dismissing those with differing opinions
Having a holier-than-thou attitude
Intolerance for mistakes
Believing that duty is more important than freedom
Viewing anyone less disciplined than oneself as weak
Associating with like-minded people
Believing that one's role is to educate others on what is correct and acceptable
Being more concerned with facts or truth than with people
Intolerance and prejudice
Disdain for those who don't measure up to one's ideals
Having unrealistic expectations
Perfectionism
Forming opinions about people based on appearances
Clinging to first impressions
Using criticism to change the behavior of others
Doubting that others can truly change for the better
Assuming the worst of others

Difficulty displaying positive emotions
Rarely offering praise or pride in another's accomplishments
Being unsympathetic; believing that hardship builds character
Pursuing conversations that 'instruct or inform' rather than engage others

ASSOCIATED THOUGHTS:
Look at him. I can't believe he'd go out in public like that.
She could stop smoking if she really wanted to.
Once a liar, always a liar.
I would never do something like that.

ASSOCIATED EMOTIONS: annoyance, contempt, defensiveness, envy, fear, hatred, insecurity, pride, resentment, scorn, smugness, unease

POSITIVE ASPECTS: Most judgmental characters aren't afraid to speak up, which can help clear the air if it's needed. This can lead to open discussion and planning to change a difficult situation, rather than letting dissatisfaction fester. Because they believe themselves to be right, they say what they feel, even if it's unpopular or hurtful. Their vigilance for flaws makes them good at analyzing projects and processes, where they are adept at spotting issues before they become bigger problems.

NEGATIVE ASPECTS: Judgmental characters attempt to push their own ideals upon others, make snap decisions about people based on arbitrary criteria, and assume that everyone should be just like them. Their compulsive need to categorize everyone can hurt others and create unfair biases. While their actions are sometimes based on the belief that they're right, other times it comes from a darker place of fear, envy, insecurity, or hatred.

EXAMPLE FROM LITERATURE: Holden Caulfield (*Catcher in the Rye*) spends a great deal of time thinking about and passing judgment on others. They're phony, nosy, boring, moronic, slobs, or jerks. In Holden's mind, no one, with the sole exception of his sister, is any good. This constant negativity toward others is a major flaw that makes it difficult for him to accept his peers and develop normal relationships with them. **Other Examples from Film:** Comte de Reynaud (*Chocolat*), Kate Moseley (*The Cutting Edge*)

OVERCOMING THIS TRAIT AS A MAJOR FLAW: Judgmental characters are almost always intolerant and convinced of their own rightness. A good way to help these characters change is to prove them wrong in a big way by the person they judged to be inferior or incorrect in the first place. But change doesn't come easily, especially for a stubborn character who's used to being right all the time. This transformation will be more realistic if there were some niggling doubts already at work in his mind before the big showdown.

TRAITS IN SUPPORTING CHARACTERS THAT MAY CAUSE CONFLICT: childish, easygoing, flamboyant, ignorant, irresponsible, just, lazy, tolerant

KNOW-IT-ALL

DEFINITION: one who claims to know more than everyone else

SIMILAR FLAWS: braggart, windbag

POSSIBLE CAUSES:
An inherent need to prove oneself to others
Insecurity
The desire to share one's knowledge with others
Feeling inferior in other areas (physically, materially, etc.) and choosing to excel intellectually
High intelligence
Extreme pride in one's own intellectual abilities
A competitive nature
The need to dominate

ASSOCIATED BEHAVIORS AND ATTITUDES:
Being the first to answer a question
Talking over others
Interrupting
Compulsive studying and researching
Taking pride in always knowing the right answer
Speaking as an expert on whatever topic is being discussed
Eagerly participating in various opportunities to gain experience and knowledge
Frequenting the library
Always having a book close at hand
Keeping up with current events (reading the paper, watching the news, etc.)
Pondering and discussing big issues
Always wanting to have the last word
Arguing to defend one's point of view
Being a tattle-tale
Joining multiple groups, clubs, and societies to increase one's influence
Name-dropping
Being confrontational
Automatically assuming the leadership role
Speaking to teachers, professors, and tutors as if they were one's equal
Scoffing when others make mistakes or show their lack of knowledge
Becoming impatient when others are slower or inept
Being a loner
Having trouble relating to others
Feeling angry when one is left out of a decision-making process
Being achievement-focused
Reluctance to admit that one is wrong or doesn't know something
Frantically researching when one realizes that knowledge is lacking
Answering with certainty, even when one is unsure of the answer

Being bossy or pushy

Haughtiness or conceit; wanting to "rub it in"

Telling others how to do something better

Criticizing others for their poor dedication or lack of progress

Taking offense when someone else is consulted for information

Being hyper aware of one's image and the way one is perceived by others

Feeling less certain when emotions are involved

Being hard on oneself if one doesn't meet or exceed expectations

Overcommitting to others; taking on more responsibility than one can handle

ASSOCIATED THOUGHTS:

How can she not know this?

Lisa answered more questions than I did in physics class. I need to study more.

Why are they asking him? I know more about this than anyone.

Margret think she's the expert? Right. She didn't spend summer studying Latin like I did.

ASSOCIATED EMOTIONS: confidence, curiosity, desire, eagerness, excitement, pride, satisfaction, scorn, smugness

POSITIVE ASPECTS: Know-it-alls are often quite knowledgeable in their preferred areas of expertise and are eager to share what they've learned with others. Many of them have a love of learning and will spend much time and energy researching topics that interest them.

NEGATIVE ASPECTS: Know-it-alls are pushy in their efforts to prove their knowledge. In their eagerness to share how much they know, they can easily insult, dismiss, or scorn the people around them. When their credibility is threatened, they take it personally, becoming defensive and belligerent. Their need to always be the expert makes it difficult for them to learn from others or forge friendships.

EXAMPLE FROM LITERATURE: Hermione Granger knows the answer to every question and is eager to show it. Her tone often implies smugness and self-satisfaction, driving a wedge between her and the other students. Throughout the *Harry Potter* series, she matures into a true intellectual with a love of learning and thirst for knowledge, but in the beginning, she's simply a know-it-all. **Other Examples from Film and TV**: C3PO (*Star Wars*), Brainy Smurf (*The Smurfs*)

OVERCOMING THIS TRAIT AS A MAJOR FLAW: The difference between intellectuals and know-it-alls is that the former values knowledge for knowledge's sake while the latter craves recognition for her learning and insight. A know-it-all who can come to value knowledge over the recognition it brings will be more self-confident and no longer need to push her expertise upon others.

TRAITS IN SUPPORTING CHARACTERS THAT MAY CAUSE CONFLICT: cocky, controlling, haughty, insecure, intelligent, irresponsible, lazy, skilled, studious

LAZY

DEFINITION: disinclined to exercise or work; not energetic or vigorous

SIMILAR FLAWS: idle, inactive, indolent, languid, lethargic, shiftless, slothful, sluggish

POSSIBLE CAUSES:
Physical limitations
Illness
Growing up in an environment where one didn't have to work
An attitude of entitlement
A fear of failure (using laziness as an excuse to avoid applying oneself)
Valuing comfort over all else

ASSOCIATED BEHAVIORS AND ATTITUDES:
Resisting changes that would require more work
Ducking responsibility
Not volunteering for anything extra
Excessive sleeping
Sitting sedately for long periods of time
Avoiding all physical exertions (asking someone to bring them a phone or TV remote)
Taking elevators and escalators instead of using the stairs
Circling a parking lot, waiting for a better spot to become available
Ordering out instead of cooking
Wearing dirty clothes because none are clean
Procrastination
Doing a job the easiest way possible
Being content to let things remain the way they are
Lowering one's standards
Over-indulging in sedate activities (watching TV, reading, playing games on the computer, etc.)
Completing tasks in a sloppy, half-hearted fashion
Languid movements; moving at a slow pace
Selfishness
Expecting to be served by others
Waiting for other people to do necessary work (cooking dinner, completing a project, etc.)
Exhibiting no sense of urgency
Playing on the sympathies of others: *My back is still troubling me. Can you walk the dog?*
Having a messy car, house, or work space
Growing a beard because shaving takes too much effort
Having overgrown hair because one is too lazy to make an appointment to cut it
Borrowing items and not returning them
Poor hygiene
Poor eating habits
Obesity
Minimizing friends' problems to avoid having to get involved

Bumming rides when one lives a walking distance away
Encouraging others to relax and hang out to distract them from their problems
Going without rather than taking the trouble to fix something
Staying in rather than going out because it takes too much effort to get oneself ready
Believing one's critics have impossibly high standards and simply need to loosen up a bit

ASSOCIATED THOUGHTS:
Man, I'm so tired. I'm not moving unless I have to.
Pretty soon, someone else will come along and take care of it.
Emily is so picky. I think it's good enough the way it is.
That's too much work.

ASSOCIATED EMOTIONS: indifference, loneliness, peacefulness, resignation

POSITIVE ASPECTS: Lazy characters aren't easily rattled or shaken, and they tend to be fairly easygoing. Because change requires work, these characters don't rock the boat and are unlikely to willingly cause conflict or tension.

NEGATIVE ASPECTS: Because they're more concerned with conserving energy than with doing their best, lazy characters don't often fulfill their duties to the satisfaction of others. They tend to have a fixed mindset rather than a growth mindset and are unconcerned with improving themselves or their projects. Their selfish desire for comfort means that they don't usually pull their own weight; their work ethic is lacking and offensive to those who bear the brunt of the imbalanced load.

EXAMPLE FROM FILM: The opening monologue from *The Big Lebowski* identifies its hero as the laziest man in all of Los Angeles County, and possibly in the whole world. This is proven true when we meet The Dude and realize that he's an unemployed slacker with a penchant for bowling and smoking weed. When circumstances propel him into action, instead of embracing the opportunity for change, he spends the rest of the movie trying to regain his former lazy existence. **Other Examples from Literature and TV**: Templeton (*Charlotte's Web*), the supporting characters in *The Little Red Hen*, Mister Monday (*Keys to the Kingdom*), Peggy Bundy (*Married with Children*)

OVERCOMING THIS TRAIT AS A MAJOR FLAW: As with many flaws, laziness is rooted in selfishness. For a character to overcome it, he needs to see the negative effects of his actions. Perhaps his poor work ethic contributes to the downfall of his employer or co-worker. Or, if he truly cares about no one but himself, he might see that his laziness is destroying his health or keeping him from achieving other goals.

TRAITS IN SUPPORTING CHARACTERS THAT MAY CAUSE CONFLICT: enthusiastic, industrious, inflexible, judgmental, nagging, passionate, proper, severe, workaholic

MACHO

DEFINITION: aggressive pride in one's manly qualities, including a belief in one's right to dominate

POSSIBLE CAUSES:
Being raised by traditional people with traditional ideas
A fear of being perceived as feminine or unmanly
Overcompensation for masculine-focused insecurities (virility, being height-challenged, etc.)
A history of being bullied
Having an overly critical father figure

ASSOCIATED BEHAVIORS AND ATTITUDES:
Obsessively working out
Aggression
Bullying others
Steroid use
Domineering behaviors
Attending live sporting events or getting together with the guys to watch the game
Participating in extreme sports (bungee jumping, skydiving, drag racing, etc.)
Not backing down from a perceived threat or insult
Competitiveness; having to be the best
Refusing to ask for help
Getting into fights and arguments
Embracing danger as a way to prove oneself as manly
Taking excessive pride in one's possessions (showing off a new truck or one's trophies, etc.)
Chauvinistic tendencies
Using the "I'm the head of the household" reasoning to behave as one sees fit
Doing anything to avoid losing face in front of other men (lying, starting a fight, etc.)
Womanizing behaviors; ogling women, harassing women
Playing in fantasy leagues
Drinking to prove how much liquor one can hold
Proudly belching, farting, spitting, etc.
Eating large quantities of food
Eating "manly" foods (red meat, wings, chili, spicy foods, etc.)
Refusing to do "women's work" (cooking, cleaning, shopping, child-rearing, etc.)
Playing noisy, competitive, and violent video games
Subscribing to man-centric magazines (*ATV World, Penthouse*, etc.)
Boasting about sexual conquests
Cockiness
Telling dirty, racist, and otherwise inappropriate jokes
Domestic abuse
Watching action-packed or violent movies
Listening to aggressive music
Encouraging boys to be macho and girls to be subservient

Being possessive of the women in one's life
Reluctance to express intimate feelings
Using anger or rage to process uncomfortable emotions
Enduring pain rather than seeking help
Being jealous of other men's achievements (although not admitting it)
Living by a *do as I say, not as I do* mentality: *I can sleep around, but my girl better not.*

ASSOCIATED THOUGHTS:
As a matter of fact, I AM God's gift to women.
The house better be clean when I get home or Amy's gonna be sorry.
Those UFC guys aren't so great. I could take 'em.
It's 6:00. Why isn't dinner on the table?

ASSOCIATED EMOTIONS: confidence, envy, insecurity, pride, satisfaction, smugness, rage

POSITIVE ASPECTS: Many macho characters see nothing wrong with acting the way they do. Somewhere, they have seen or heard that this is the way real men behave, and they're trying to live up to that standard.

NEGATIVE ASPECTS: Macho characters are offensive on a number of levels. Their proprietary attitudes toward women stem from the belief that women are frail beings who need someone to take care of them. Most of these men have learned this lesson from macho role models in their lives who taught them that this is the way men relate to women and to each other. Their need to be the best and constantly prove their prowess hints at overcompensation and often does come from a place of insecurity—the need to prove their worth as a man.

EXAMPLE FROM FILM: In *Beauty and the Beast*, Gaston is as macho as they come. He shoots, fights, and spits better than anyone. Well aware of his strength and good looks, he realizes that only the most beautiful girl in town is good enough for him, and he's confident that any woman would be grateful for the chance to cook his meals, wash his socks, and provide him with a house full of strapping young boys. The only possible catch is his No-Thinking-For-Yourself rule. But since no woman in Gaston's mind has ever done that, he doesn't consider it to be a sticking point.
Other Examples from Film: Chet Donnelly (*Weird Science*), Joe Fusco Jr. (*While You Were Sleeping*)

OVERCOMING THIS TRAIT AS A MAJOR FLAW: Machismo is simple masculinity taken too far, usually out of a need to prove something. This character will need to recalibrate his idea of manliness—possibly through a positive male role model or a woman who refuses to accept his behavior.

TRAITS IN SUPPORTING CHARACTERS THAT MAY CAUSE CONFLICT: nagging, cocky, confrontational, controlling, timid, whiny

MANIPULATIVE

DEFINITION: attempting to influence the behavior of others for one's own benefit

SIMILAR FLAWS: finagling, maneuvering

POSSIBLE CAUSES:
An inflated ego
Exposure to conditional love (especially growing up)
Selfishness
A lack of self-esteem; insecurity
A need for power and control
The fear that one can't get what one wants through acceptable means

ASSOCIATED BEHAVIORS AND ATTITUDES:
Telling people what they want to hear
Passive-aggressiveness
Using subversive methods
Denying any accusations of manipulation
Putting the blame on others
Laying guilt-trips on people
Feigning hurt feelings
Using other people's secrets and weaknesses against them
Asking questions when one already knows the answers
Lying
Choosing which truths to share to encourage certain conclusions to form
Giving people the silent treatment to make them feel guilty
Buttering someone up before requesting something of them
Exhibiting highly emotional responses (anger, rage, vengeance) when one's bluff is called
Expecting immediate compliance
Preying on the weak or vulnerable
Repeatedly making the same requests until one's desires are met
Not taking *No* for an answer
Reconstructing past events to suit one's desires
Putting people down in attempts to gain control over them
Using threats
Living according to a dysfunctional sense of morality and ethics
Believing that the ends justify the means
Encouraging codependence
Using another's sense of guilt or shame to get them to comply
Having a *tit-for-tat* mentality: *I did this for you, so you owe me.*
Flattery; using one's charm to disarm people
Being confrontational
Distancing people from loved ones and others who might influence them
Attempting to cause people to doubt their own memories
Believing one's own lies

ASSOCIATED THOUGHTS:
I want that, and he's going to get it for me.
Dad will never let me spend the night at Jane's. Maybe if I get her parents to call and ask...
After everything I've done for them!
Being so nice makes me want to puke, but it's the only way to score an invite to her party.

ASSOCIATED EMOTIONS: denial, determination, doubt, fear, frustration, impatience, insecurity

POSITIVE ASPECTS: Manipulators are pragmatic and very good at succeeding at whatever they set out to do. They understand the complexities of emotion and how to use it to achieve a goal, and can easily read most situations. They're also able to cut off personal feelings that stand in the way of what they want. Manipulators are often found in positions of influence and power, where they can better use their skills to bring about a desired result.

NEGATIVE ASPECTS: Many manipulators think in terms of collateral damage, meaning that they get what they want even if bodies are left behind. Their "friendships" tend to be based on an exchange of power and influence, not on transparency and honesty. It can be difficult to trust someone who is manipulative, as there will always be doubt as to whether their words, actions, and emotions are genuine. Manipulators will often avoid asking questions or seeking help out of a fear of appearing weak, but will obtain aid through influential methods to get what they need.

EXAMPLE FROM LITERATURE: Becky Sharp (*Vanity Fair*) shamelessly and tirelessly manipulates others to further her own social standing. She pursues a number of men before landing a proposal, and then uses her wiles to further her husband's career by flirting with influential men and sucking up to rich relatives. She continues this pattern through the end of the story, when she finagles her son into financially supporting her despite her past neglect and apathy toward him. **Other Examples from Film, Literature, and TV:** Napoleon the pig (*Animal Farm*), Fagin (*Oliver Twist*), Marie Barone (*Everybody Loves Raymond*)

OVERCOMING THIS TRAIT AS A MAJOR FLAW: Manipulation is about control and achieving desired outcomes using subversive means. To overcome this flaw, these characters need to be confronted with their actions in a way that they can't slip out of or deny. Pairing them with a strong character who sees through their deceit and isn't afraid to challenge them may help them recognize their actions as self-serving and controlling and provide a catalyst for change.

TRAITS IN SUPPORTING CHARACTERS THAT MAY CAUSE CONFLICT: controlling, flaky, gullible, honorable, melodramatic, nagging, perceptive, unintelligent, weak-willed

MARTYR

DEFINITION: one who frequently takes on the victim role as a means of manipulation or to gain validation

POSSIBLE CAUSES:
Control issues
Having one or more caregivers who assumed the victim role
Living in an environment where one's value is determined by what a person can offer
Low self-esteem
Long-term resentment from an unfulfilled desire to be recognized for one's sacrifices
Needing empathy from others to validate oneself
A desire for love and acceptance

ASSOCIATED BEHAVIORS AND ATTITUDES:
Frequent complaining
Blaming other people for one's problems
Assuming that coincidental events have been done deliberately
Attempting to influence others by reminding them of what one has done for them
Blowing events out of proportion
Remembering events incorrectly
Never forgiving or forgetting
Being dissatisfied but taking no steps to fix the problem
Creating new complaints when old ones have been addressed
Encouraging dependence in one's children or family to ensure one will always be needed
Serving others, but expressing resentment when sufficient gratitude isn't expressed
Passive-aggressiveness
Depending upon others to make one happy or feel validated
Criticism and high standards
Difficulty forming healthy, balanced relationships
Feeling unappreciated by others
Volunteering to assist but later grousing that others never help out
Refusing help because one doesn't trust others to follow through or do the job as well
Begrudgingly accepting help, then complaining about the form it takes
Accusing others of not pulling their weight, but not affording them the chance to do so
Verbally cataloguing one's duties, responsibilities or past sacrifices
Expressing primarily negative emotions (anger, resentment, frustration, scorn, etc.)
Instigating arguments
Taking on too many responsibilities and then whining about being overwhelmed
Taking excessive pride in one's abilities or accomplishments
Complaining about aches and pains
Listing one's health problems
Using the needs of others as an excuse to avoid working on personal development
Using guilt to control others: *When I'm gone, I hope you'll appreciate what I've done for you.*
Reminding others of how much money one has spent on them

ASSOCIATED THOUGHTS:
Mary never offers to help organize these events. It always falls to me, year after year.
Sure, go ahead and play golf while I stay home and take care of the kids. Again.
They have no idea how much I do around here. Without me, this place would fall apart.
After all the things I've done for her, is a little appreciation too much to ask?

ASSOCIATED EMOTIONS: anger, annoyance, denial, determination, frustration, loneliness, overwhelmed, resentment, scorn

POSITIVE ASPECTS: Martyrs are often hard workers who will take on extra jobs that others turn down. They form strong attachments to the people in their lives and are generous when it comes to their time and energy.

NEGATIVE ASPECTS: The martyr's need for love is often met by the empathy or attention of others, which they hope to receive by proving how unappreciated they are. But their constant complaining quickly becomes a drain when those around them realize that the martyr will never be satisfied, that any resolved problem will merely be replaced with a new one. Although a martyr will express dissatisfaction with life, they usually refuse help, since their problems are necessary for them to gain the empathy they seek. After a while, they lose credibility and people begin to placate or ignore them, which heightens the martyr's need for validation.

EXAMPLES FROM FILM: Commodus (*Gladiator*) is a Roman emperor at the top of the political game in ancient Rome. Yet he is bitter and dissatisfied and blames the people around him for his difficulties. His father didn't understand him or appropriately reward him for his years of subservience. His sister doesn't appreciate him the way he thinks she should. The Roman people fail to adore him the way they adored his father, and instead turn their fickle affections to his enemy. In reality, Commodus' problems are of his own making, but he puts the blame on others, refusing to change or take responsibility for his actions. **Other Examples from TV:** Mrs. Wolowitz (*The Big Bang Theory*), Marie Barone (*Everybody Loves Raymond*)

OVERCOMING THIS TRAIT AS A MAJOR FLAW: The martyr's need for validation and empathy is what drives him to act the way he does. If he realizes that his actions aren't bringing about the desired result, it may be a motivation to change. It may also help to introduce a character who can show true caring to the martyr, proving that love isn't conditional upon how much the martyr does or gives.

TRAITS IN SUPPORTING CHARACTERS THAT MAY CAUSE CONFLICT: apathetic, callous, cruel, inattentive, independent, inflexible, selfish, perceptive

MATERIALISTIC

DEFINITION: overly concerned with acquiring material things; tying one's value to what one has or can display to others

POSSIBLE CAUSES:
A desire to maintain a certain image
A shopping addiction
Wanting to have what others have
A sense of entitlement
A low sense of self-worth
Growing up in a materialistic family or society
Growing up in poverty
Peer pressure
Being spoiled as a child; always being given what one wants

ASSOCIATED BEHAVIORS AND ATTITUDES:
Insisting on buying brand-name products
Thinking in superficial terms: *I wouldn't be caught dead in those jeans.*
Buying what one's peers have purchased
Dissatisfaction with one's own possessions
Being trendy (in regards to fashion, pop culture, etc.)
Making judgments about others based on their possessions: *What is she, destitute?*
Buying the latest technological gadgets
Using manipulation to get what one wants
Going on shopping sprees when feeling down or discouraged
Running up credit card debt
Living beyond one's means
Throwing extravagant parties
Driving luxury cars
Spending a great deal of money on spa treatments and hair and skin products
Engaging in expensive hobbies
Having a spending mentality rather than a saving one
Replacing items that are in perfectly good working condition
Wastefulness
Having a high-profile job
Attending an Ivy League college because it's considered prestigious
Enrolling one's children in costly private schools
Only shopping at certain stores
Critical of one's own body image
Showing off one's possessions
Choosing one's friends based on their social status
Constantly looking to upgrade one's things (cars, houses, jewelry, etc.)
Employing others (drivers, nannies, maids, chefs. etc.) as a means of firming up one's status
Social climbing

Being overly concerned with what others think
Taking great pains with one's appearance
Having plastic surgery done

ASSOCIATED THOUGHTS:
I'm getting the new iPhone as soon as it comes out.
Claire's going to be so jealous when she sees this!
They can't ignore me in this suit.
I'm so bummed about failing that test. I know what will cheer me up: shopping!

ASSOCIATED EMOTIONS: anticipation, desire, disappointment, elation, envy, excitement, impatience, jealousy, resentment, smugness, worry

POSITIVE ASPECTS: Materialistic characters take their image very seriously, so they're often fit and well-groomed. Their need to keep up with others can make them competitive in other areas, too, which can become a driving force to help them achieve their goals.

NEGATIVE ASPECTS: Characters who are materialistic are seldom satisfied with what they have and are always wanting more; while a recent purchase may keep them happy temporarily, they're soon back to needing another fix. These characters often play the comparison game, which leads to feelings of disappointment, envy, and low self-worth. Their system of validation (based on who has what) can make many of these characters judgmental and haughty, causing them to look down on, dismiss, or mistreat those who don't live up to their expectations.

EXAMPLE FROM FILM: Patrick Bateman (*American Psycho*) seems to have it all: a job on Wall Street, a high-end apartment, all the latest gadgets, and a platinum American Express card. But his impressive acquisitions leave him unfulfilled and empty. Overall, it is his excess and its pointlessness that drives him over the edge and into madness. **Other Examples from Film:** Cher Horowitz (*Clueless*), Daisy Buchanan (*The Great Gatsby*), Heather and Megan Vandergeld (*White Chicks*)

OVERCOMING THIS TRAIT AS A MAJOR FLAW: Materialism often develops when a character equates self-value with personal possessions. But the acquiring of things isn't effective in raising a person's self-esteem. Instead, it would help for the materialistic character to find pride and purpose in something that does matter: a talent or skill, charitable work, generosity, or serving others. Once self-worth can be connected to something that truly does build one's sense of value, the materialistic character can give up his fruitless pursuit and embrace something worthwhile.

TRAITS IN SUPPORTING CHARACTERS THAT MAY CAUSE CONFLICT: devout, efficient, jealous, judgmental, resentful, responsible, sensible, stingy, thrifty

MELODRAMATIC

DEFINITION: overly emotional; exhibiting overblown responses to situations or stimuli, often to create drama or draw attention

SIMILAR FLAWS: histrionic, sensational

POSSIBLE CAUSES:
A need for attention
A flair for the theatrical
Being self-absorbed
Being spoiled as a child
Paranoia
A desire to control the behavior of others
Being overly sensitive
Having melodramatic caregivers
Being praised for shallow or theatrical behavior as a child (being a child beauty queen, etc.)

ASSOCIATED BEHAVIORS AND ATTITUDES:
Making a big deal out of a small slight
Playing the victim
Using rapid speech and hand gestures
Speaking in an emotion-clogged tone
Raising one's voice to draw attention
Complaining and whining
Talking about oneself
Taking everything personally
Being overly sensitive to smells, shifts in temperature, and environmental changes
Making grand gestures and statements
Quick, extreme mood shifts
Difficulty being objective
Not prioritizing well
Avoiding situations that negatively affect one's comfort level
Manipulation
Not being able to let something go when one is upset
Being highly aware of others and their emotions
Making memorable exits
Believing that one's opinions and beliefs are the most important
Being energized by the admiration of others
Talking a mile a minute when upset
Speaking one's thoughts without hesitation or filter
Jumping to conclusions
Making scenes
Being overly sentimental
Giving in to overblown responses (screaming, crying, railing at God, etc.)

Believing that one's pain is deeper and more important than anyone else's
Hysterics
Being oversensitive to criticism or advice
Doing outrageous things to gain attention

ASSOCIATED THOUGHTS:
How could she say something so HATEFUL? I can't believe she would wound me like that!
Where is Andrew? I've left him THIRTEEN messages! He better call me, or it's over.
I'd rather DIE than wear that shirt.
I really hate my boss. Why can't he get fired or something?

ASSOCIATED EMOTIONS: depression, excitement, fear, frustration, worry

POSITIVE ASPECTS: Melodramatic characters are energized by being the center of attention, which makes them life-of-the-party individuals. They feed off of excitement and often have a good sense of humor and wit. Melodramatic characters have no qualms about sharing their feelings, so their moods are usually transparent to others.

NEGATIVE ASPECTS: Melodramatic characters can shift moods rapidly, leaving the people around them to wonder what happened. When upset, they can be reckless with their words and cause hurt feelings. If ruffled, their wit can turn biting and cut offenders down to size, regardless of whether the offense was intended or not. While some friends may be entertained by the drama for a while, many people find it stressful and will eventually abandon the melodramatic character to avoid the volatility.

EXAMPLE FROM FILM: Norma Desmond (*Sunset Boulevard*) is a has-been silent movie star determined to make a Hollywood comeback. She lives in a fantasy world, refusing to recognize her washed-up status and overreacting to any criticism. When jilted, she attempts suicide in an effort to regain her lover's affections. When that doesn't work, she ends up shooting him dead. **Other Examples from Film**: Anna Harrison (*Stepmom*), Allie Hamilton (*The Notebook*), Ruby Rhod (*The Fifth Element*)

OVERCOMING THIS TRAIT AS A MAJOR FLAW: For a character to break free of her melodramatic patterns, she needs to learn that life isn't all about her, that other people need attention, too. Getting to know someone who isn't normally in the spotlight but would benefit from a little extra recognition may help a melodramatic character to turn her focus from herself to others. It would also be beneficial for her to develop innate skills and talents that bring her joy, so she can see that her value isn't based solely on the attention she receives.

TRAITS IN SUPPORTING CHARACTERS THAT MAY CAUSE CONFLICT: controlling, gentle, humorless, inattentive, introverted, proper, inhibited, timid

MISCHIEVOUS

DEFINITION: maliciously or impishly troublesome

SIMILAR FLAWS: devilish, impish, tricky

POSSIBLE CAUSES:
Overconfidence; believing oneself to be more clever than others
Desiring power; liking to push people's buttons
A playful nature; wanting to have fun
Boredom
Curiosity; wanting to see how far one can go without getting caught
High intelligence
Immaturity

ASSOCIATED BEHAVIORS AND ATTITUDES:
Playing practical jokes
Easy laughter
Coming up with crazy ideas
Getting oneself and others into frequent trouble
Talking others into mischievous behavior
Leading a crew or gang of one's peers
Competitiveness
Embellishing stories of one's activities
Being fidgety or restless
Curiosity; wondering what will happen
Becoming easily bored
Needing constant stimulation
Taking foolish risks
Being charismatic
Taking a prank too far
Cockiness
Not seeing how practical jokes can cause others pain or frustration
Engaging in petty actions meant to inconvenience others (pulling a fire alarm, etc.)
Deliberately doing things that annoy another person
A fascination with rules, limits and boundaries, and the desire to push past them
Playing one parent or authority figure against the other
Having strong problem-solving skills
Vindictiveness
Making jokes at the expense of others
A lack of seriousness
Poor judgment
Impatience
Playing ill-timed jokes or pranks on purpose to get a bigger reaction
Claiming that weak or stupid people deserve to be duped

Being entertained when others are upset or in a state of chaos
Viewing one's behavior as harmless when it isn't
Escalating behaviors; needing to outdo one's last prank or activity
Damaging the reputations of others
Using trickiness to get back at others for perceived wrongs

ASSOCIATED THOUGHTS:

Dad never uses the shed, so he won't notice that the tractor's missing.
So Mara is being Miss Bossypants today, is she? Wait until she finds the mouse under her pillow.
The firecracker prank was good, but this time, let's try a bomb!
I'm so bored! There has to be something fun to do around here.

ASSOCIATED EMOTIONS: amusement, anticipation, confidence, curiosity, eagerness, smugness

POSITIVE ASPECTS: Mischievous characters are fun-loving. Often highly intelligent and curious, they're constantly thinking, their brains churning out new and inventive ways to pass the time. Their fearlessness and enthusiasm are enviable qualities, drawing others to them. When they do get into trouble for their mischief, they're often able to charm their way out of it.

NEGATIVE ASPECTS: Whatever the reason behind it, mischievous behavior almost always negatively impacts others, causing inconvenience, embarrassment, or minor chaos. Though mischievous characters may downplay the results or plead ignorance, there's often a not-so-nice reason for their continued engagement in these activities. Because they're good at reading others, these characters can be adept manipulators, and on the occasions when they do get caught, they're not above using deceit to escape consequences.

EXAMPLE FROM TV: Bart Simpson (*The Simpsons*) is a rebellious boy whose penchant for mischief frequently causes trouble. His shenanigans include prank calling Moe the bartender, writing messages on the school chalkboard, shoplifting, and streaking. While he isn't bad-hearted, his impatient and rowdy nature often spurs him into mischievous behavior. **Other Examples from TV and Literature**: Dennis Mitchell (*Dennis the Menace*), Peeves the Poltergeist (*Harry Potter* series)

OVERCOMING THIS TRAIT AS A MAJOR FLAW: While most mischievous characters aren't cruel, they do get a kick out of creating chaos and seeing people lose their cool. This disrespect for others is the root of the problem and must be overcome for these characters to be taken seriously. Recognizing the long-term hurt or humiliation that one has caused through selfish or thoughtless pranks may encourage a mischievous character to rethink his actions.

TRAITS IN SUPPORTING CHARACTERS THAT MAY CAUSE CONFLICT:

apathetic, cowardly, fussy, humorless, inflexible, melodramatic, nervous, sensitive, worrywart

MORBID

DEFINITION: having a bleak or gruesome outlook or an unhealthy interest in death

SIMILAR FLAWS: bleak, depressing

POSSIBLE CAUSES:
Depression
Being raised in an environment where death and disease was a matter of course
Having a deep (or dark) interest in the unknown or one's own mortality
Having experienced more than one's share of death and loss
Curiosity about the afterlife

ASSOCIATED BEHAVIORS AND ATTITUDES:
Asking questions or making death-related observations that cause others discomfort
A lack of fear regarding death
Closely examining a person or animal in a stage of illness, pain, or death
Maintaining strong eye contact when most would avert their gaze from something unpleasant
Reaching out to touch or handle the dead or dying
Excitement at viewing some aspect of death
Isolation
Having few friendships
A negative or bleak outlook
Difficulty relating to other people
Collecting items that symbolize death in some way (books on illnesses, pinned insects, etc.)
Discussing death or pain in a matter-of-fact way
Expressing interest in the afterlife and/or reincarnation
Expecting or hoping for bad things to happen
Staring into the eyes of something dying or dead
Wondering what happens after death
Researching death and different cultural beliefs surrounding it
Frequenting gravesides and graveyards
Wanting to attend funerals (especially if one has never done so)
Thinking about the preparations a body goes through before burial
Planning one's own "final arrangements" (cremation, burial, etc.)
Questioning people who are close to death
Showing an interest in near-death experiences
Imagining and fantasizing about different types of death (drowning, burning, poisoning, etc.)
Not being grossed out by decay
Feeling "alive" at the sight of blood
Wanting to touch a dead body to know how it feels
Depression
Feeling that there is no point to life
Desiring death
Thoughts of suicide
Creating a suicide plan or attempting it to see if one could actually go through with it

ASSOCIATED THOUGHTS:

I wonder if it hurts when you die.

I sure hope the afterlife is better than this one.

I'd rather die in a fire than drown. With smoke, you pass out, but in water, you feel everything.

Lilly is different since her dad died. It must be hard to know he's never coming back.

If I were going to kill myself, how would I do it?

ASSOCIATED EMOTIONS: apathy, curiosity, depression, disgust, somberness

POSITIVE ASPECTS: Characters with morbid interests are often able to derive answers to questions that most people are too unnerved to explore. Death is a natural occurrence, and sometimes through trying to understand it, morbid characters can reach a deeper appreciation of life.

NEGATIVE ASPECTS: While curiosity is one thing, morbid characters often become fixated on death and the dead. Their obsession may take an unhealthy turn whereby they become more interested in the next life than this one, opening them up to a flirtatious relationship with death. This dark fascination is unsettling to others, who may eventually fear and exclude morbid characters, further isolating them and reinforcing their thoughts of escaping this world.

EXAMPLE FROM LITERATURE: Victor Frankenstein, the mad scientist from Mary Shelley's *Frankenstein*, was so obsessed with life and death that he experimented on the dead, combining the organs from different donors and reanimating a corpse, thereby creating life. **Other Examples from Literature and Film**: Hamlet (*The Tragedy of Hamlet, Prince of Denmark*), Hades (*Greek Mythology*), Lydia Deetz (*Beetlejuice*)

OVERCOMING THIS TRAIT AS A MAJOR FLAW: If morbidity is the major flaw a character must overcome to achieve his goals, it might help for him to be exposed to something incredibly life-affirming and meaningful. This experience may bring about a transformation that turns him away from obsessing about death to embracing life. Love, friendship, personal fulfillment, or discovering a higher purpose might help him make the change.

TRAITS IN SUPPORTING CHARACTERS THAT MAY CAUSE CONFLICT: energetic, flamboyant, funny, gentle, happy, idealistic, kind, optimistic, wholesome, worrywart

NAGGING

DEFINITION: continually scolding and verbally prodding others in an unwelcome fashion

SIMILAR FLAWS: shrewish

POSSIBLE CAUSES:
Being highly devout
Believing that it's one's job to guide and correct others for their own good
A lack of trust
Control issues
Insecurities that cause one to live vicariously through others

ASSOCIATED BEHAVIORS AND ATTITUDES:
Continually checking up on others to monitor their progress
Using guilt or other underhanded techniques to manipulate behavior
Assuming that people will fall short of one's expectations
Projecting a desire for achievement and acclaim onto others
Never being content; always wanting more from others
Watching for signs that others are not dedicated to their duties
Being hyper aware while watching a student or protégé
Using uptight body language (arms crossed, stiff posture, tense muscles)
Infrequent smiles
Asking questions that contain reminders: *You promised to call Dad after work tonight, right?*
Expressing anger and frustration when others don't immediately comply
Giving criticism and instruction rather than encouragement
Having high expectations and standards
Using abrupt hand signals and gestures
Speaking rapidly, in a stiff tone
Worrying about the future: *I just want you to get into a good college one day!*
Voicing anger or frustration
Being highly organized and focused
Venting to others
Playing the martyr
Bringing up past failures
Forcing others to adhere to one's own timetable
Using hurtful comparisons: *Alice finished her homework ten minutes ago. Why are you so slow?*
Repeating instructions or warnings
Judging others
Having an eye for detail
Reminding people of what they're supposed to do
Relentlessly badgering others until the desired outcome is produced
Hurting relationships by pushing people too hard
Making threats when someone doesn't follow through
Being so preoccupied with what others should be doing that one's own tasks are forgotten

Strong persistence and dedication
Worrying about the perceptions of others

ASSOCIATED THOUGHTS:

Jimmy's late again. How many times have I asked him to call when he can't make it for dinner?
If Diana doesn't clean this room, I'm tossing everything into the garbage.
I can't believe Tonya failed that test. I've been after her all week to study.
Sheldon is nothing like his brother. How can someone so orderly have such a disorganized twin?
I'm going to wait right here until Alan gets home from his shift. He'll have to listen to me then.

ASSOCIATED EMOTIONS: anger, disappointment, frustration, irritation

POSITIVE ASPECTS: Naggers have a clear vision of how something should be and they go after it with great persistence. They often believe that they are teaching others manners and appropriate behavior by sharing their opinions about what's acceptable. While many people may not like the constant prodding, those who lack focus and organization may appreciate a nagger's reminders.

NEGATIVE ASPECTS: Naggers are dictatorial. Their subjects often feel that their personal freedoms are being cast aside. Some may choose to rebel, refusing to follow through out of protest, while others may placate the nagger by doing the bare minimum in an attempt to stop the badgering. Since nagging characters tend to be judgmental, those closest to them may be reluctant to share their feelings or opinions, instead choosing evasion or dishonesty to avoid the inevitable scolding.

EXAMPLE FROM LITERATURE: In Grimm's *Hansel and Gretel*, the impoverished woodcutter is having difficulty providing for his family of four. His wife heartlessly suggests that he abandon his son and daughter in the woods. When he resists, she points out that either the children die in the forest, or they'll all die of hunger at home. Though he is reluctant, she continues to pester him until he gives in and leads his children away to starve. **Other Examples from TV and Film:** Lois Wilkerson (*Malcolm in the Middle*), Momma Lift (*Throw Momma from the Train*)

OVERCOMING THIS TRAIT AS A MAJOR FLAW: For a character to overcome nagging, she would need to have an epiphany regarding how her behavior is damaging her relationships with others. It might also help if she experienced it herself in an extreme way. Naggers must be made to see the unhealthy nature of believing that their value is tied to the performance of the people in their lives. Finding fulfillment through rediscovering one's own interests and talents will lessen the need to seek validation from others.

TRAITS IN SUPPORTING CHARACTERS THAT MAY CAUSE CONFLICT:
apathetic, callous, controlling, defensive, independent, mischievous, needy, rebellious, resentful, rowdy

NEEDY

DEFINITION: emotionally fragile; requiring constant attention and support

SIMILAR FLAWS: clingy, dependent

POSSIBLE CAUSES:
Needing human connection
The fear of rejection or abandonment
Poor health
Anxiety disorders
Codependency
Insufficient nurturing or neglect during childhood
Overprotective parents or caregivers
Low self-worth; a need for constant reassurance
Deep insecurity
Loneliness
A traumatizing past event
A debilitating disease (Alzheimer's, etc.)
Immaturity

ASSOCIATED BEHAVIORS AND ATTITUDES:
Sharing worries and fears with others in an effort to lessen the burden
Seeking frequent reassurance
Over-sharing one's personal history, especially any traumatic events
Asking for advice and opinions before making decisions
Offering compliments
Tying one's own value to others: *I've supported Bill all the way, and look at him now!*
Frequent phoning and texting
Feeling overwhelmed if the subject of one's clinginess isn't around
Hinting for invites to events and social gatherings
Working to insert oneself into the personal lives of others
Exhibiting unhealthy levels of trust for one's loved ones and friends
Perfectionist tendencies; needing everything to be just so in order to avoid anxiety
Feeling abandoned when others aren't around
Talking often about one's own problems and circumstances
Making others feel valued and strong in an effort to win favor and tighten bonds
Sharing one's secrets, hopes, and desires
Not respecting the boundaries and privacy of others
Wearing someone's favorite color in the hopes that they'll notice
Showing kindnesses (making someone's favorite meal, buying them gifts, etc.)
Feeling relaxed and happy in the company of friends
Fishing for compliments: *Oh, I'm such a burden to you.*
Exhibiting anger or frustration when a friend is with others or not available
Desiring one's relationships to be stronger and more intimate

Smothering others; draining their energy with one's neediness
Wanting to spend every minute with the person who makes one feel complete
Wanting to be taken care of and loved
Arranging get-togethers so there is always something to look forward to
Engaging in comforting routines (going to ball games together, establishing a movie night)

ASSOCIATED THOUGHTS:

I feel so good when Sarah is here. I wish we could spend every minute together.
Why isn't Mark home yet? He said he'd be here by seven-thirty.
Nobody knows what it's like to be me. Why is it so hard to deal with everything?

ASSOCIATED EMOTIONS: anxiety, disappointment, doubt, fear, nervousness, worry

POSITIVE ASPECTS: Needy characters enjoy being with others. In the company of loved ones, they're able to reveal their fears and worries and feel more at ease than when they are alone. A needy character's friends may sometimes benefit from the relationship by feeling important through providing support and encouragement.

NEGATIVE ASPECTS: Needy characters are a drain on the people around them, monopolizing large amounts of time and attention. They often have problems that require solving and are in constant need of guidance. Friends may feel that the relationship is mostly about rescuing the clingy character, and that they are giving more than they're receiving. Although they may secretly wish to escape the relationship, their guilt often keeps them from following through.

EXAMPLE FROM FILM: Bob Wiley (*What About Bob?*) has no concept of boundaries. When his psychiatrist goes on vacation, Bob is so afraid of being without him that he follows the doctor and his family to their New Hampshire getaway. Although Dr. Leo asks, begs, and orders Bob to leave him alone, Bob only wiggles his way further into the doctor's life by befriending his family and beginning a romantic relationship with Leo's sister. Though Bob is clearly the hero of this story, his clinginess makes him a somewhat annoying one. **Other Examples from Film**: Hedra Carlson (*Single White Female*), Bridget Jones (*Bridget Jones's Diary*)

OVERCOMING THIS TRAIT AS A MAJOR FLAW: For a character to overcome this flaw, he would need to slowly build up a sense of self-worth to gain the confidence to face situations independently. Rather than burdening friends with his problems and needs, this character would need to realize that he cannot always control things, and that the welfare of others is just as important as his own. Increasing his self-esteem will help a flawed character see that he has something to offer, and that he has value to others. Friends could help the character by discussing strategies that would enable him to solve his own dilemmas and problems.

TRAITS IN SUPPORTING CHARACTERS THAT MAY CAUSE CONFLICT:
apathetic, haughty, independent, judgmental, inhibited, spoiled, uncooperative, withdrawn

NERVOUS

DEFINITION: having an uneasiness of the mind or a brooding fear

SIMILAR FLAWS: anxious, edgy, skittish, uneasy

POSSIBLE CAUSES:
Having caregivers who worried and fussed over every little thing
Control and trust issues
Chemical imbalances in the brain
Hyperthyroidism
Paranoia or an over-active imagination
Pessimism
Anxiety disorders or social phobias
Believing in superstitions
Being victimized in the past; repressed traumatic memories
An important loss (a family death, etc.) at a critical stage in development
Surviving a natural disaster or war
Substance abuse or side effects from medications

ASSOCIATED BEHAVIORS AND ATTITUDES:
Constantly dwelling on the worst-case scenario
Panic attacks and profuse sweating
Stuttering or rushed speech
Second guessing one's decisions
Negative self-talk: *I should have known this would happen. How could I be so stupid?*
A darting gaze that quickly marks exits
Sensitivity to noise and movement
An unhealthy zeal for protecting those in one's care
Arriving late to social events and leaving early
Inappropriate social responses (laughing too loudly or at the wrong time)
Tics and unnatural gestures (touching one's hair, grimaces that one can't control, pacing, etc.)
Difficulty following a conversation or paying attention
Asking questions that reveal one's worries: *Dean should have called by now, don't you think?*
Fearing perceived risks or dangers
Watching too much news
Avoiding people, groups, or events
Staying at home; isolation
Poor communication skills
Wondering what other people are thinking and doing
Feeling judged or watched
Avoiding triggers for anxiety (public transit, alleys, family gatherings, etc.)
Having few deep friendships
Visible signs of discomfort (plucking at clothes, fiddling with one's rings, etc.)
Hypervigilance

Difficulty sleeping

Overprotectiveness

Hypochondria

Needing to be on schedule; sticking to routines and being constantly aware of the time

Simple worries that quickly grow into full blown fears

Difficulty relaxing or enjoying social situations

ASSOCIATED THOUGHTS:

Something bad is going to happen, I can feel it.

I should have stayed at home! Why didn't I stay at home?

I can't catch my breath. I'm going to pass out.

No way am I going downtown. I'll get mugged for sure.

Please don't let me catch whatever she's got.

ASSOCIATED EMOTIONS: anxiety, fear, nervousness, paranoia, worry

POSITIVE ASPECTS: Because nervous characters are aware of their surroundings, they're often the first to sense danger. Their sensitivity allows the fight-or-flight response to kick in quickly, giving them the best chance for survival. Because they frequently worry about what could be, they avoid risky behaviors and can be counted on to play it safe.

NEGATIVE ASPECTS: Nervous characters' ever-present fears make it difficult for them to enjoy life and connect with others. They don't often understand the cause of their feelings, which adds an extra layer to their anxiety. Characters with this flaw also tend toward negative thoughts and a fixation on the terrible things that could happen. This mindset generally interferes with all aspects of their life, stealing their enjoyment.

EXAMPLE FROM FILM: In *Zombieland*, college student Columbus' nervous nature causes him to hole up in his apartment and avoid the outside world. His paralyzing fear of what might happen almost causes him to miss the Zombie Apocalypse, and in the aftermath, his neurotic ways keep him alive but create challenges when it comes to trusting people and forging relationships. Faced with fight-or-flight scenarios, he consistently flees until he comes to care more about a group of strangers than for his own safety. While his nervousness never fully disappears, it also no longer controls him. **Other Examples from Literature and Film:** Piglet (*Winnie-the-Pooh*), Ichabod Crane (*Sleepy Hollow*)

OVERCOMING THIS TRAIT AS A MAJOR FLAW: A character who finds himself highly nervous may have a mental disorder or a physical issue requiring diagnosis. Medication and/or cognitive behavioral therapy will help the character to control symptoms and learn new thought patterns to avoid anxiety and negativity. Other milder forms of nervousness may lessen with repeated "safe" exposure to triggers, friends who understand the condition and work to help the character through it, meditation and relaxation techniques, and a conscious effort to focus on life's positives.

TRAITS IN SUPPORTING CHARACTERS THAT MAY CAUSE CONFLICT: bold, catty, confident, cruel, extroverted, flamboyant, independent, mischievous, pushy

NOSY

DEFINITION: intrusive; prying into the affairs of others

SIMILAR FLAWS: interfering, meddlesome, prying, snooping

POSSIBLE CAUSES:
Needing to feel superior, to be more in the know
Dissatisfaction with one's life
Avoidance of one's own shortcomings and problems
Loneliness
Being overly curious
Boredom
A suspicious nature; trust issues
A genuine sense of caring for others
A tendency to worry too much
Assuming responsibility for the welfare of others

ASSOCIATED BEHAVIORS AND ATTITUDES:
Asking pointed, inappropriate questions
Utilizing charm and kindness to make one seem approachable and trustworthy
Disrespecting personal boundaries
Spying and snooping on others
Reading over someone's shoulder
Disregarding the privacy of others
Watchfulness
Inserting oneself into another's life without permission
Making assumptions and jumping to conclusions
Chiding others or offering unwanted advice
Gossiping
Being intrigued by rumors
Reading into situations and actions
Proactively thinking of where something may lead
Gathering information (internet searches, etc.) under the guise of protecting oneself
Judging others
Having an opinion on everything
Sneakiness
Eavesdropping
Pretending to hang up a phone extension while staying on the line
Acting friendly while hiding one's true agenda
Inviting people over with the ulterior motive of eliciting information
Using guilt trips
Lying to gain insight
Promising that one can keep a secret
Steering the conversation

Ignoring the signs that one's interest is making others feel uncomfortable
Offering to help out in order to glean insight or gain a foothold in the situation
Making excuses to be in a place where one can listen in
Changing one's routine to keep tabs on someone else
Citing similar interests: *I love to hike. Maybe we could go together this Saturday?*

ASSOCIATED THOUGHTS:

That handyman is here almost every week. What's going on next door?
Why does Mara go through the mail before taking it inside?
That's the moving van. I should go over and see where the new neighbors are from.
Funny, how Bill and Carol don't come to church together any more. Trouble in paradise?

ASSOCIATED EMOTIONS: curiosity, disappointment, envy, hopefulness, suspicion

POSITIVE ASPECTS: Nosy characters have intimate knowledge of the people and places around them and can be a source of information when it's needed. Because they enjoy gossip and conjecture, many are willing to reveal their information with minimal prompting.

NEGATIVE ASPECTS: Nosy characters may not see their insatiable need to know as a problem and can become hurt when they're rebuffed by others. Because friends don't appreciate being spied on or interrogated, they may avoid or lie to a nosy neighbor to maintain privacy. This can lead to loneliness, self-doubt, and frustration for the meddlesome character. Nosy characters can also be easily manipulated by others, who may use them to become an unwitting spy or to spread information.

EXAMPLE FROM FILM: In the movie *Disturbia*, a bored teen under house arrest spies on his neighbors and witnesses what he believes to be a murder at the house next door. His obsessive desire to know if his neighbor is a serial killer or not nearly destroys him and his friends. **Other Examples from Film and Literature**: Jeff Jeffries (*Rear Window*), Gail Weathers (*Scream*), Rita Skeeter (*Harry Potter* series)

OVERCOMING THIS TRAIT AS A MAJOR FLAW: Honesty can often be used to help a nosy character see the discomfort his snooping causes. If the character with this flaw values the friendship and respect of others, he will take this advice to heart and restrain his curiosity in the future, even if he feels he has a legitimate reason to pry. Another method would be to turn nosiness back on the character. Having a victim respond to prying by become obnoxiously probing himself might help the character see what it feels like to have one's privacy invaded.

TRAITS IN SUPPORTING CHARACTERS THAT MAY CAUSE CONFLICT: dishonest, evasive, hostile, introverted, judgmental, stubborn, uncooperative, withdrawn

OBSESSIVE

DEFINITION: fixated; being subject to recurring thoughts that take over

SIMILAR FLAWS: neurotic

POSSIBLE CAUSES:
Fear of making a mistake
Fear of failure or loss
The need to control
A mental disorder
A life-altering loss or trauma
A brain chemical imbalance
Growing up with perfectionist parents or role models
Having a strong creative bent (artists, musicians, etc.)

ASSOCIATED BEHAVIORS AND ATTITUDES:
Constantly thinking about the source of one's obsession
Emotional extremes (love, hate, fear, etc.)
Focusing on one thing and building a life around it (a love of trains, fear of germs, etc.)
Talking incessantly about the obsession
Having ideas that take root and won't let go
Rationalizing one's obsession to others: *If I shake hands, I'll get a disease.*
Losing sense of one's identity because the obsession takes over
Extreme protectiveness of anything to do with the obsession
Difficulty sleeping or insomnia
Thoughts that won't turn off (anorexics obsessing about weight and food, etc.)
Needing to touch or hold a symbol of one's obsession
Possessiveness
Stalking (if the obsession is a person)
Attributing emotions to a possession or thing
Feelings of self-loathing or disgust
Engaging in mental rituals that comfort or relieve stress from one's obsessive thoughts
Difficulty making decisions
Avoiding places or circumstances where one believes harmful things may happen
Isolation
Keeping secrets
Making excuses or lying to others to hide one's obsessive nature
Latching onto a specific thing or activity and shutting out everything else
Changing one's routine to accommodate the obsession
Making personal sacrifices to devote more time and energy to one's obsession
Spending vast amounts of time and money on the obsession
Impaired reasoning skills
Pulling away from family and friends
Believing in superstitions
Losing one's job, income, or family as the obsession gains control over one's life

ASSOCIATED THOUGHTS:

If I don't get a 4.0, everyone will be disappointed.

Mark is the one. I know it. No matter what, I'm going to make him love me too.

If Emmy and I go to the movies, what will Anna say? Will she hate me? Break up with me?

People think it's weird that I bleach everything, but it's the best way to avoid getting sick.

ASSOCIATED EMOTIONS: anxiety, desire, fear, love, paranoia, worry

POSITIVE ASPECTS: Obsessive characters are driven, focused, and can account for some amazing contributions to society. Advances in science, new art forms, cures for diseases, and discoveries about the past, present, and future have all been the result of someone passionately following an idea or thought process.

NEGATIVE ASPECTS: Characters with this flaw are often prisoners to their own thoughts. Deep fears of failure and inadequacy drive obsessions and can lead to poor eating and sleeping habits, withdrawal from society, and unfulfilled goals. Those closest to these characters often resent taking a backseat to their fixation and may choose to distance themselves or end the relationship. If an obsession becomes strong enough, it may require compulsive rituals to offer relief (counting, touching objects, organizing belongings in a specific way, etc.), which only drive the obsessive character further into a lifestyle of isolation and secrecy.

EXAMPLE FROM LITERATURE: Iconic Captain Ahab in Melville's *Moby Dick* is as obsessive as they come in his hunt for the great white whale. In his quest to kill Moby Dick, his willingness to sacrifice everything for revenge eventually leads to his own death. **Other Examples from Film**: Mitch Leary (*In the Line of Fire*), Joan Crawford (*Mommy Dearest*), Alex Forrest (*Fatal Attraction*).

OVERCOMING THIS TRAIT AS A MAJOR FLAW: An obsession will last as long as the character fixates on it, and he may not be able to overcome his neurotic thought patterns alone. Cognitive therapy and medication may be necessary to break through his deeply embedded worries and fears. In order to want to change, the character would also need to recognize the fixation as unhealthy. If it's goal-oriented, achieving success may alleviate the obsession, but the root cause would still remain. Understanding what fear drives an obsession will allow the character to seek help for and deal with the cause.

TRAITS IN SUPPORTING CHARACTERS THAT MAY CAUSE CONFLICT: controlling, efficient, fussy, nagging, nosy, sensible

OVERSENSITIVE

DEFINITION: overly perceptive to emotion; easily hurt by external influences

SIMILAR FLAWS: hypersensitive, thin-skinned, touchy

POSSIBLE CAUSES:
High intelligence or giftedness
Low self-confidence and self-esteem
Fears and phobias
A chemical imbalance in the brain that causes an easily triggered fight-or-flight reflex
Growing up or living in an unsafe environment
Poor body image; believing oneself to be outside the norm (overweight, underweight, etc.)
A trauma in one's childhood (being bullied or suffering other abuse)
Domineering, callous parents
Autism
Drug or alcohol abuse
An overly excitable nervous system
Paranoia
Perfectionism
A real or perceived lack of control
An obsessive need for the approval of others

ASSOCIATED BEHAVIORS AND ATTITUDES:
Crying or other emotional displays
Shutting down and becoming unresponsive
Leaving in haste and without reason
Reading into what another said or did in a way that was not intended
Growing silent during banter or conversation
Reacting explosively to teasing
Seeing criticism where there is none
Paranoia
Being overly sensitive to sounds and smells
Moodiness, depression
Obsessing about a past situation where one's feelings were hurt
Being pulled in by another's emotion
Holding grudges
Extreme curiosity
Being deeply loyal to those who've proven themselves trustworthy
Deep empathy
Displays of kindness and compassion
Defensiveness
Avoiding critical or opinionated people
Worrying about disappointing others
Isolation

Insecurity
Difficulty opening up to or trusting others
Disliking and avoiding social events
Feeling euphoria when receiving a compliment or positive reinforcement
Difficulty understanding or expressing sarcasm
Frequent apologizing
Misreading body language or expressions and making assumptions based on what one "sees"

ASSOCIATED THOUGHTS:
How could she say such a horrible thing?
Why are they all making fun of me? Don't they know how much it hurts?
It was Anna's cat that died, but I think I feel as sad as she does.

ASSOCIATED EMOTIONS: anxiety, depression, fear, overwhelmed, sadness, worry

POSITIVE ASPECTS: Oversensitive characters are empathetic and make good caregivers. They are capable of great compassion and are often creative or gifted in some way. They see the extremes around them—including the wonder and beauty of the world—that most miss or don't take time to enjoy. When it comes to friendship and relationships, these characters are incredibly loving and loyal.

NEGATIVE ASPECTS: Oversensitive characters often read into the actions of others and become hurt by things that wouldn't bother most people. They struggle with playful banter and have difficulty accepting advice without taking it personally. When these characters recognize their own sensitivity and inability to cope, they often turn their frustration inward, which only increases their feelings of low self-worth. Supporting characters may choose to treat these characters with kid gloves because of their emotional volatility. Others may view them as immature or weak and mark them as targets for bullying. Either response can make a character with this flaw feel alone and misunderstood.

EXAMPLE FROM LITERATURE: Moaning Myrtle (*Harry Potter* series) of Hogwarts lives out her afterlife in the pipes of the first floor girls' bathroom. Though death has freed her from the bullying that plagued her earthly existence, she continues to wail and cry at the slightest provocation, taking offense where none is given.

OVERCOMING THIS TRAIT AS A MAJOR FLAW: To grow, a character with this flaw would need to acknowledge that her oversensitivity is controlling her in ways that she doesn't want or need. She may use techniques such as meditation, breathing exercises, and realistic self-talk to cope with situations and gain control of her feelings. Role-playing potentially problematic situations with a trusted friend may also help her learn how to handle day-to-day situations and criticisms and not become overwhelmed by them.

TRAITS IN SUPPORTING CHARACTERS THAT MAY CAUSE CONFLICT: controlling, cruel, cynical, evil, honest, hostile, judgmental, nagging, pessimistic, pushy, tactless, vindictive

PARANOID

DEFINITION: inclined to excessive worrying and irrational suspicion

POSSIBLE CAUSES:
Drug or alcohol abuse
Insomnia
Stressful life events or past traumas (surviving a kidnapping, abuse, etc.)
Growing up in a situation where one was constantly criticized or ridiculed
Schizophrenia, paranoid delusions, bipolar and paranoid personality disorders
Intense feelings of inferiority
A head trauma or brain damage
Extreme trust issues
Growing up with untreated mentally ill caregivers
Frequent exposure to suspicious ideas and negative thinking

ASSOCIATED BEHAVIORS AND ATTITUDES:
Becoming socially isolated
Living a life that is overly safeguarded and secure
Obsessive behaviors (cleaning one's guns, looking through the front door's peephole, etc.)
Making accusations
Watching, following, and stalking others
Adhering to certain routines for safety (eating the same carefully prepared food day after day)
Changing routines in an effort to avoid detection (leaving the house at odd times, etc.)
Tics and other nervous actions
Reacting defensively
Jumping to conclusions
Muttering and mumbling
Poor hygiene
Pessimism and negativity
Believing that one has been singled out or targeted in some way
Asking questions that suggest paranoid thoughts: *Do you ever feel like you're being followed?*
Believing in conspiracy theories
Being suspicious of those offering kindness or friendship
Refusing to forgive real or imagined insults or wrongs
Arming oneself for protection
Stockpiling (food, water, weapons, batteries, medical supplies, etc.)
Explosive anger or aggression
Being confrontational
Honing one's survival skills
Refusing to join group activities or events
Hostility and unfriendliness
Poor eating habits
Assuming that everyone has a hidden agenda
Hypervigilance

Being sensitive to change
Dismissing legitimate news as propaganda
Feeling watched or spied on
Believing nothing is mere coincidence

ASSOCIATED THOUGHTS:

Someone's been in here messing with my stuff!
My neighbor's spying on me. Why else would he 'accidentally' end up with my mail?
The boss thinks she's so slick with her compliments. She's just trying to get us to work harder.
I don't look anything like mom or dad. Maybe they're not my real parents.
I know I locked that window. Someone must have tried to break in!

ASSOCIATED EMOTIONS: anger, frustration, paranoia, suspicion

POSITIVE ASPECTS: Paranoid characters are concerned with safety and security, meaning that danger is unlikely to catch them unawares. They are watchful and notice things that others miss or disregard.

NEGATIVE ASPECTS: Paranoid characters take risks that most people wouldn't in an effort to remain safe. If they see a person as a threat, they may react with aggression or violence. Even low-level paranoia can lead these characters to sabotage people or projects, cause disruptions, and act in irrational or irresponsible ways. Paranoid characters have difficulty engaging socially with others, maintaining balanced relationships, and supporting the people in their lives. Everyone around them is suspect, and the smallest slight may turn a friend into a foe.

EXAMPLE FROM FILM: John Nash (*A Beautiful Mind*) is a brilliant mathematician who suffers from paranoid schizophrenia. In the early years of his career, he believes himself to be a spy for the Department of Defense and sees danger everywhere. Even after his diagnosis and treatment, he continues to see and hear people who don't exist, and struggles with doubt as to what is real and what isn't. **Other Examples from Film**: Howard Hughes (*The Aviator*), Jerry Fletcher (*Conspiracy Theory*), Marvin Boggs (*Red*)

OVERCOMING THIS TRAIT AS A MAJOR FLAW: Most paranoid characters will not seek out help on their own because they are mistrustful of everyone. Friends or family who encourage the character to get help may in fact be playing into the paranoid's fantasy of everyone being against him. Therapy and medication may be needed to overcome this flaw.

TRAITS IN SUPPORTING CHARACTERS THAT MAY CAUSE CONFLICT: analytical, confrontational, evasive, impatient, mischievous, nosy, reckless, secretive, sensible, uninhibited

PERFECTIONIST

DEFINITION: perceiving anything less than perfection as failure

POSSIBLE CAUSES:
Being raised by caregivers with unrealistic expectations
A compulsion to be the best
Low self-esteem; the need to prove oneself to others
The belief that one's value is directly related to one's results or level of achievement
A fear of failure
Childhood trauma

ASSOCIATED BEHAVIORS AND ATTITUDES:
Meticulousness
Checking one's work, looking for ways to make it better
Difficulty delegating; having to do everything oneself
Control issues
Hypersensitivity to criticism
Reluctance to admit when one has made a mistake
Setting unrealistic goals
Chastising oneself for falling short
Expecting perfection from others
Being highly critical and judgmental of others
Following rules and regulations to the letter
Being open with one's disappointment when others do not measure up
Dissatisfaction with the status quo; always seeking to improve
Inefficiency caused by the need to keep trying until one's work measures up
Seeking to improve through education or practice
Focusing on one's weaknesses rather than on strengths
Competitiveness
Not settling for less than perfection
Comparing oneself to others
Missing the forest for the trees
Placing undue pressure on oneself or on others
Obsessing over one's performance or project
Workaholic tendencies
Experiencing envy when someone else excels in a given area
Negative thoughts
Excessively working or practicing
Difficulty sleeping
Neglecting one's personal needs
Refusing to attempt something that one can't do perfectly
Underachieving as a way of avoiding failure and disappointment
Depression
Reluctance to try new things

Difficulty letting something go and move onto something new

Growing angry at praise when one feels it is underserved

Complete commitment to a task or project

ASSOCIATED THOUGHTS:

It's still not good enough.

Why would she turn in such a shoddy project?

If I can succeed in this area, Mom will see how good I am.

I can do better. I'll just have to work harder.

ASSOCIATED EMOTIONS: anxiety, defeat, depression, desperation, doubt, frustration, insecurity, overwhelmed, shame, worry

POSITIVE ASPECTS: Perfectionists are active rather than passive. Never satisfied with the status quo, they're always looking for ways to make things better. These characters are diligent and persistent, doing whatever it takes to achieve their goals. They set high standards and often challenge others to do better.

NEGATIVE ASPECTS: Many perfectionists fail to see that their goals are unattainable. Their inability to settle for anything less than perfection sets them up for failure and creates a vicious cycle of disappointment, self-loathing, and defeatism. Their compulsive need for perfection can render them inefficient and unproductive, making them difficult to work with. Because these characters also expect perfection from others, co-workers and family members may chafe under their unrealistic expectations.

EXAMPLE FROM FILM: Nina Sayers (*Black Swan*) has found success as a ballerina through perfect technique and control on stage. This makes her the obvious choice to play the White Swan in Swan Lake. But to dance the perfect Swan Queen, she must also be able to play the Black Swan, which requires her to lose control and give herself over to the part. Desperate for perfection, she embraces her inner darkness so completely that she ends up going mad as a result. **Other Examples from TV and Literature:** Bree Van de Kamp (*Desperate Housewives*), Hermione Granger (*Harry Potter* series)

OVERCOMING THIS TRAIT AS A MAJOR FLAW: To overcome perfectionism, one must realize that one's expectations are not only unrealistic but impossible to reach and, therefore, self-defeating. The perfectionist must learn to set reasonable goals and change her mindset from one of criticism and blame to one of grace and forgiveness, allowing room for the less-than-perfect.

TRAITS IN SUPPORTING CHARACTERS THAT MAY CAUSE CONFLICT: disorganized, easygoing, flaky, forgetful, frivolous, lazy, oversensitive, playful, temperamental

PESSIMISTIC

DEFINITION: inclined to focus on the negative and expect the worst possible outcome

SIMILAR FLAWS: negative

POSSIBLE CAUSES:
Cynicism from having experienced much negativity
Fear of disappointment
Living with a chronic disability, ailment, or difficult situation
Repeated failures over the course of one's life
Having been victimized or otherwise traumatized through no fault of one's own
Depression

ASSOCIATED BEHAVIORS AND ATTITUDES:
Passivity
Giving up control
Having and using negative thoughts and words
Believing the worst of people
Expecting the worst possible outcome to occur
Being argumentative or sarcastic
Anticipating failure
Chronic worrying
Believing that a situation will never change
Apathy and resignation
Focusing on the negatives in one's life and in the lives of others
Frequent gloomy, grumpy moods
Self-criticism
Resentment
Decreased productivity at work or school
Being unmotivated
Losing interest in hobbies or favorite pastimes
Bemoaning what's gone wrong rather than being grateful for what went right
Withdrawing from others
Difficulty focusing
Constant complaining
Ingratitude
An inability to trust others
Counteracting another's happy news by voicing one's own bad experience in the same area
Feeling that there is little or no point; just going through the motions
Dampening the good moods of others
Harping on one's weaknesses rather than focusing on one's strengths
Suspecting others of selfishness or hidden agendas
Not being able to take something at face value
Viewing change with trepidation or resentment

Putting in minimal effort; believing that nothing will make a difference
Believing that good things come with a price
A need to bring optimistic people down to one's own reality

ASSOCIATED THOUGHTS:
It's never going to change, so what's the point in trying?
We can't beat this team. They're just better than we are.
Sure, the weather's beautiful now, but wait until winter kicks in.
Just watch. As soon as we get to the beach, it'll start raining.

ASSOCIATED EMOTIONS: anguish, defeat, depression, disappointment, doubt, guilt, hurt, indifference, resignation, sadness

POSITIVE ASPECTS: Pessimists tend to look beyond the present to the long-term. They see not only the immediate possible results of a given situation but its effects far into the future.

NEGATIVE ASPECTS: Pessimism is a vicious cycle of negative thinking producing negative results. The more a character believes that he will fail, the more he will fail, proving himself right. This pattern of negative thinking makes it difficult for him to succeed in any area. Like a disease, the negativity associated with pessimism is catching; it brings others down. For this reason, many people will avoid these characters, leaving them lonely and disconnected. Many pessimists also experience health problems like heart disease and a shortened life span due to their intense negativity.

EXAMPLE FROM LITERATURE: No doubt about it: Eeyore (*Winnie-the-Pooh* series) is a gloomy Gus. Whether he's losing his tail or receiving popped balloons as a birthday gift, he never seems quite surprised when bad luck strikes, as if he expects these things to happen. Even when life is good, he's glum and sarcastic and in a dour mood. Thank goodness A.A. Milne chose to give Eeyore upbeat friends like Tigger and Roo, or the donkey's negative outlook might bring readers down. **Other Examples from TV**: Charlie Brown (*Peanuts*)

OVERCOMING THIS TRAIT AS A MAJOR FLAW: The sad thing about pessimism is that the negativity is all in the character's head. To change, the pessimist must learn to reprogram his thinking: notice the good instead of the bad, be grateful instead of complaining, and choose to think positively rather than negatively. Only then will he be able to experience contentment and happiness.

TRAITS IN SUPPORTING CHARACTERS THAT MAY CAUSE CONFLICT: friendly, humorous, idealistic, kind, optimistic, playful, wholesome, trusting

POSSESSIVE

DEFINITION: needing to own (a thing) or dominate (a subject)

POSSIBLE CAUSES:
The need to control
Codependence
Jealousy
Paranoia
Low self-esteem
Fear of being alone

ASSOCIATED BEHAVIORS AND ATTITUDES:
Selfishness
Not respecting boundaries or privacy
Obsessive behavior regarding a person or thing
Having high expectations of others
Questioning the motives of others
Laying guilt trips on one's subject at the first sign of emotional independence
Becoming aggressive if one's control or ownership is threatened
An untrusting nature
Showing negativity towards those who wish to interact with one's possession
Running down others to the subject: *Your neighbor Larry needs to learn what deodorant is.*
Calling, dropping by, or texting more than is reasonable
Objectifying people to use or manipulate them
Growing angry if the subject makes independent decisions
Studying the subject's interests and using them to integrate oneself into their life
Attempting to increase the subject's isolation: *Lisa is so needy. You don't need friends like that.*
Spending vast amounts of time thinking about the object
Feeling resentful of responsibilities that take one away from one's possession
Unreasonable protectiveness: *You shouldn't go to the library alone. I'll come with you.*
Negativity
Utilizing emotional blackmail: *Quit hanging out with Barry, or it's over!*
Showing undue concern and attentiveness for the subject
Offering compliments and gifts to the subject
Believing one knows the subject's needs best
Needing to know where the person is and what they are doing at all times
Checking up on the person (following him at lunch, reading his personal email, etc.)
Controlling who the subject sees and when
Showing strong affection for the loved one
Acting unreasonably and demanding compliance
Irrational suspicion and jealousy
Verbal, emotional, or physical abuse
Encouraging codependency in an effort to control the subject
Using the excuse: *I'm doing this for your own good.*

ASSOCIATED THOUGHTS:

Beth's brother has too much influence with her. She needs to stay away from him.
The book club is taking up too much of Jane's time. I'm going to tell her to quit.
Why does Luke need to hang out with the guys when he has me?
Jill's parents are so controlling. I'm giving her an ultimatum—them or me.

ASSOCIATED EMOTIONS: annoyance, desire, fear, jealousy, love, suspicion, uncertainty

POSITIVE ASPECTS: Possessive characters are protective and will keep the ones closest to them under their control at all costs. If a loved one is being mistreated and finds it difficult to rectify the situation, a possessive character will step in and make the hard decisions on their behalf. This kind of low-level possessiveness can make a person feel loved and secure.

NEGATIVE ASPECTS: Possessive characters are very controlling, slowly dominating every aspect of their loved ones' lives. Characters with this flaw will grow angry when the people they care about spend time with others or engage in personal interests. Jealous flare-ups and aggression can make loved ones fearful, forcing them to give up their passions and cut themselves off from other people to keep the peace.

EXAMPLE FROM LITERATURE: Moose, from the *Archie* comics, is very possessive of his long-time girlfriend, Midge. Always on the lookout for guys who might be ogling her, he flies into a rage at the barest hint of interest, beating the suspects black and blue. This frightening level of jealousy sometimes results in Midge's own anger and her temporary rejection of Moose as a boyfriend. **Other Examples from Film and Literature**: Martin Burney (*Sleeping with the Enemy*), Norma Bates (*Psycho*), Norman Daniels (*Rose Madder*)

OVERCOMING THIS TRAIT AS A MAJOR FLAW: Sometimes, only through loss can a person really understand how their possessive actions contributed to the outcome. That said, it can be dangerous for the person leaving an extremely possessive relationship, even temporarily, as the controlling character may adopt an "If I can't have you, no one can" viewpoint.

TRAITS IN SUPPORTING CHARACTERS THAT MAY CAUSE CONFLICT: disloyal, independent, rebellious, ungrateful, unselfish

PREJUDICED

DEFINITION: being strongly opinionated without sufficient knowledge; having a bias for or against

SIMILAR FLAWS: biased, bigoted, racist

POSSIBLE CAUSES:
Growing up in a household with strong opinions and bias
Having a strong need for order, to place things into categories (right and wrong, good and bad)
Loyalty to a belief due to conditioning: *We're all Democrats in this family.*
An intolerant upbringing
Ignorance; a lack of information or experience with diversity
A group mentality or cultish thinking: *Hazing is just part of the process. Everyone's got to do it.*
Fear
Desiring to fit in and belong

ASSOCIATED BEHAVIORS AND ATTITUDES:
Discrimination
Making snap judgments and decisions
Refusing to listen to other theories or alternative ideas
A reluctance to interact with a person or group that opposes one's beliefs
Telling racial jokes; making racial slurs and comments
Ignoring facts or common sense in favor of acting on one's emotional reactions
Making assumptions based on biases
Negative stereotyping
Hate-mongering
Adopting a group's beliefs and practices as part of one's identity
Viewing everything that opposes one's beliefs as a threat
Holding onto deep, enduring beliefs
Being overly judgmental
Self-righteousness
Repressing individuals or groups out of bias and hatred
Deeming certain groups as being unworthy of respect
Making fun of an individual or group's belief system: *There go the Bible thumpers!*
Denying the rights of a specific group
Showing disrespect for a group or person (spitting in their direction, etc.)
Jumping to conclusions
Acting with suspicion and wariness
Creating rules for others that align with one's beliefs: *Stay away from that family, you hear?*
Giving preferential treatment to loyal, like-minded individuals
Ignoring the individual and only seeing him in light of his race, religious affiliation, etc.
Pressuring others to share one's way of thinking
Blaming a group, organization, or race for the world's problems

ASSOCIATED THOUGHTS:

The immigrants are to blame, coming over here and messing things up.
Look at her—the way she's dressed and wearing all that makeup; she was asking for it.
The world would be better off without the whole lot of them.
All those people from up north are so pushy.

ASSOCIATED EMOTIONS: agitation, fear, hatred, rage, scorn, suspicion

POSITIVE ASPECTS: Prejudiced characters draw confidence from the knowledge that they can quickly make judgments of right, wrong, good, and bad based on their individual beliefs. They are highly loyal and have great determination, which enables them to cling to ideas that are often patently wrong.

NEGATIVE ASPECTS: Prejudiced characters think they're better in some way than the people they judge, and so come off as self-righteous. Through intolerance, they dismiss individuals and groups, cheating themselves of possible friends, lovers, and mentors as well as missing out on the knowledge and experiences those people would share. Another problem with prejudice is that it often occurs in groups. The mob mentality encourages biased thinking, making it difficult for these characters to see their errors and change their ways. Their unfriendliness or even hateful actions toward others can make them very unlikable.

EXAMPLE FROM FILM: When the father of Derek and Danny Vinyard (*American History X*) is murdered, elder son Derek joins a neo-Nazi gang and pursues a life categorized by violence and hatred. He eventually kills someone himself and goes to prison, where his experiences lead to a change of heart. Paroled, he returns home a transformed man but discovers that his bigotry and cruelty have infected his younger brother. In the end, he frees himself but is unable to save Danny. **Other Examples from Literature and TV**: The Malfoys (*Harry Potter* series), Archie Bunker (*All in the Family*), Charlie Dillon (*School Ties*)

OVERCOMING THIS TRAIT AS A MAJOR FLAW: Prejudice can be overcome when one's bias is proven false. If the character believes that a group of people are bad but then directly witnesses their doing great good, cracks in his value system will form. He may then recognize that putting a label on others and dismissing their individuality is shortsighted and hurtful.

TRAITS IN SUPPORTING CHARACTERS THAT MAY CAUSE CONFLICT: bold, intelligent, just, socially aware

PRETENTIOUS

DEFINITION: characterized by a showiness meant to emphasize one's inflated sense of importance

SIMILAR FLAWS: flashy, grandiose, ostentatious, pompous, showy

POSSIBLE CAUSES:
Being spoiled as a child
Having a life of privilege
Having a rich benefactor
Being a high achiever
Being overly worried about what others think
Narcissism

ASSOCIATED BEHAVIORS AND ATTITUDES:
Using big words to sound important
Name-dropping
Overconfidence
Speaking loudly to draw attention
Wearing flashy or expensive clothing
Having a sense of entitlement
Believing that people should adhere to a social caste system
Lavish displays of wealth or influence (a party packed with celebrities, etc.)
Making bold claims or grand promises
Acting overwhelmed by attention while secretly reveling in it
False modesty
Preening
Ego trips
Having a "what's in it for me?" attitude
Believing that one's time and attention are more important than others'
Preening under lavish attention
Telling people how much something costs or how difficult it was to obtain
Talking constantly about oneself and one's achievements
Surrounding oneself with admirers
Refusing to do unpleasant tasks or manual labor
Carefully adhering to current styles, trends, and fashions
Having an entourage of followers and hangers-on
Pursuing hobbies and interests because they are highly regarded
Requiring others to come to one's location rather than going to them
Attending or hosting events only for people with connections and means
Offering ideas and expecting others to be grateful for them
Selectively paying attention to individuals to either reward or punish
Demanding rather than asking
Expecting to be obeyed

Lamenting one's busy schedule
Expecting one's needs and privacy to be valued above others'

ASSOCIATED THOUGHTS:
I hope I get into the Key Club this year. Everybody who's anybody is a member.
I wouldn't be caught dead in any car but a Rolls.
Everyone must be dying to hear about my trip to France.
I suppose I should pick a charity to endorse this year, but which one?

ASSOCIATED EMOTIONS: insecurity, overconfidence, pride, smugness

POSITIVE ASPECTS: Pretentious characters have a desire to be seen and heard and, with a little ego-stroking, will eagerly champion causes, charities, and forward-thinking initiatives. As long as they're made to look good, they can easily be influenced into doing what others want them to do.

NEGATIVE ASPECTS: Pretentious characters are vain, materialistic, and hyper aware of their reputation in the community. Position and prestige are very important to them, and they will go to great lengths to gain and maintain them. Similarly, people who are attracted to pretentious characters often plan on using them for their influence. This can make it difficult for a character with this flaw to trust the motives of others and develop true friendships.

EXAMPLE FROM TV: As a renowned psychiatrist and Seattle celebrity, Dr. Frasier Crane (*Frasier*) has a very high opinion of himself. He hobnobs with the rich and famous, seeks membership in elitist clubs, is an opera and wine snob, and only buys the very best of everything. It's ironic that as a physician who's able to help many people with their difficulties, he's blind to his own elevated sense of self and the problems that it causes. **Other Examples from Film**: Doyle Standish (*Dutch*), Louis Winthorpe III (*Trading Places*)

OVERCOMING THIS TRAIT AS A MAJOR FLAW: One thing most pretentious characters rarely experience is actual hardship and failure. If someone with this flaw came face-to-face with the raw and terrible hurts of this world, he might realize just how shallow his own reality is and feel a deep need for change, leading to personal growth.

TRAITS IN SUPPORTING CHARACTERS THAT MAY CAUSE CONFLICT: catty, cocky, competitive, haughty, jealous, lazy, needy, oversensitive, rowdy, uncouth, vindictive

PROMISCUOUS

DEFINITION: engaging in casual sexual behavior that is not restricted to one partner

SIMILAR FLAWS: licentious, loose, wanton

POSSIBLE CAUSES:
A strong libido and enjoyment of sexual contact
A desire for empowerment
The desire for sexual independence
Fear of being alone
Low self-esteem
Anxiety caused by feeling unloved
Sexual addictions
Fear of commitment and long-term relationships
Disdain for social or cultural rules
Loneliness
Intoxication or drug use
A history of sexual abuse
Trust issues

ASSOCIATED BEHAVIORS AND ATTITUDES:
Participating in one-night stands
Avoiding commitment
Dressing provocatively
Caving in to loneliness by going out to meet someone
Provocative movements and actions meant to draw sexual interest
Sex for the sake of sex, with no emotional attachments
Focusing heavily on one's appearance
Playful sexual banter
Being open-minded to trying different things
Enjoying the attention and interest of others
Adding an element of risk to keep things interesting
Controlling a potential partner's attention in an effort to gain power
Making the first move
Playing cat and mouse to heighten the foreplay
Not asking probing questions or getting too personal
Flirting in the workplace
Engaging in affairs
Encouraging "friends with benefits" relationships
Having multiple partners in a short period of time
Visiting places where sexual partners are readily found (bars, frat parties, etc.)
Engaging in sex while intoxicated
Prostitution
Swinging

Belonging to a dating hook-up site
Paying for escorts or hookers
Getting tested for sexually transmitted diseases
Experiencing guilt or regrets in the aftermath

ASSOCIATED THOUGHTS:
I wonder who I'll be going home with tonight.
She better not be the clingy type. Fun and done, that's my motto.
I don't want to spend another night alone. Maybe I'll head out and see who's at the bar.

ASSOCIATED EMOTIONS: anticipation, desire, excitement, insecurity, shame

POSITIVE ASPECTS: Promiscuous characters avoid being caught up in the drama and responsibility of committed relationships. By staying emotionally unattached during encounters, there is no fear of being rejected or hurt by the other person.

NEGATIVE ASPECTS: Promiscuous characters put themselves at risk for sexually transmitted infections and unwanted pregnancies. Other people frequently judge them for their actions or use them for sex. If the behavior is a result of a past trauma, prolonged activity will only add to a promiscuous character's self-esteem deficit, creating a spiral effect of loneliness, depression, and possibly self-loathing. Depending on the core reasons behind the promiscuity, these characters may find that their long-term emotional needs are not satisfied through these types of relationships.

EXAMPLE FROM FILM: In *Wedding Crashers*, John Beckwith and Jeremy Grey work together as divorce mediators who enjoy crashing wedding parties as a way to sleep with women with no risk of commitment. They adopt false identities and charm lonely bridesmaids into one-night stands, enjoying all of the fun and none of the responsibility. Ultimately, this becomes a lonely endeavor, especially for John, who longs for something deeper and more meaningful. **Other Examples from TV and Film**: Charlie Harper (*Two and a Half Men*), Susanna Kaysen (*Girl, Interrupted*)

OVERCOMING THIS TRAIT AS A MAJOR FLAW: If promiscuity is keeping the character from achieving a balanced, fulfilling life and is creating low self-worth, he will need to find ways to break his dependence on sexual encounters for emotional gratification. Meeting someone who offers unconditional love and friendship may create a bridge to trusting the other person enough to try a monogamous relationship if he desires it.

TRAITS IN SUPPORTING CHARACTERS THAT MAY CAUSE CONFLICT: catty, cautious, controlling, evil, immoral, jealous, judgmental, needy, nosy, overbearing, inhibited

PUSHY

DEFINITION: overly assertive; in-your-face

SIMILAR FLAWS: aggressive, bossy, demanding, forceful, overbearing

POSSIBLE CAUSES:
A drive to excel or succeed
Needing to control or be in charge
Exhibiting taught behavior (domineering parents, siblings, friends, etc.)
Having an overindulged childhood
Insecurity that results in a need to prove something (intelligence, knowledge, being right, etc.)
Self-righteousness
Poor communication skills
Impaired social skills
Narcissism
Overconfidence

ASSOCIATED BEHAVIORS AND ATTITUDES:
Having high standards
Not taking *No* for an answer
Disrespecting the personal space and boundaries of others
Making judgments
Using shame or guilt trips to get one's way
Prying, hounding, and nagging
Making verbal threats or insults
Intimidation
Brazen forwardness
Ignoring social cues of discomfort
Pushing others to excel in areas one did not (especially one's children)
Employing pressuring tactics
Pushing one's own beliefs or opinions onto others
Belittling others
Rudeness
Impatience
Emotional manipulation
Overprotectiveness
Dominating the conversation; talking too much
Making demands
Giving ultimatums: *Finish the report or don't bother coming in on Monday.*
Dismissing those deemed unworthy
Projecting opinions onto others; telling them what they should feel
Being opinionated and argumentative
Meddling in other people's affairs
Bullying

Negativity
Always being ready with an answer
Growing angry and aggressive when challenged

ASSOCIATED THOUGHTS:
What a stupid idea. I better step in before Oliver makes a mess of things.
Why is Ben being so stubborn? I'm always right about stuff like this.
If I pressure Alice enough, she'll give in. She always does.
I wish Rick would grow a pair. It gets old, having to convince him to stand up for himself.

ASSOCIATED EMOTIONS: agitation, confidence, contempt, frustration, impatience, pride

POSITIVE ASPECTS: Pushy characters are usually comfortable in leadership roles. While some are incompetent, others are legitimately good at what they do—efficient, and always striving to be and do better. They are bold and outspoken and know which buttons to push to get a reaction. Many characters will follow someone who's pushy if he is charming, successful, or strong in other areas.

NEGATIVE ASPECTS: Pushy people do not respect boundaries. To get what they want, they can be demeaning or insulting, ignoring cues from others that enough is enough. Believing that they can do things better than anyone else often results in impatience, self-righteousness, and snobbery. Many of these characters lack the social skills necessary to develop meaningful relationships, which is ironic since most of them really want to be in charge of others.

EXAMPLE FROM FILM: Biff Tannen from *Back to the Future* is aggressive and in-your-face and isn't afraid to throw a few punches to get what he wants. His specific target is George McFly, who he intimidates into doing his homework for him. Biff uses pushiness to manipulate others because he isn't smart enough to achieve success on his own. This continues into adulthood and, as a result, Biff is not liked or respected, only feared. **Other Examples from Film and TV:** Melanie Carmichael (*Sweet Home Alabama*), Marie Barone (*Everybody Loves Raymond*)

OVERCOMING THIS TRAIT AS A MAJOR FLAW: Characters with this flaw may need to be emotionally shoved around themselves in order to understand how their behavior affects others. Suffering the loss of a friendship or position at work may be a wake-up call that they've finally gone too far.

TRAITS IN SUPPORTING CHARACTERS THAT MAY CAUSE CONFLICT: fanatical, hostile, inflexible, lazy, oversensitive, patient, perfectionist, rebellious, resentful

REBELLIOUS

DEFINITION: flouting the law or resisting authority

SIMILAR FLAWS: defiant, disobedient, insubordinate, mutinous

POSSIBLE CAUSES:
Having domineering parents
Living in a strictly-controlled culture or society
Repression
Being denied creative expression
Discrimination
Being at war or living in a policed state
Being strong-willed
Having been independent and answering to no one for a long time
A history of abuse or mistreatment by those in authority
Needing control and freedom, to be independent
Believing that respect must be earned, not automatically granted

ASSOCIATED BEHAVIORS AND ATTITUDES:
Backtalk; insolent or impudent retorts
Arguing
Silent protests
Flouting the rules of one's parents or society
Ignoring warnings
Risky behavior
Stubbornness
Lying
Doing something because it is forbidden or illegal
Participating in marches, sit-ins, protests, or revolutions
Deliberately engaging in activities that annoy those in charge
Joining a group with like-minded ideals and beliefs
Getting a tattoo or piercing to symbolize one's freedom to do so
Eschewing trends or popularity
Smoking
Refusing to answer a question, account for one's whereabouts, etc. on principle alone
Exploring beliefs of right and wrong, good and evil, moral and immoral, etc.
Questioning facts
Pushing boundaries and testing limits
Aggression that may lead to violence
Encouraging others to challenge authority
Sneaking around to get one's way
Fighting for personal freedoms and rights
Passive-aggressiveness; acting as if one is on board while secretly planning to rebel
Becoming easily angered

Saying things deliberately meant to hurt those in authority
Ignoring orders
Being uncooperative
Keeping secrets to deny someone information

ASSOCIATED THOUGHTS:
Who put her in charge? I could run this class better than she does.
They can't treat me this way. I won't put up with it.
If he wants my respect, he has to earn it.
He might be running this project, but he's not running me. I'll do things my own way.
Let him try and tell me what to do. We'll see who wins that fight.

ASSOCIATED EMOTIONS: anger, determination, excitement, frustration, rage

POSITIVE ASPECTS: Rebellious characters are able to set their own moral compass and follow it without fearing where it may lead. They're also open to new experiences and are fairly tolerant of others. These kinds of characters are often magnets for those who feel shoehorned into a particular mold, beaten down by parental expectations, and constricted to a certain path.

NEGATIVE ASPECTS: Rebellious characters often have impaired judgment, seeing the allure of what they want and missing the possible consequences. Risky behavior means putting themselves and others into danger or doing irreparable damage as a result of following their whims. Other people may take advantage of a rebellious character's zeal for independence by urging them to participate in harmful or immoral activities, and prodding them into behavior that aligns with their own agendas.

EXAMPLE FROM FILM: John Bender (*The Breakfast Club*) rebels against authority whenever possible, which frequently lands him in Saturday detention. In one memorable scene when he's challenged by the teacher in charge, John doesn't back down but repeatedly defies him, racking up week after week of detentions to come. While his rebellion may look like strength, it's really just a distorted attempt to gain some kind of control of his world, which is largely ruled by a verbally and physically abusive father. **Other Examples from Film:** Randle McMurphy (*One Flew over the Cuckoo's Nest*), Merida (*Brave*)

OVERCOMING THIS TRAIT AS A MAJOR FLAW: To overcome a rebellious nature, a character would have to come face-to-face with the ugly side of his actions. Seeing the negative consequences for something that cannot be undone may open the character's eyes to the importance of limits, rules, and boundaries in society.

TRAITS IN SUPPORTING CHARACTERS THAT MAY CAUSE CONFLICT: controlling, courteous, cowardly, evil, immoral, inflexible, mature, obedient, possessive, timid

RECKLESS

DEFINITION: marked by a lack of proper caution; being careless of consequences

SIMILAR FLAWS: careless, heedless, imprudent

POSSIBLE CAUSES:
Conceit
A rebellious nature
Needing to prove something to others
Needing to be accepted or liked
Being an adrenaline junkie
Perceived invulnerability
A naturally fearless nature
An utter lack of care or concern for oneself
Impulsivity
Immaturity; the lack of ability or desire to make careful decisions
ADHD or ADD
Suicidal tendencies; believing that there's nothing to live for
Guilt or shame
Long-term anger or rage
Excessive pride and self-confidence
Addictions
Being raised by adventurous and fearless parents

ASSOCIATED BEHAVIORS AND ATTITUDES:
Driving too fast
Driving while intoxicated
Engaging in unprotected sex
Endangering others
Having a sense of fun and adventure
Committing to an action and then following through no matter what
Being irresponsible with one's possessions
Buying into the mistaken belief that everything will be fine because it always has been in the past
Chasing adrenaline rushes without considering the risks
Engaging in foolhardy actions (jumping off a roof, racing a train, etc.)
Participating in pranks
Breaking the law
Shoplifting
Car surfing
Volunteering to go first in a dangerous situation
Chasing the thrill of the unknown
Not taking safety precautions (wearing a helmet or life jacket, taking a cell phone, etc.)
Diving off bridges or cliffs without checking for rocks or other dangers
Gambling with funds that one can't afford to lose

Carrying weapons
Using stolen credit cards
Defacing property or stealing things for kicks
Messing around with explosives
Sexting or posting inappropriate photos online
Goading others into participating in reckless activities
Giving in to one's desires and whims without using common sense
Being highly spontaneous

ASSOCIATED THOUGHTS:
Nothing bad's gonna happen. It never does.
A little risk makes everything more exciting.
Driving Daddy's car, huh? Let's see if Al is man enough to play chicken.
People worry too much.

ASSOCIATED EMOTIONS: confidence, excitement, impatience, pride, satisfaction, smugness

POSITIVE ASPECTS: Reckless characters often thrive on attention and aren't afraid to do things that terrify others. These characters can be entrepreneurial in nature, thinking outside of established norms and coming up with new ideas. They are often determined, decisive, and brave. Although dangerous, they provide fun and excitement for the people around them.

NEGATIVE ASPECTS: Reckless characters are a danger to themselves and others. They're self-involved, often knowing that their behavior is dangerous but being compelled to still pursue whatever it is they seek. Because people can confuse recklessness with free-spiritedness or adventurousness, a character with this flaw is often admired by others and can lead weaker-minded people astray.

EXAMPLE FROM FILM: Martin Riggs (*Lethal Weapon*) is a reckless and impulsive police detective who is just short of suicidal in his pursuit of criminals. Driven half-mad since the death of his wife, he often shows a complete disregard for his own safety. This behavior masks his pain as he struggles to cope with his loss. **Other Examples from Literature and Film:** Dally Winston (*The Outsiders*), Axel Foley (*Beverly Hills Cop* series)

OVERCOMING THIS TRAIT AS A MAJOR FLAW: A grave injury as a result of recklessness might sober a character enough to think twice about this type of behavior. Alternatively, if the character's actions caused hurt, damage, or loss of life to another, he would have to feel the weight of responsibility and recognize the foolishness of his reckless actions.

TRAITS IN SUPPORTING CHARACTERS THAT MAY CAUSE CONFLICT: cautious, cowardly, flaky, nervous, obedient, oversensitive, proper, responsible, timid, worrywart

RESENTFUL

DEFINITION: marked by bitterness

SIMILAR FLAWS: bitter, rancorous, sour, waspish

POSSIBLE CAUSES:
Inequality in the workplace
Experiencing preferential treatment within society (racial profiling, discrimination, etc.)
Having parents who played favorites with their children
Injustice
A traumatic humiliation
Long-standing envy or jealousy
Family feuds
Rejection by a lover, family member, or close friend
Oppression
Desiring to be recognized or appreciated
Losing one's freedom
A deeply embedded sense of fairness

ASSOCIATED BEHAVIORS AND ATTITUDES:
Edginess
Being judgmental of others
Reliving the past; picking at old wounds
Sarcasm
Running others down
Deliberately sabotaging someone in order to make him look foolish or lose face
Unfriendliness
Constantly talking about how one was wronged
Desiring to make the offending party pay
Poor communication skills
Touchiness about certain topics associated with the source of one's resentment
Impaired judgment that is colored by one's negative experience
Cutting someone out of one's life
Overreacting (quitting a job or group in a fit of anger, etc.)
Negativity
Isolation
Trust issues
Happiness or satisfaction that is temporary at best
Insomnia and restless sleeping habits
Difficulty concentrating on tasks
Mistrusting others
Fixating on the actions and choices of the person involved
An inability to forgive or forget
Employing guilt trips in an effort to manipulate others

Withholding praise, even when it's deserved
Difficulty accepting change
Angry outbursts when the resentment can no longer be contained
Obsessive thoughts regarding the person or event that caused the resentful feelings
Stubbornness
A warped viewpoint (taking things out of context, seeing offense where none was meant, etc.)

ASSOCIATED THOUGHTS:
Why do I always have to do the dishes while Brad and Tim get to watch TV?
Even if Miranda apologizes for taking my bracelet, I'll never forgive her.
Every time I go out with Alex, he's broke. I'm sick of paying for everything!
Bill gets a ticket and he's allowed to go out? If I did that, I'd be grounded for a year.

ASSOCIATED EMOTIONS: anger, envy, frustration, jealousy, resentment, scorn

POSITIVE ASPECTS: Resentful characters tend to be cautious and wary, protecting themselves from hurt. They also are likely to appreciate close friends and trusted family members, and are grateful for the support of loved ones who won't betray them.

NEGATIVE ASPECTS: Characters who are resentful often have trust issues and may cast suspicion on people who don't deserve it. Their fixation on past betrayals and wrongs can make them quite negative. Peripheral characters may grow tired of listening to their complaints and secretly wish that the resentful character would just move on. Happiness is fleeting for a character with this flaw, his mood instantly souring at any reminder of his betrayal.

EXAMPLE FROM LITERATURE: Loki, adoptive brother of the god Thor, is raised in a society where Thor is worshipped for his strength and courage in battle. Loki feels inferior because he lacks the physical attributes that would bring him the same acclaim. Although skilled as a sorcerer, he harbors resentment over not receiving the credit due him. This bitterness and hostility eventually builds into a quest for revenge. **Other Examples from Literature and Film**: Grendel (*Beowulf*), Ron Kovic (*Born on the Fourth of July*)

OVERCOMING THIS TRAIT AS A MAJOR FLAW: To overcome resentment, the character would need to understand the toll his bitterness is taking on his happiness. If forgiveness can be achieved, the character can reclaim control of his life and will no longer be ruled by the past event.

TRAITS IN SUPPORTING CHARACTERS THAT MAY CAUSE CONFLICT: cocky, cooperative, friendly, haughty, happy, know-it-all, optimistic, trusting, vindictive

ROWDY

DEFINITION: boisterous and disorderly; a nuisance

SIMILAR FLAWS: boisterous, rambunctious, raucous, rough, unruly

POSSIBLE CAUSES:
Immaturity
Poor parental discipline, a lack of boundaries growing up
Consistently escaping the consequences of one's actions
Behavioral problems and conditions
Impulsiveness
Alcohol or drug use
A lack of social ties to the community
Family or environmental conflict
A lack of respect for authority or general disrespect for others
Adrenaline surges
Being repressed and controlled by past caregivers

ASSOCIATED BEHAVIORS AND ATTITUDES:
Throwing loud parties
Defacing property with graffiti
Not respecting privacy or boundaries
Minor theft (shoplifting, etc.)
Pushing and shoving in a group
Talking loudly or shouting when it isn't appropriate to do so
Poor social graces
Feeling a sense of power when causing disruptions and chaos
Being inconsiderate (playing music too loudly, smoking in someone's house, etc.)
Making a mess in someone else's home
Setting off fireworks
Starting fires for fun
Not understanding why limits are in place
Smashing bottles and littering
Belligerence, rudeness, and telling crude jokes
Ranting, shouting, or arguing in a disruptive way
Inappropriate behavior (ripping one's shirt off and shouting at a business cocktail party, etc.)
Drunken behavior
Intimidating or harassing others for fun
Pulling pranks
Showing basic disrespect for others
Mobbing places and events with the intent to be disruptive
Inciting riots
Egging or toilet papering someone's house
Getting into fights

Public indecency

Interrupting others

Embarrassing friends or family with one's antics

ASSOCIATED THOUGHTS:

Let's crank the music 'til the house shakes!

Is that a siren?

It would be hilarious if we stole all the hubcaps off these cars!

Everyone's all jacked up after the game. I wonder what would happen if I yelled "Riot!"

ASSOCIATED EMOTIONS: amusement, anticipation, eagerness, excitement, happiness

POSITIVE ASPECTS: Rowdy characters take risks, are high energy, and can encourage others to release their inhibitions and cut loose. They're often the life of the party and are fun to be around—as long as their moods don't turn ugly.

NEGATIVE ASPECTS: Rowdy characters are impulsive and don't always recognize limits. A bit of fun can turn into an all-out destruction spree, a rude comment can lead to a shoving match, or a dare can become a life-threatening activity. Rowdy characters are likely to take risks and use peer pressure to encourage others to join in, which can result in injury or worse.

EXAMPLE FROM TV: Cosmo Kramer (*Seinfeld*) always makes his presence known by bursting into rooms uninvited (often knocking himself down) and talking at the top of his lungs. His hand and body gestures are a danger to himself and anyone within reach. From urinating in public to committing mail fraud, his impulsivity and lack of common sense consistently get him and others into trouble. **Other Examples from Literature**: Max (*Where the Wild Things Are*), the Weasley twins (*Harry Potter*), Jo March (*Little Women*), Dennis Mitchell (*Dennis the Menace*)

OVERCOMING THIS TRAIT AS A MAJOR FLAW: Characters who are rowdy to the point of disturbing others or causing chaos need to understand that there is a time and place for boisterous behavior. There is also a difference between having fun and being a public nuisance. Having one's own property vandalized or feeling the hurt and frustration that accompany a loss may make the character more aware of the negative impact of rowdy behavior.

TRAITS IN SUPPORTING CHARACTERS THAT MAY CAUSE CONFLICT: calm, childish, disciplined, fussy, gentle, haughty, introverted, meticulous, oversensitive, proud, responsible, sensible, timid

SCATTERBRAINED

DEFINITION: exhibiting thoughts that are not logical or connected

SIMILAR FLAWS: airheaded, bewildered

POSSIBLE CAUSES:
Difficulty thinking more than one step ahead
Disdain for structure and responsibility
Immaturity
Brain damage
Growing up in a disorganized household
Having a free-spirited personality
A degenerative brain disease
Attention disorders

ASSOCIATED BEHAVIORS AND ATTITUDES:
Missing meetings and appointments
Tardiness
Messiness
Going off on conversational tangents that make no sense
Constantly losing one's phone, keys, etc.
Making excuses for one's behavior
Poor planning skills
Distraction
Disorganization
Poor decision-making
Ineffective attempts at gathering one's thoughts (grocery lists that are left at home, etc.)
Focusing so much on one area that others are neglected
Forgetting birthdays and other events
Arguing in a way that doesn't make sense
Minimizing the importance of items that one has forgotten
Not getting jokes
Trailing off in the middle of a sentence; forgetting where one was going
Sending emails or texts that contain embarrassing typos
Talking badly about a person who happens to be present
Having a slow learning curve; repeating the same mistakes
Backing out of the garage when the door is closed
Locking one's keys in a running car
Mixing up the names of people one has known for years
Missing sarcastic comments or hidden meanings
Accidentally sending an email to everyone on a list instead of to just one person
Showing up for an event on the wrong night or in the wrong place
Forgetfulness that impacts other people (forgetting to pick someone up for work, etc.)
Thoughts that skip from topic to topic
Being unable to follow what someone is saying

ASSOCIATED THOUGHTS:
Man, I really need to study... Oh, I like that dress Betty's wearing.
Blah, blah, blah. This class is so boring. How long until lunch?
Did I leave my curling iron on this morning?
Am I supposed to pick up the kids today or was Mike grabbing them?

ASSOCIATED EMOTIONS: anxiety, conflicted, contentment, frustration, overwhelmed, scorn, worry

POSITIVE ASPECTS: Scatterbrained characters are usually free-spirited and easy to get along with. They often enjoy being with people and like to have fun. Because of their easygoing nature, they can be fairly open-minded and welcome change.

NEGATIVE ASPECTS: Scatterbrained characters are disorganized. Their forgetfulness affects others in a negative way when they're late for appointments or forget their duties. Events planned by a scatterbrained person are likely to frustrate attendees when necessary elements are forgotten. While a character with this flaw might take pride in her free-spirited ways, anxiety can set in when she's put in a leadership position or when she's around others who are highly organized.

EXAMPLE FROM TV: Lucy Ricardo (*I Love Lucy*) is a scatterbrained housewife whose thoughts and decisions don't always make sense. When a tabloid suggests that her husband might be interested in a girl at work, instead of confronting him, Lucy disguises herself and heads to his club to spy on him. On numerous occasions, she tries to wheedle her way into Ricky's limelight though she lacks the necessary skills, like applying as a saxophone player when she can't play the instrument, or auditioning as a Parisian Apache dancer when she doesn't know the dance. Her scatterbrained habits make for much trouble and hilarity—a great example of choosing the perfect trait for the character and the story. **Other Examples from Literature and TV**: Sybill Trelawney (*Harry Potter*), Vern Tessio (*Stand By Me*), Phoebe Buffay (*Friends*), Luna Lovegood (*Harry Potter*)

OVERCOMING THIS TRAIT AS A MAJOR FLAW: To overcome a lack of focus, a character with this flaw would need to incorporate some form of organization. Keeping a day planner, making notes, and setting one's alarm are all small ways to make sure things don't get lost or fall through the cracks. Thinking before reacting, and a steady routine combined with the act of simplifying one's life, will aid this character in keeping track of the important things.

TRAITS IN SUPPORTING CHARACTERS THAT MAY CAUSE CONFLICT: alert, analytical, disciplined, melodramatic, meticulous, obsessive, organized, sensible, paranoid

SELF-DESTRUCTIVE

DEFINITION: inclined toward actions and choices that hurt oneself

SIMILAR FLAWS: destructive, ruinous

POSSIBLE CAUSES:
Depression, eating disorders, or other mental disorders
Addiction
Emotional pain
Low self-esteem
Extreme guilt or shame as a result of a defining past event
A desperate need for attention
A fear of failure or success
Learned behavior from role models
A lack of attachment to others
Loss of hope

ASSOCIATED BEHAVIORS AND ATTITUDES:
Making unwise decisions with one's friends and relationships
Unreliability
Impulsiveness
Showing up late
Missing events or blowing people off
Sabotaging friendships
Wasting opportunities
Excessive or restless sleep habits
Poor nutrition
Taking sexual risks (having frequent partners, not protecting oneself, etc.)
Embracing excess (drinking too much, dangerous drug experimentation, etc.)
Dangerous driving
Pushing people away, refusing help
Placing oneself in risky situations
Punishing oneself or self-harming (cutting, scratching, etc.)
Bulimia or anorexia
Snapping at others or acting mean to push people away
Shirking one's responsibility
Betraying the trust of others by stealing, lying, etc.
Believing that one is unworthy and deserving of punishment
Keeping secrets
Refusing to confide in others about one's emotional pain
Passive-aggressiveness
Self-doubt and second-guessing
Negativity
Expecting the future to be as bleak as the present

Having suicidal thoughts; desiring one's pain to end
Wanting to confess one's sins to others but being unable to do so
Acting inappropriately in order to be fired from a job or get kicked out of a group

ASSOCIATED THOUGHTS:
Why can't Steve leave me alone? I'm not worth the trouble.
This is fun, and I don't want to think or feel anymore.
Mom needs to realize that I'm long past saving.
So what if it's dangerous?
If they knew what I did, they'd all hate me.

ASSOCIATED EMOTIONS: conflicted, defeat, depression, frustration, hurt, resignation, sadness

POSITIVE ASPECTS: Characters who are self-destructive trigger a desire to help in the people around them, propelling them to try and save these characters from themselves.

NEGATIVE ASPECTS: Self-destructive characters make choices that harm themselves and sabotage their happiness. Many times, they make poor decisions (like choosing to smoke) because of a believed positive benefit (it calms the nerves). If a mental disorder is present, destructive choices stemming from a lack of self-esteem can escalate quickly, especially if these characters are withdrawn or isolated. Their negativity and self-defeating behavior can also attract other people who suffer from mental disorders or low self-esteem, leading to a codependent relationship that encourages a continued downward spiral. Characters with low self-worth who refuse to protect themselves are at risk of being taken advantage of by those who thrive on hurting others.

EXAMPLE FROM FILM: Ben Sanderson (*Leaving Las Vegas*) has allowed alcohol to ruin his life. In despair, he goes to Las Vegas with the goal of drinking himself to death, and eventually succeeds. **Other Examples from Film and Literature:** Colonel Frank Slade (*Scent of a Woman*), Lincoln Rhyme (*The Bone Collector*), Parker Fadley (*Cracked Up to Be*)

OVERCOMING THIS TRAIT AS A MAJOR FLAW: To overcome a highly self-destructive trait, the character would need to build esteem through things like friendships, achievable goal-setting that leads to increased confidence, and a positive frame of mind. The caring and patience of friends or family may help with this, or a deeper level of therapy might be required to break the destructive patterns. The character would also need to explore the causes of his low self-worth and begin to deal with the contributing event(s). If guilt is the root cause, the character must find a way to forgive himself in order to heal. Avoiding negative forces (such as self-destructive friends) will also aid in recovery.

TRAITS IN SUPPORTING CHARACTERS THAT MAY CAUSE CONFLICT: adaptable, controlling, disciplined, empathetic, evil, kind, needy, nurturing, optimistic, vindictive

SELF-INDULGENT

DEFINITION: satisfying one's appetites, passions, and whims without restraint

SIMILAR FLAWS: uncontrolled, undisciplined, unrestrained

POSSIBLE CAUSES:
Laziness
Poor judgment
A live-in-the-moment attitude that dismisses consequences down the road
A spoiled or entitled upbringing
A rebellious nature
A history of overindulgence without negative consequences
Lacking willpower
Having worked hard and exhibited discipline with little or no positive outcome
Low self-esteem
Depression

ASSOCIATED BEHAVIORS AND ATTITUDES:
Overeating
Not exercising
Going to bed late
Oversleeping
Doing what one wants at the moment without thinking of the future
Overindulging in a hobby (playing video games, watching TV, surfing the web, etc.)
Getting sick from indulging in an excess of unhealthy foods or drinks
Knowing the consequences of overindulging but feeling powerless to stop
Guilt and shame
Arriving late to work, school, and appointments
Not taking care of one's appearance
Poor time management
Procrastination
Refusing to do the things one doesn't want to do, even when others will have to pick up the slack
Acting according to what one wants rather than thinking of what's best for oneself or for others
Expressing impatience when gratification is delayed
Seeing no need to change oneself
Living for the moment
Focusing on immediate gratification
Pickiness, needing things to be exactly as one likes them to be
Over-socializing (going to too many parties, staying out too late, etc.)
Racking up debt
Feelings of deep hopelessness
Sabotaging one's health and relationships (obesity getting so out of hand one is bedridden, etc.)
Doing the bare minimum on work projects or activities that aren't one's favorite
Spending more money than is wise
Setting limits, then breaking them

Unrestrained sexual activity
Extravagance and waste

ASSOCIATED THOUGHTS:
I know I should work out but I really don't want to.
This project is due tomorrow, but why should I have to work when everyone else is going out?
I love these shoes, but they're over my budget. I'll put them on my credit card.
I'll regret this tomorrow, but right now I don't care.

ASSOCIATED EMOTIONS: conflicted, defeat, denial, eagerness, frustration, guilt, indifference, satisfaction

POSITIVE ASPECTS: Self-indulgent characters are often easygoing and laid back. They do what they want and encourage others to do the same, making them fun companions. Unconcerned with long-term consequences, these characters are able to fully live in the here-and-now.

NEGATIVE ASPECTS: Characters who overindulge are usually self-centered, focusing on what they want rather than what's best for them and for others. They continue along this path despite negative consequences such as health problems, broken relationships, and lost jobs. These characters can also be difficult to work with, doing only the tasks that please them and leaving the unpleasant jobs for others. Their reluctance to delve into activities that don't interest them can lead to poor performance at school and at work.

EXAMPLE FROM LITERATURE: Templeton (*Charlotte's Web*), the rat who lives under Wilbur's trough, is a self-professed glutton who does nothing unless there's some intrinsic benefit for him. As the only barnyard animal able to go to the dump and bring back the words that can save Wilbur's life, one would think he would gladly go. But it takes the promise of food to motivate him to do this important thing. Similarly, when he learns that he alone can bring Charlotte's egg sac home from the fair, he only agrees after being guaranteed first dibs on the food trough forever. He lives a solitary, sedentary life, without a care for anyone but himself. **Other Examples from TV and Literature**: Homer Simpson (*The Simpsons*), Friar Tuck (the *Robin Hood* legend), Hawkeye Pierce (*M*A*S*H**)

OVERCOMING THIS TRAIT AS A MAJOR FLAW: The self-indulgent character has to realize that his behavior is having a negative impact—on himself, others, his relationships, his success, the environment, etc. Many times, these characters don't care enough about themselves for a personal consequence to elicit change; in this case, seeing how one's lack of discipline is hurting others may spur them to alter their habits.

TRAITS IN SUPPORTING CHARACTERS THAT MAY CAUSE CONFLICT: disciplined, fussy, haughty, judgmental, lazy, sleazy, stingy, stubborn, unethical

SELFISH

DEFINITION: overly or solely concerned with one's own needs

SIMILAR FLAWS: self-absorbed, self-centered, egocentric

POSSIBLE CAUSES:
Insecurity
Greed
Having a weak emotional connection to society
Personality disorders
Fear of sacrifice
A desire for personal comfort
Unmet goals or needs
Control issues

ASSOCIATED BEHAVIORS AND ATTITUDES:
Rarely (if ever) thinking of others' needs
Placing one's welfare above that of others
Aligning oneself with people who make one look good or increase one's influence
Having high standards and expectations
Being preoccupied with one's needs, priorities, and goals
Viewing others as a means to an end
Manipulation
Difficulty trusting others
Acting altruistic only when there's a benefit from doing so
Only sharing information that will benefit oneself in some way
Plotting, planning, or scheming a way to get what one wants
Lying or only telling part of the story
Difficulty compromising or finding middle ground with others
Becoming highly protective of one's property and possessions
Hoarding one's resources
Difficulty sharing
Lack of charity
Assuming that others are only out for themselves
Being able to turn a blind eye to the needs of others in order to keep what one has
Struggling with team-based activities
Having a cagey attitude
Keeping secrets
Making excuses to avoid the things one doesn't want to do
Using people to get ahead
Difficulty committing to others
Refusing to be inconvenienced to help another
Avoiding responsibility if one believes it will lead to failure or consequences
Minimizing risks in one's personal and professional life

Arrogance

Becoming petulant when one doesn't get one's way

Experiencing anger or even rage when thwarted

Believing one's time is more valuable than another's

ASSOCIATED THOUGHTS:

I don't care what play Coach calls; this time, I'm taking the ball.

Hmm, I need an excuse. No way am I giving up my weekend to help Marty move.

If I volunteer this time, they'll ask me to help every time.

Maybe I can sweet-talk Anna into sitting on the board so I don't have to.

ASSOCIATED EMOTIONS: anger, anguish, desire, desperation, determination, envy, jealousy, pride

POSITIVE ASPECTS: Selfish characters are survivors. They are very protective of their time and money; because of this, they're able to focus on goals that result in their enjoying the fruits of their labors.

NEGATIVE ASPECTS: Selfish characters have a "me first" attitude and become disgruntled when having to do something that isn't on their agenda. Every decision they make is calculated and self-promoting; they don't derive benefit from the rush of well-being that comes from kindness and giving. Their tunnel vision may result in them ignoring the desires of others, causing frustration and hurt feelings. Because most people view selfishness as an unlikable trait, these characters may have difficulty forming meaningful connections with others.

EXAMPLE FROM FILM: Charlie Babbitt (*Rain Man*) is an unethical, narcissistic car dealer. When his estranged father dies and leaves the bulk of his estate to Charlie's autistic brother, Charlie sets out to reclaim his fortune. With no knowledge of or empathy for Raymond's disability, Charlie abducts his emotionally fragile sibling, drags him across the country, and attempts to exploit Raymond's money-making capabilities. The only thing he cares about is getting what he's due; everyone and everything else is secondary. **Other Examples from Literature and Film**: Scarlett O'Hara (*Gone with the Wind*), Will Freeman (*About a Boy*), Phil Connors (*Groundhog Day*)

OVERCOMING THIS TRAIT AS A MAJOR FLAW: For a character to become less selfish, he would have to practice his empathy skills and try to discern what the people around him are feeling. It would also help to engage in activities that benefit others instead of only seeking to indulge himself. Through seeing how kindness is received and appreciated, a selfish character might begin to understand how he can make an impact on other people's lives and, in turn, experience a surge of positivity that will encourage more caring and giving behaviors.

TRAITS IN SUPPORTING CHARACTERS THAT MAY CAUSE CONFLICT: cocky, competitive, fair, jealous, just, manipulative, mature, spoiled, suspicious, unselfish, vain

SLEAZY

DEFINITION: sordid and corrupt; creepy

SIMILAR FLAWS: degenerate, insidious

POSSIBLE CAUSES:
A lack of dignity for oneself or others
Low self-esteem
A lack of morality
Having experienced or witnessed victimization in the past
A pessimistic view of humanity
A mental disorder
Brain damage
A sociopathic nature

ASSOCIATED BEHAVIORS AND ATTITUDES:
Vulgarity
Low body image
Poor hygiene
Dishonesty
Stealing
Drug trafficking
Enjoying how one makes others feel uncomfortable and unsafe
Blackmailing people
Liking to watch or spy unseen
Justifying one's actions by claiming that everyone is immoral on some level
Using someone's weaknesses for one's own gain
Providing free drugs in order to create addicts
Betraying the privacy of others (placing hidden cameras in a washroom, etc.)
Making others uncomfortable through one's actions (leering, ignoring boundaries, etc.)
Acting with a lack of compassion or empathy
Seeking out opportunities to take advantage of others
Frequenting strip clubs and sex shows
Criminal behavior
Viewing people as sheep
Having corrupt or perverted thoughts (abusing women, pedophilia, etc.)
Showing little or no respect for privacy or boundaries
Enjoying the debasement and humiliation of others
Viewing child pornography
Exhibiting a use-and-abuse philosophy
Mistrusting others
Sadism
Committing acts of sexual abuse
Enslaving people

Human trafficking
Kidnapping
Walking away from people in need
Feeling no social responsibility
A lack of common decency
Sexual harassment
Feeling no loyalty to one's community or country

ASSOCIATED THOUGHTS:
I hope Mandy's working tonight. She knows how to put on a good show.
A cute kid like that...his parents would pay a lot to get him back.
That guy should be grateful I didn't take his girlfriend along with his wallet.
If he's stupid enough to park his car in this alley, he deserves to lose it.
So I scam them out of a little pension money. They're so old, they'll never use it all anyway.

ASSOCIATED EMOTIONS: confidence, contempt, desire, desperation, scorn, suspicion, smugness

POSITIVE ASPECTS: Characters who come off as sleazy or creepy instantly create feelings of discomfort and mistrust. For authors, these characters make great scapegoats and can be used as effective red herrings when one wants to throw the reader off.

NEGATIVE ASPECTS: Sleazy characters don't elicit empathy, which will make it difficult for authors to create that important reader-character bond. Readers will wish to remain distant from them, as will the peripheral characters in the story.

EXAMPLE FROM FILM: Sean Nokes (*Sleepers*) works as a guard at the Wilkinson Home for Boys, where he routinely sexually abuses his charges. His treatment of them is so foul that ten years after their release, two of the former inmates happen to see him in a restaurant and shoot him dead on the spot. **Other Examples from Film**: Franklin Hart, Jr. (*9 to 5*), Daryll Lee Cullum (*Copycat*), Boss Tweed (*Gangs of New York*), Nils Bjurman (*The Girl with the Dragon Tattoo*)

OVERCOMING THIS TRAIT AS A MAJOR FLAW: If the character, once unaware of the feelings he or she evoked in others, becomes aware of them, shame may push him to make life changes. Humanizing the people this character victimizes could also allow him to see how his attitudes, beliefs, and actions are hurting others. If any sordid behavior is a result of a mental disorder, therapy and possibly medication would likely be needed to create pathways to empathy and respect for the human condition.

TRAITS IN SUPPORTING CHARACTERS THAT MAY CAUSE CONFLICT: devout, gullible, honorable, just, kind, proud, timid, trusting, wholesome

SPOILED

DEFINITION: having an attitude of entitlement due to excessive coddling and pampering

SIMILAR FLAWS: bratty, entitled

POSSIBLE CAUSES:
Having overindulgent caregivers
A history of always getting what one wants
Immaturity
Being the baby of the family
Being the only boy in a family of girls, or vice versa
A low sense of self-worth
Believing that one's value is directly related to what one has

ASSOCIATED BEHAVIORS AND ATTITUDES:
Greediness
Seeing what one wants and demanding it
Using manipulation to control and take advantage of others
Throwing tantrums
Manufacturing crocodile tears
Having a sense of entitlement
Using another's love or affection to get what one wants: *If you loved me, you'd take me to Paris.*
Feeling put upon when others request help
Putting self-gratification first
Wanting things without having to work for them
Wastefulness
Using excuses to avoid responsibility: *I'm too sick to babysit.*
Pitting people against one another: *Mom says I'm too young, but you don't think so, do you Dad?*
Whining and complaining
Having high expectations: *I hope Joey knows that anything less than a carat is unacceptable.*
Using compliments to get one's way
Having a conveniently forgetful memory: *I don't remember saying I'd walk Annie's dog.*
Citing ultimatums when one doesn't get one's way
Speaking rudely to others
Refusing to speak, socialize, or eat as a means of control
Being quick to anger
Expressing resentment when others steal the limelight
Talking back to those in authority
Letting emotion rule over reason
Stubbornness
Melodrama
Jealousy
Bringing up the past: *You bought Steven a car for his graduation, remember?*
Comparing what one has to what others have

Losing interest in one's possessions when something new becomes available
Wanting what other people have
Living above one's means
Possessiveness
Becoming resentful when asked to share with others
Being ungrateful
Acting as if one is better than one's peers
Disparaging other people's possessions
Treating one's possessions with a lack of care since they're easily replaced

ASSOCIATED THOUGHTS:
Why does he bother arguing? We both know I'll get what I want eventually.
She got the job instead of me? That's not fair!
I don't want to wait! I want it now!

ASSOCIATED EMOTIONS: anger, desire, frustration, insecurity, irritation, scorn

POSITIVE ASPECTS: Spoiled characters are transparent with their feelings and desires, so there's no second-guessing what they want. They're often bold and will go after what they feel they deserve. This kind of character can be useful when the author needs someone to speak up or make demands.

NEGATIVE ASPECTS: Spoiled characters are ruled by their wants and needs rather than by objective good sense and graciousness. If they feel wronged or treated unfairly they will lash out with their words and actions in ways that hurts others. Acquisitions are often more important to a spoiled character than relationships, most of which remain superficial or become broken due to their treatment of others.

EXAMPLE FROM FILM: Veruca Salt (*Willy Wonka & the Chocolate Factory*) is a spoiled, bratty girl who is used to getting just what she wants. She looks down on the other children on the Wonka factory tour, seeing herself as superior due to her wealth. Materialistic and overindulged, Veruca demands that her parents give her whatever she fancies. When she sets her eye on the goose that lays golden eggs, her pompous attitude sees her dropped down the garbage chute and labeled a "bad egg." **Other Examples from Literature and Film**: Scarlett O'Hara (*Gone with the Wind*), Dudley Dursley (*Harry Potter* series), Eric Bates (*The Toy*)

OVERCOMING THIS TRAIT AS A MAJOR FLAW: If a character is shamed in a way that allows her to see her bratty behavior for what it is, she will likely feel enough embarrassment or humiliation to want to change. Many spoiled characters do not realize how others view them, so exposure to others' perceptions (through an overheard conversation, for instance) may be hurtful but can also lead to the self-awareness that precedes a desire to change.

TRAITS IN SUPPORTING CHARACTERS THAT MAY CAUSE CONFLICT: courteous, extravagant, fair, honest, jealous, selfish, stingy, thrifty, weak-willed

STINGY

DEFINITION: exhibiting miserly tendencies

SIMILAR FLAWS: cheap, miserly, parsimonious, tightfisted

POSSIBLE CAUSES:
Living through a financial crisis
Experiencing a situation where one was grossly taken advantage of
A devastating financial loss
Selfishness or a desire to amass wealth at all costs
Viewing generosity as a weakness

ASSOCIATED BEHAVIORS AND ATTITUDES:
Haggling to get the best price, even when it means taking advantage of someone
Reusing items well past what is normal or healthy (eating expired food, etc.)
Refusing to buy new products even when one can afford to do so
Accusing a service provider of taking advantage simply because one doesn't want to pay
Not leaving a tip
Having a generally negative attitude about people
Being protective of one's time and money
Refusing to help others
Bemoaning the high prices of goods and services
Imposing one's experiences onto others: *I worked for minimum wage as a kid, so he should, too.*
Not celebrating Christmas or birthdays because one is too cheap to buy gifts
Re-gifting
Refusing to donate to charities or those in need
Checking one's receipt in calculated detail
Always supplying correct change, even when paying a bill with friends
Reluctance to split the bill, especially if the other person's meal was more expensive
Suggesting that the other party should treat because of a favor done in the past
Keeping mental track of who owes one money
Resenting people who ask to borrow money or possessions
Clipping coupons
Charging high interest for loans
Shopping only during a sale
Refusing to pay full price for anything
Purchasing items that come with something free even if one doesn't need them
Limiting one's driving due to the high price of gas
Reluctance to attend functions where gifts are given (weddings, retirement parties, etc.)
Eating half a meal then returning it in the hopes of getting a discount or refund
Stealing
Hoarding tendencies

ASSOCIATED THOUGHTS:

Three bucks for a pound of butter? No way am I paying that.

Pay full price? He must think I'm an idiot.

I'm almost out of shampoo, but it isn't on sale yet. Guess I'll have to make it last.

If I sit through the carpet cleaning demo, I get a free set of knives? Sweet!

It's been two weeks. When is Rick going to pay me back for lunch?

ASSOCIATED EMOTIONS: annoyance, contempt, frustration, irritation, scorn, suspicion, worry

POSITIVE ASPECTS: Stingy characters derive pleasure from chasing a bargain and take pride in their ability to control their finances. They're recyclers and creative thinkers, reusing or repurposing old goods rather than buying new. These characters, determined to make do with what they have, are excellent savers and rarely waste money on frivolous things.

NEGATIVE ASPECTS: The stingy person's determination to save every penny is all-important, influencing everything from business deals to gifts purchased for others. This obsession with money even extends to dealings within the family, causing bad feelings and lingering resentment. Stingy characters can also be so devoted to saving that they develop hoarding tendencies, refusing to give up anything that they deem useful.

EXAMPLE FROM LITERATURE: Ebenezer Scrooge, the despised character from Charles Dickens' *A Christmas Carol*, is a miserly yet wealthy man who ignores the suffering of others and looks down on poor people. He regularly mistreats his employees and takes advantage of others for his own gain. On Christmas Eve, he is visited by three ghosts who show him both the dark future that awaits if he is to continue his stingy ways, and the possible redemption if he can change in time. **Other Examples from TV**: Mr. Burns (*The Simpsons*), Frank Barone (*Everybody Loves Raymond*)

OVERCOMING THIS TRAIT AS A MAJOR FLAW: Like Ebenezer, a character would need to experience a major perception-altering event to change him from greedy to generous. Suffering a huge financial loss, becoming homeless or dependent on others to survive, or losing something incredibly personal and important as a result of miserly behavior are all possible scenarios.

TRAITS IN SUPPORTING CHARACTERS THAT MAY CAUSE CONFLICT: extravagant, generous, greedy, judgmental, mischievous, superficial, trusting

STUBBORN

DEFINITION: unyielding or obstinate

SIMILAR FLAWS: bullheaded, headstrong, mulish, obstinate, stiff-necked, willful

POSSIBLE CAUSES:
Growing up spoiled and accustomed to getting one's way
Control issues
Being fiercely independent
Having an intense drive to succeed, win, or be right
Excessive pride
Selfishness
Fear of appearing weak to others

ASSOCIATED BEHAVIORS AND ATTITUDES:
Reluctance to compromise
Defending one's ideas and beliefs
Having a strong moral compass
Reacting negatively to criticism, even if it's offered kindly
Being touchy about past mistakes
Refusing to admit defeat
Being highly opinionated
Tenaciousness and determination
Seeing one's flaws as being part of oneself and refusing to change
Difficulty communicating when upset
Rarely admitting to being wrong
Not asking for help when one needs it
Citing past events when one was right
Feeling misunderstood
Having a high opinion of one's views and beliefs
Being resistant to new ideas that don't coincide with one's beliefs
Arguing when opposed
Sticking with a decision despite overwhelming evidence it is a mistake
Not working well with others
Difficulty empathizing with opposing views
Retreating when one is challenged or pushed too far
Citing examples of why one is right
Refusing to explain one's reason for resistance
Feeling like one's opinions aren't valued or taken seriously
Not letting others help, instruct, or take over
Struggling with collaborative activities
Being judgmental of others
Choosing to do more work rather than admit one was wrong
Being loyal to causes and people who have earned one's respect and trust

Pushiness
Competitiveness

ASSOCIATED THOUGHTS:
Mary needs to stop nagging at me to eat healthier. I'm an adult—I'll do what I want.
Jeez, Alyssa! Stop bugging me about the dance! I'd rather die than see Bill and Amy together.
She needs to shut up about being lost. The house is around here somewhere, I'm sure.
Does Rick think he knows how to do my job better than I do?
I don't care how much experience he has; I'm doing this my way.

ASSOCIATED EMOTIONS: anger, confidence, contempt, determination, fear, frustration, pride

POSITIVE ASPECTS: Once bullheaded characters pick a course of action, they can be trusted to see it through to the end. Because of this, they often make good leaders. When this trait is applied to relationships, these characters become fiercely loyal to those who win their affections. Stubborn characters with an unparalleled sense of morality will always fight for what is right, no matter the obstacles.

NEGATIVE ASPECTS: Characters with this flaw do not always know when enough is enough, and can push people to the breaking point with their inability to meet others halfway. They often struggle with adaptability and miss the forest for the trees because they can only view problems from a single angle. They may hold to a goal even when it is no longer prudent to do so and have a hard time letting others contribute or be in charge. Letting stubbornness dictate their actions can cause challenges and ruin relationships, bringing pain to everyone involved.

EXAMPLE FROM FILM: In the second installment of the *Star Trek* movie franchise, the villain Khan unexpectedly escapes lifelong exile. In charge of a Federation starship, he has the freedom to go anywhere and create a new life for himself and his crew. Instead, he decides to chase down and destroy his old nemesis. Despite being advanced in years, never having piloted a starship, and knowing that he's risking the lives of everyone on board, he insists on his course of action. In the end, stubborn pride overpowers his "superior intellect," leading to his defeat. **Other Examples from Literature and Film**: Katniss Everdeen (*The Hunger Games*), Captain James T. Kirk (*Star Trek*), Rooster Cogburn (*True Grit*)

OVERCOMING THIS TRAIT AS A MAJOR FLAW: For a character to overcome his stubborn nature, he would need to see that he doesn't know everything and that others have valid ideas and opinions, too. Not becoming defensive when advice or gentle criticism is given is a good step, along with seeking wise counsel from others. By asking for help and seeing a quick resolution to a problem, the character may be more open to collaboration and advice in the future.

TRAITS IN SUPPORTING CHARACTERS THAT MAY CAUSE CONFLICT: controlling, courteous, helpful, honest, nagging, nosy, pushy, sensible, uncooperative

SUBSERVIENT

DEFINITION: extremely compliant and obedient

SIMILAR FLAWS: obsequious, servile, slavish

POSSIBLE CAUSES:
A history of codependence
A desperate need for acceptance, love, or inclusion
A lack of self-esteem; believing that worth is gained solely by serving others
Gratitude
A fear of losing the favor of others
Believing that one is incapable of surviving or succeeding on one's own
Desiring to make up for a perceived failing in the past
Sexual masochism

ASSOCIATED BEHAVIORS AND ATTITUDES:
Timidity
Following orders without question
Not thinking for oneself
Never disagreeing with those in charge
Adopting the opinions of the person being served
Living in fear of doing something wrong or upsetting those in charge
Blind loyalty
Believing in something bigger than oneself and being willing to sacrifice for it
Difficulty making independent decisions
Obsessing over what one's idol thinks and feels
Striving to meet unrealistic expectations
Neediness
Being a rule-follower
Jumping to the defense of the person in charge
An inability to cut loose and have fun
Protectiveness of one's few secrets
Being a yes-man
Setting poor boundaries within relationships; having an unhealthy attachment to others
Feeling guilty if one believes he is failing in some way
Being highly observant
Incessantly worrying and obsessing about the person one idolizes
Growing upset if too much time has passed without seeing the person one is committed to serve
Being eager to please
Being a peacemaker
Indecisiveness
Fanaticism
Putting one's wants and needs aside in order to serve others

Neglecting one's health
Measuring one's success by the success of the people one serves
Becoming indignant when someone disrespects the person in charge
Experiencing a loss of identity
Feeling guilt when thinking of oneself

ASSOCIATED THOUGHTS:
I don't know what to do. I'll ask Tom; he'll know.
Mrs. Jackson is almost out of coffee. Let me get her some more.
He's a brilliant man. I'd do anything for him.

ASSOCIATED EMOTIONS: anxiety, denial, guilt, insecurity, uncertainty, unease

POSITIVE ASPECTS: Subservient characters are usually perceptive. They can pinpoint needs and will go out of their way to meet them. They willingly put their own wants and desires aside so they can better serve others. Often timid, they are unswervingly loyal and will become bold and defensive when someone they respect is being maligned.

NEGATIVE ASPECTS: Though very cognizant of the needs of others, subservient characters have a somewhat skewed view of themselves. In their eyes, their value is wrapped up in the person they serve; as such, they often lack a sense of their own identity. Through their compulsion to care for others, they put themselves at risk by entering into toxic relationships. Their own needs, dreams, and desires usually go unmet, which can lead to repressed resentment and depression.

EXAMPLE FROM FILM: Aaron Stampler (*Primal Fear*) is a timid, stuttering altar boy who falls victim to one of the most powerful men in Chicago. Though sexually abused by the archbishop, Aaron mourns his passing, defending his memory by recalling his philanthropy and all of the positive things he had done. **Other Examples from Film and TV**: Waylon Smithers (*The Simpsons*), Scott Pritchard (*No Way Out*), the house elves from the *Harry Potter* series

OVERCOMING THIS TRAIT AS A MAJOR FLAW: To recover, a subservient character must recognize his own value and worth and come to understand that serving and thinking for himself isn't selfish, but healthy. Because of ingrained habits, certain skills will need to be learned, like assertiveness, basic problem solving and decision making skills, and how to productively communicate.

TRAITS IN SUPPORTING CHARACTERS THAT MAY CAUSE CONFLICT:
controlling, independent, judgmental, manipulative, reckless

SUPERSTITIOUS

DEFINITION: believing that omens and symbols can have specific prophetic meaning and that certain ritualistic practices will influence events

POSSIBLE CAUSES:
Obsessive-compulsive disorders
Paranoia
Being highly influenced by the concept of luck
Growing up in a religious or superstition-influenced environment
Having a strong imagination
Belonging to a culture steeped in folklore or mythological beliefs
Fear of failure or death
Needing to explain things that seem unexplainable

ASSOCIATED BEHAVIORS AND ATTITUDES:
Carrying symbols of one's superstitions
Adhering to ritualistic behavior (throwing salt over a shoulder if spilled, etc.)
Visiting psychics, having one's palm read, reading tea leaves, etc.
Abiding by horoscopes
Not believing in coincidences
Becoming attached to an object, person, or place and associating good or bad things with it
Crossing oneself or making the sign of the evil eye when frightened
Avoiding danger because of superstitious beliefs (not walking under a ladder, etc.)
Blaming luck for an outcome: *Three broken dishes in one day? Talk about bad luck.*
Using superstition to avoid blame: *I told you parking in spot thirteen was a bad idea!*
Seeing "signs" and making decisions based on the information
Adhering to unproven patterns: *I always bet on seven; it's my favorite number.*
Embracing sport-related superstitions: *If I shave during playoffs, my team will lose.*
Knocking on wood, crossing fingers, or adopting other widely used habits
Avoiding symbols of bad luck (black cats, cracks in the sidewalk, etc.)
Difficulty coping with change
Giving advice based on superstition instead of fact
Speaking a mantra in order to comfort oneself and create a sense of peace
Taking coincidence as proof: *Told you my rabbit's foot would help me win at slots!*
Adhering to patterns that bring comfort (visiting the same places, eating certain foods)
Associating a favorite piece of clothing with good luck
Being comforted that a larger force is at work in one's life
Uncertainty about what to do, and so seeking out omens to help steer one's course
Believing that signs and symbols are everywhere and one's fate is controlled by them
Believing that superstition is tied to one's fortune or survival

ASSOCIATED THOUGHTS:
Full moon tonight. No wonder the kids are so crazy.
I can't believe David bought a snake. Doesn't he know they're bad luck?
Maybe I should wear my horseshoe earrings to help with the big exam.
I hate to cancel, but after breaking that mirror, it's safer to stay home.
My horoscope says to be wary of strangers, so I think I'll skip my run through the park today.

ASSOCIATED EMOTIONS: fear, paranoia, peacefulness, worry, unease

POSITIVE ASPECTS: Characters with this flaw are comforted by superstitious beliefs that help give them a measure of control in an uncertain world. Performing rituals can allow them to feel calm and focused, offering security and peace when their mind is in turmoil.

NEGATIVE ASPECTS: Some of these characters take their beliefs to an unhealthy extreme, allowing their superstitions to impair judgment, damage relationships, and render them unable to adapt to change. A character incapable of controlling the urge to act on a superstition may find himself crossing moral lines in order to satisfy his compulsion.

EXAMPLE FROM FILM: In the movie *The Village*, the inhabitants adhere to many superstitions, most of which revolve around specific colors. Yellow represents safety while anything red must be buried, covered, or destroyed. These beliefs have been encouraged by the leaders as a means of controlling the people and keeping them from leaving. As with many superstitions, the practices are fear-based with no basis in truth, and what is meant to liberate the practitioners instead serves to limit them. **Other Examples from Film:** Pat Solitano Sr. (*Silver Linings Playbook*), Adrian Monk (*Monk*)

OVERCOMING THIS TRAIT AS A MAJOR FLAW: When superstitions begin to take over, the character will not be able to enjoy life to the fullest without intervention. Sometimes simple education is all that is needed. Approaching events logically in a way that shows the superstition in an irrational light may help. Also, challenging the character to forego his rituals and see what happens without them may help him overcome any illogical beliefs.

TRAITS IN SUPPORTING CHARACTERS THAT MAY CAUSE CONFLICT: analytical, compulsive, devout, disrespectful, fanatical, intelligent, obsessive, paranoid, proper, studious

SUSPICIOUS

DEFINITION: suspecting others without proof or evidence

SIMILAR FLAWS: disbelieving, doubtful, leery, mistrustful, wary

POSSIBLE CAUSES:
Suffering a past betrayal or painful trauma
Living in a corrupt society or environment
Growing up with abusive parents or other adults
Feeling unsafe
A mental disorder rooted in anxiety, depression, or paranoia
Witnessing unethical activity by those in positions of power
Paranoia as a result of long-term drug use
Consistently catching others in lies, especially people who should have been trustworthy
Witnessing two-faced behavior in others
Being scammed or taken advantage of
Being raised in a home that was riddled with paranoia

ASSOCIATED BEHAVIORS AND ATTITUDES:
Asking pointed questions that suggest suspicion
Obsessing over man-made tragedies and world events in the news
Being on the lookout for inconsistencies in people's stories
Not taking anything at face value
Demanding evidence; needing proof before believing
Keeping one's distance from others
Needing time to investigate before committing to an action
Assuming that the past will repeat itself
Singling anything out that doesn't fit a pattern
Strong gut instinct that is often correct, reinforcing that one should pay attention to it
Difficulty relaxing and being open unless the people present have earned one's trust
Suspecting another of a transgression that one has committed in the past: *I bet he stole that watch.*
Keeping one's distance from strangers or new acquaintances
Protecting one's personal information
Obsessing over security (changing passwords frequently, turning on lights, etc.)
Having few close friends
Steering conversations away from anything personal
Being overly cautious
Watching for warning signs
Jumping to conclusions
Expecting people to not follow through on their promises
Taking the forgetfulness of others personally
Adhering to routines and sticking to familiar places that are considered safe
Maintaining ample personal space

Being uncomfortable in enclosed spaces and crowds
Impatience
Thinking too much
Negativity

ASSOCIATED THOUGHTS:
What did Bess mean by that? Was that a dig at what I'm wearing?
He smiles too much, like he's hiding something.
John expects me to take him at his word? Yeah, right.
Why is he so eager to help? What's in it for him?

ASSOCIATED EMOTIONS: anxiety, desperation, fear, wariness, worry

POSITIVE ASPECTS: Suspicious characters have a shield in place, making them less likely to be taken advantage of. They think before they act and question rather than assume. Hyper aware and keenly attuned to danger, they rarely find themselves in situations as victims.

NEGATIVE ASPECTS: These characters rarely let their guard down, which can make them seem unfriendly or unapproachable. Because of their wariness, they have a hard time creating and maintaining lasting relationships, and once friendships do form, it's difficult for them to make themselves vulnerable. Suspicious characters often view others as being too trusting or naïve and may make I-told-you-so statements when bad things happen.

EXAMPLE FROM FILM: Sister Aloysius Beauvier (*Doubt*) is such a mistrusting person that when Father Flynn preaches a sermon on doubt, she wonders why he felt compelled to do so, and encourages her fellow nuns to keep an eye on him. Her suspicious nature sets in motion a chain of events that, despite her not having a shred of evidence, ends up costing Father Flynn his job. The story ends with Sister Aloysius first defending her actions, then breaking down, admitting that she is consumed by doubts. **Other Examples from Film**: Myra Fleener (*Hoosiers*), Walt Kowalski (*Gran Torino*)

OVERCOMING THIS TRAIT AS A MAJOR FLAW: To overcome suspicion, the character must learn to let go of any past events that have left her in this jaded state. Through the patience of others who are open and honest, a suspicious character will see that not everyone is painted with the same brush. By witnessing kindness and trust in action and experiencing the freedom they bring, she can learn to see people as individuals, not potential abusers-in-waiting.

TRAITS IN SUPPORTING CHARACTERS THAT MAY CAUSE CONFLICT: bold, cautious, cocky, cowardly, cruel, flaky, forgetful, gullible, lazy, mischievous, optimistic, weak-willed

TACTLESS

DEFINITION: lacking tact

SIMILAR FLAWS: indelicate, indiscreet, insensitive, thoughtless, undiplomatic

POSSIBLE CAUSES:
Self-centeredness
A lack of empathy
Taking pride in speaking one's mind
Having a high regard for candor and honesty
Immaturity
Impulsivity
A lack of concern for what others may think
Being unobservant

ASSOCIATED BEHAVIORS AND ATTITUDES:
Saying things that hurt people's feelings
Telling offensive jokes
Interrupting others
Speaking the whole truth regardless of one's audience
Being unobservant
Not listening when others speak
Bringing up topics that distress others
Saying whatever comes to mind
Giving one's opinion straight and unfiltered
Not picking up on social cues, such as when people become uncomfortable or want to leave
Asking inappropriate questions
Monopolizing the conversation; not giving others a chance to speak
Saying something that minimizes another's pain or difficult experience
Publicly confronting others
Frequent complaining
Speaking in a loud voice
Making hurtful observations: *Your yard looks terrible. I guess you and Ken split up, huh?*
Boisterous laughter
Discussing social taboos: *Holy cow, Amy, you've gained a ton of weight! What happened?*
Not respecting the wishes of others
Occasionally enjoying one's ability to make others uncomfortable
Revealing confidential information
Feeling bad if one's thoughtless words caused unintentional hurt to a loved one or friend
Changing the topic during a serious discussion or debate
Asking for favors or networking at inappropriate times: *Can I borrow the car after the funeral?*
Pointing out another's shortcomings: *Your breath is awful. You need to brush.*
Stealing attention during someone's special moment (arguing during a graduation ceremony, etc.)

A lack of self-restraint
Becoming frustrated when one is inconvenienced

ASSOCIATED THOUGHTS:
Some people are just too sensitive.
I'm not going to sugar coat things.
Sometimes the truth hurts.
Forget all that "politically correct" nonsense.
If she didn't want the truth, she shouldn't have asked my opinion.

ASSOCIATED EMOTIONS: contempt, determination, indifference, satisfaction, surprise

POSITIVE ASPECTS: Many times, tactless characters feel that they're doing the right thing by telling an unpleasant truth or honestly answering a question. These characters are dedicated to candor above all else. Because of their insensitivity, they're not overly bothered or swayed by what others think. An author can utilize these characters to impart information that others are reluctant to share.

NEGATIVE ASPECTS: Tactless characters are often either deliberately or indifferently oblivious to the feelings of others. They're more concerned with furthering their own agendas (speaking truth, getting their point across, etc.) than they are with pleasing people. They always seem to say the wrong thing and cause others grief. When they do upset the people around them, they don't usually notice.

EXAMPLE FROM FILM: Pat Healy (*There's Something about Mary*) is so caught up in getting Mary's attention that everyone else becomes secondary. He regularly degrades the mentally handicapped people that she works with and insults her friends. In his relentless pursuit, he's repeatedly insensitive to Mary herself; if he truly listened to her or took the time to get to know her, he would see the importance of the people in her life and make more of an effort to treat them with care. **Other Examples from Film and TV:** Paulie Pennino (*Rocky*), Ouiser Boudreaux (*Steel Magnolias*), Archie Bunker (*All in the Family*), Cosmo Kramer (*Seinfeld*)

OVERCOMING THIS TRAIT AS A MAJOR FLAW: The best way to overcome this trait is to see the effect that it has on others. The lesson is particularly obvious when the person harmed is someone vulnerable or innocent. If tactless behavior leads to a friend's shame or humiliation, it would make a character with this flaw see how his thoughtlessness brought about unintended pain.

TRAITS IN SUPPORTING CHARACTERS THAT MAY CAUSE CONFLICT: abrasive, cautious, discreet, honest, judgmental, needy, oversensitive, proper

TEMPERAMENTAL

DEFINITION: marked by unpredictable changes in mood

SIMILAR FLAWS: capricious, erratic, mercurial, moody

POSSIBLE CAUSES:
Insomnia or poor sleep habits
Prolonged illness or stress
Excessive social or financial responsibilities
A mental disorder (bipolar disorder, oppositional defiant disorder, etc.)
Behavioral issues
High anxiety
Dysfunctional family dynamics
Being bullied or abused
Alcoholism or drug abuse
Being highly creative
Paranoia
Hormonal shifts (menopause, etc.)

ASSOCIATED BEHAVIORS AND ATTITUDES:
Erratic mood changes
Growing angry when others voice disagreement
Having a low tolerance for the mistakes of others
Venting
Being highly opinionated
Overreacting to slights, comments, and opinions
Outbursts (shouting, laying blame, etc.)
Low-level violence (breaking objects, bumping into things and knocking them over, etc.)
Mild violence against people and animals (pushing, hitting, pulling with too much force, etc.)
Using unnecessary force (gripping someone's wrist painfully)
Being easily provoked
Difficulty taking criticism
Blowing mistakes out of proportion
Apologizing for one's outbursts
Poor communication when one is upset
Always having an excuse for one's behavior
Being sensitive to specific stressors (one's mother-in-law, a co-worker's annoying laugh, etc.)
Using risk and danger to blow off steam
Seeing one's opinions, needs, and feelings as being more important than others
Assertiveness
Feeling hemmed in or trapped by responsibility
Frustration at delays or a lack of organization
Acting before thinking
Being happy one minute and depressed or cranky the next

Becoming touchy and argumentative when certain topics are broached
Taking offhanded comments as personal criticisms
Feeling overwhelmed
Taking everything personally

ASSOCIATED THOUGHTS:
Why did she make meatloaf for dinner when she knows I hate it?
I was so excited about this weekend but now Brandy's going. She ruins everything!
I can't believe I bruised her arm. She must have sensitive skin, because I barely touched her.
Why did he pick The Burger Joint for dinner? They'll probably give me food poisoning.

ASSOCIATED EMOTIONS: anger, depression, elation, excitement, happiness, overwhelmed, sadness

POSITIVE ASPECTS: This flaw breeds wariness, so others will watch their step with a moody character, often choosing to cater to their preferences. People with this flaw have high expectations and can challenge others to improve by demanding only the best from those in their charge.

NEGATIVE ASPECTS: A temperamental character can behave erratically and explosively, leaving relationship shrapnel in his wake. Friends don't always know what will set him off, and many will avoid the character rather than deal with his outbursts. Others will placate the character in order to head off drama, thereby enabling his erratic tendencies. Those who stick around are always walking on eggshells, taking great care in what they say or do in order to avoid conflict.

EXAMPLE FROM LITERATURE: Sherlock Homes is a complex, moody character in book and film. His emotions swing quickly—first brooding and dismal, then manic in his desire to acquire knowledge and information. An abuser of both drugs and alcohol, he is an eccentric who pushes the limits, and very likely suffers from a mental disorder of some kind. **Other Examples in Literature**: The Queen of Hearts (*Alice in Wonderland*), Tinkerbell (*Peter Pan*), Edward Cullen (*Twilight* saga)

OVERCOMING THIS TRAIT AS A MAJOR FLAW: For a character to avoid this level of emotional touchiness, he would need to examine his life and see what stressors are prompting his reactive behavior, then work at lightening the load. Yoga, meditation, and therapy all might help the character learn to better accept the world for what it is and his own place within it. Taking up a hobby that brings joy will help him find fulfillment and make him feel more centered and able to deal with what life throws his way.

TRAITS IN SUPPORTING CHARACTERS THAT MAY CAUSE CONFLICT: abrasive, confrontational, disciplined, flaky, needy, oversensitive, tactless, volatile

TIMID

DEFINITION: easily cowed; lacking courage, bravery, and self-assurance

SIMILAR FLAWS: intimidated, mousy, timorous, unassertive

POSSIBLE CAUSES:
A past trauma
Phobias (especially social phobias)
Abuse or neglect
Shame
A history of isolation
An overly sheltered childhood
Fragile health
Insecurity and low self-esteem

ASSOCIATED BEHAVIORS AND ATTITUDES:
Avoiding change
Isolation
Nervousness around strangers
Flinching at too much noise
Hiding or withdrawing when one is uncomfortable
Choosing activities that one can do alone
Becoming tongue-tied
Always going along with what others want
Freezing under pressure or stress
Avoiding scary movies and TV shows
Being extremely self-conscious around other people
Being ruled by insecurities that prevent one from enjoying life to the fullest
Preferring to stay in rather than go out
Self-doubt; low self-esteem
Shakiness
Using a quiet voice
Speaking less than others
Imagining the worst-case scenario
Running away from danger
Fainting
Living vicariously through other people and the Internet
Negative self-talk
Preferring to read or hear about exciting moments rather than experience them oneself
Having panic attacks at the thought of being the center of attention
Fearing the rejection of one's peers
Social awkwardness (difficulty conversing, maintaining eye contact, joking, etc.)
Not volunteering when help is needed
Not going after goals if doing so will require assertiveness

Being content to let others win or receive recognition
Difficulty sharing one's opinions or ideas

ASSOCIATED THOUGHTS:
If the winners have to go up on stage, I hope I lose.
Where are those police cars going?
Why do I freeze up when Mrs. Taylor calls on me? Why can't I just answer like a normal person?
If Donnie also wants the job, I'll withdraw my application.

ASSOCIATED EMOTIONS: anxiety, conflicted, doubt, dread, fear, resignation, unease, worry

POSITIVE ASPECTS: Timid characters tend to be careful thinkers; they can see deeper into situations and problems than those who are more reactive and simply want to act. Unthreatening by nature, these characters are very approachable, even by the most wily or volatile of personalities.

NEGATIVE ASPECTS: Timid characters are often so afraid of life that they fail to experience it. They allow fear to control their decision making, and rarely venture into challenging situations or try new things. Because of their vulnerability, they are a target for abuse and are taken advantage of by those who prey on the weak or easily manipulated.

EXAMPLE FROM FILM: Petrie, the pteranodon in *The Land Before Time*, is panicky and timid and too scared to use his wings to fly. He is fearful of trying anything new and is dependent on others for friendly nudging and support. If not for their prodding help, he would have perished during the "great earthshake." **Other Examples from Literature and Film**: Mole (*The Wind in the Willows*), Adrian Pennino (*Rocky*)

OVERCOMING THIS TRAIT AS A MAJOR FLAW: To move past this flaw, characters would have to understand how much they are limited by their lack of bravery. Slowly exposing themselves to new situations and trying new things will help build self-confidence and diminish fear. Through stretching themselves and experiencing positive results, confidence will build. Achieving small goals that previously seemed out of reach will further allow these characters to leave the chains of their timidity behind.

TRAITS IN SUPPORTING CHARACTERS THAT MAY CAUSE CONFLICT: adventurous, ambitious, bold, confrontational, manipulative, melodramatic, pushy, temperamental

UNCOMMUNICATIVE

DEFINITION: reluctant to impart information or share one's feelings and thoughts

SIMILAR FLAWS: closemouthed, guarded, reserved, unresponsive

POSSIBLE CAUSES:
Growing up with closed-off adults
Fear (of rejection, making oneself vulnerable, consequences)
Having a secret to protect
Paranoia
Being emotionally repressed
Low self-esteem; believing that one has nothing to offer
Pain (emotional or physical)
Trust issues

ASSOCIATED BEHAVIORS AND ATTITUDES:
Keeping secrets
Desiring connection but not wanting to open up to others
Diverting attention away from oneself
Staying in the background
Having an unemotional outward demeanor
Speaking in a quiet voice
Giving one-word answers
Responding awkwardly (letting silences linger, walking away, etc.)
Avoiding people who press for information
Not answering the phone or door
Not making eye contact
Engaging in solitary activities (video games, reading, hiking alone, etc.)
Using a diary, YouTube channel, or an anonymous blog as an outlet for expression
Disengaging when someone probes for answers
Replying with nonverbal responses (nods, head shakes, shrugs, etc.)
Lackluster body movements
Pretending disinterest
Letting emotions build internally rather than expressing them
Listening in on conversations without engaging
Covertly observing others
Lying to avoid telling the truth
Agreeing or disagreeing but refusing to elaborate
Being content to watch and listen at social events
Becoming self-sufficient to avoid having to rely on others
Refusing to speak
Avoiding social situations
Giving answers that don't reveal anything

ASSOCIATED THOUGHTS:
Why does she want to discuss every little thing?
I'll get yelled at for saying what I think, so why bother?
Nag, nag, nag. I should have taken the bus home.
No way am I saying anything. It'll just make things worse.
I can't tell the truth; she'd never forgive me.
I'll never tell what happened.

ASSOCIATED EMOTIONS: agitation, annoyance, defensiveness, irritation, reluctance, scorn

POSITIVE ASPECTS: Characters with this flaw are able to maintain strict control over their tongues, choosing carefully what they're willing to share, and with whom. They are thinkers who prefer to keep their own counsel about the world and their place within it. By not sharing what they think and feel, they can avoid being drawn into heated verbal debates that lead to volatile clashes. With uncommunicative characters, actions and deeds speak louder than words.

NEGATIVE ASPECTS: It can be difficult for others to get close to uncommunicative characters. Some may assume that they have an uncaring attitude or they're self-absorbed. Others may feel rejected when their attempts to connect are rebuffed. Likewise, characters with this flaw will have a hard time reaching out to others or pursuing friendships and love interests. Their inability to let go of their fears and open up to others can cause extreme frustration.

EXAMPLE FROM LITERATURE: In *Stand by Me*, Gordie Lachance's parents are uncommunicative in the wake of his brother's death. They are so consumed by their grief that they retreat inward, going through the motions of living without interacting or showing care and concern for the son who remains. No matter how many times Gordie tries to reach through the barriers they have put up, he is unsuccessful, leaving him to struggle with feelings of low self-worth. **Other Examples from Film**: Chief Bromden (*One Flew over the Cuckoo's Nest*), John Rambo (*First Blood*)

OVERCOMING THIS TRAIT AS A MAJOR FLAW: To overcome one's uncommunicative nature, the character must move past whatever preconceived notions that have led to the belief that he must keep his own counsel. It might help to place him in a situation where another character shows unconditional caring and no judgment; this may allow him to open up a bit, learn to trust, and see that sharing oneself can bring about a positive result rather than a negative one.

TRAITS IN SUPPORTING CHARACTERS THAT MAY CAUSE CONFLICT: cocky, curious, impulsive, know-it-all, needy, nosy, paranoid, suspicious, verbose

UNCOOPERATIVE

DEFINITION: unwilling to work with others

SIMILAR FLAWS: unhelpful

POSSIBLE CAUSES:
Selfishness
Difficulty getting along with others
A fragile ego
Jealousy
Trust issues
Needing to be in charge
Stubbornness; being unable to compromise or give in to others

ASSOCIATED BEHAVIORS AND ATTITUDES:
Giving clipped answers or refusing to respond to questions
Sitting immobile; not taking action
Using closed-off body language (crossing one's arms, the body angled away, etc.)
Purposefully not being ready or prepared
Being argumentative
Ignoring other people
Feigning interest in something insignificant
Refusing to help unless one is given a leadership role
Shrewdness
Making snap judgments about others and then refusing to work with them
Emotionally shutting down
Telling half-truths
Leaving in a huff
Lacking forgiveness
Making inappropriate or unfair demands in an effort to push people away
Wanting to be alone
Thinking poorly of others
Stubbornness
Having a negative attitude
Righteousness; having strong convictions
Refusing to consider a different viewpoint if it deviates from one's own
Feeling powerful when stymieing others by refusing to cooperate
Purposely saying things to rile people up
Refusing to speak or answer
Carrying out actions that will cause delays
Bad-mouthing or slandering one's co-workers or partners
Withholding important information
Putting in minimal effort to "punish" one's teammates
Creating dissension by playing on people's personal fears and worries
Offering incorrect information with the purpose of wasting time and energy

ASSOCIATED THOUGHTS:

This is stupid. I'm not going to help.
They don't care about what I want, so why should I care about them?
If I help, something bad will happen.
What can I do to make more work for them?
He expects my help after what he did? Forget it!

ASSOCIATED EMOTIONS: anger, dread, envy, fear, frustration, jealousy, worry

POSITIVE ASPECTS: Uncooperative characters have a strong sense of right and wrong and will often act based on their own personal sense of morality and justice. When threatened, they will hold firm to their beliefs and not let the emotions of others sway their convictions. These characters can accept that there will be negative repercussions as a result of their choices, yet they remain steadfast.

NEGATIVE ASPECTS: Characters with this flaw often mistrust others and question their motives. Their unwillingness to be team players and put disagreements behind them can cause conflict with co-workers and neighbors. As frustration mounts, they may fall victim to pettiness and vindictiveness. Depending on the stakes and the stress level that a lack of cooperation causes, the situation can grow dangerous and violent if not rectified.

EXAMPLE FROM LITERATURE: In the *Harry Potter* series, house elf Kreacher is very uncooperative while serving Sirius Black. He hides family heirlooms and is rude, freely exhibiting his dislike for his master and his friends. After Sirius' death, Harry inherits Kreacher, who, for a while, continues in his open resentment and disdain—only following orders when he's forced to, in a way that produces unsatisfactory results. **Other Examples from Literature and TV**: the supporting cast of *Alice in Wonderland*, captured serial killers from *The Following*, James "Sawyer" (*LOST*)

OVERCOMING THIS TRAIT AS A MAJOR FLAW: To allow for a successful character arc where this flaw is reined in or overcome, characters must resist the urge to oppose others and, instead, see the greater good that can be achieved by working together. If trust issues lie at the heart of one's uncooperativeness, the character must learn to stop attributing past hurts to those he meets in the present, and that everyone deserves the benefit of the doubt. Understanding that someone else's vision can lead to a positive end will help the character recognize that sharing knowledge is good for all concerned.

TRAITS IN SUPPORTING CHARACTERS THAT MAY CAUSE CONFLICT: bossy, cooperative, extroverted, inflexible, nosy, nurturing, responsible, volatile

UNCOUTH

DEFINITION: lacking common social graces; uncultivated

SIMILAR FLAWS: boorish, crude, ill-mannered, loutish, vulgar

POSSIBLE CAUSES:
Being raised with a lack of social graces
Ignorance or a poor education
A lack of exposure to societal norms
Isolation
Low intelligence

ASSOCIATED BEHAVIORS AND ATTITUDES:
Eating noisily, with one's mouth open
Loud, abrasive, or inappropriate laughter
Scratching oneself
Interrupting conversations
Eating with and licking one's fingers
Picking one's nose or blowing snot rockets in public
Burping or farting and thinking it's funny or acceptable
Spitting
Speaking loudly or forcefully in a quiet venue
Ignoring suggestions to tone it down or rein in one's behavior
Making disparaging remarks at inappropriate times
Complaining
Monopolizing the conversation; refusing to let others get a word in
Not respecting other people's privacy
Changing the topic whenever one feels like it
Standing too close or leaning into another's personal space
Leering at cleavage (men) or pawing at a potential target (women)
Dressing inappropriately for the occasion
Mocking others for their politeness or social graces
Acting on impulse
Swearing
Sharing information that is highly personal
Asking embarrassing questions
Telling jokes that are uncivilized or in poor taste
Using slurs or making racial statements
Bumping into people; clumsiness that leads to embarrassment for others
Poor hygiene
Brawling
Discussing one's bowel movements
Offering unwanted sexual advances
Provoking a host about his wealth or success, hinting that he's too good for everyone else

Wiping one's hands on clothing rather than using a napkin
Putting one's elbows on the table and hunching over a plate
Drinking too much and making a spectacle of oneself

ASSOCIATED THOUGHTS:
Man, what a bunch of stiffs. They take everything so seriously.
Everybody farts. What's the big deal?
Fork? Nah, it's a drumstick. It fits your hand for a reason.
Why should I apologize? I didn't do anything wrong.
So I spit out her carrots. I couldn't swallow them—they were disgusting.

ASSOCIATED EMOTIONS: conflicted, contempt, disappointment, embarrassment, indifference, resentment, unease

POSITIVE ASPECTS: Uncouth characters are true to themselves, not conforming to society's standards or roles. They are often forthright, taking pride in speaking their minds without worrying about how others might judge them. Uncouth characters frequently view the world in black and white; because they don't get caught up in the political nature of decision-making, they can sometimes more efficiently see to the heart of the matter than those who concern themselves with what is or isn't acceptable.

NEGATIVE ASPECTS: Uncouth characters often cause offense without realizing it. They may be unfairly judged—seen as unintelligent, for example—all because they are being measured according to someone else's standard. Frustration and resentment can cause them to be emotionally reactive, which reinforces others' negative opinions about them.

EXAMPLE FROM TV: In the animated show *The Simpsons*, barfly Barney Gumble is perpetually drunk, belches often, and practically lives in Moe's bar. In addition, his personal hygiene leaves something to be desired and he often doesn't dress or act appropriately for social events. **Other Examples from Film and Literature**: Quint (*Jaws*), Shrek (*Shrek*), Eliza Doolittle (*Pygmalion*)

OVERCOMING THIS TRAIT AS A MAJOR FLAW: If a character with this flaw sees how being crude is limiting his professional or personal goals, he may be inclined to incorporate common social practices into his daily routine. As he progresses, he will likely begin to see the discomfort that his former behavior caused. This revelation can lead to a heightened respect for others, and may bring about a sense of satisfaction and increased self-worth.

TRAITS IN SUPPORTING CHARACTERS THAT MAY CAUSE CONFLICT: fussy, haughty, judgmental, meticulous, proper, proud, sophisticated

UNETHICAL

DEFINITION: rejecting accepted moral beliefs and standards of conduct

SIMILAR FLAWS: corrupt, dishonorable

POSSIBLE CAUSES:
Growing up in a society where one must do whatever it takes to survive
Social deviancy
A lack of empathy
Antisocial personality disorder
Placing a higher value on oneself than on others
Having a single-minded focus on one's goal; greed
Believing that the ends justify the means
Jealousy; a desire to have what others have regardless of the cost

ASSOCIATED BEHAVIORS AND ATTITUDES:
Theft
Cheating on taxes or tests
Lying
Bending or breaking the rules
Turning a blind eye to inhumane animal treatment or testing
Publicizing one's socially-acceptable actions while hiding those that are unconscionable
Paying for old exams
Having a sense of entitlement
Wanting to fit in or get ahead
Competitiveness
Blackmailing others
Cynicism
Insider trading, bribing others, or accepting bribes
Believing that one's actions are acceptable as long as no one finds out
Selling prescriptions for profit
Participating in scams, fraud, and phishing
Burying unfavorable statistics at the boss's request
Looking the other way when others are acting unethically
Abusing others to get one's way or to gain control
Destroying evidence or altering records
Moral lines that shift or blur
Getting in over one's head and being forced to do what one believed one was incapable of doing
Justifying one's actions: *Everyone else is doing it.*
Hiring unsavory characters to do one's dirty work
Selling products that one knows are broken or inferior
Making promises, then reneging
Buying and selling stolen or counterfeit material
Stealing office supplies and petty cash
Encouraging or coercing others to participate in unethical activities

ASSOCIATED THOUGHTS:
The company passed me over for a raise, so why shouldn't I expense this dinner?
No one's going to find out.
It's one assignment. What's the big deal?
I need the money. Besides if I don't do it, someone else will.
Legal, illegal...it's a gray area.

ASSOCIATED EMOTIONS: conflicted, contempt, cynicism, guilt, indifference, paranoia, pride, suspicion

POSITIVE ASPECTS: Unethical characters have an easier time providing for themselves and loved ones since they have less moral limitations. They have no qualms about breaking laws or violating the rights of others, and they're experts at rationalizing immoral behaviors. Unethical characters focus on the goal, not the details, and can finish a job without getting bogged down by moral concerns.

NEGATIVE ASPECTS: An unethical character has very little respect for authority or the people who stand in his way. Even if he starts with small corruptions, his ability to rationalize his behavior often leads him to bigger and worse deviations down the road. On some level, the unethical character may understand that what he's doing is wrong, but he convinces himself that the ends justify the means. He may read too much into what people say and do, and end up viewing the world with cynicism and suspicion.

EXAMPLE FROM FILM: When Andy Dufresne is wrongfully imprisoned, he falls under the control of Warden Samuel Norton (*The Shawshank Redemption*)—a man who pretends to be deeply religious, but in reality, is corrupt and unethical. When he hears about Andy's former career in finance, the warden strong-arms him into taking charge of his money-laundering operation. Upon hearing information that could prove Andy's innocence, the warden refuses to reopen the case and has the messenger killed so he can go on exploiting Andy's abilities. **Other Examples from Film:** Detective Alonzo Harris (*Training Day*), the Duke brothers (*Trading Places*), Gordon Gekko (*Wall Street*)

OVERCOMING THIS TRAIT AS A MAJOR FLAW: For an unethical character to understand the repercussions of his actions and view them as morally wrong, he would need to personally experience the dark side of a lack of ethics. Being betrayed by or seeing loved ones suffer at the hands of a corrupt person may be the catalyst that would allow such a transformation to take place.

TRAITS IN SUPPORTING CHARACTERS THAT MAY CAUSE CONFLICT: honest, honorable, jealous, lazy, needy, observant, suspicious, unselfish, vindictive, wholesome

UNGRATEFUL

DEFINITION: thankless; unappreciative

SIMILAR FLAWS: unappreciative

POSSIBLE CAUSES:
Self-importance
Pretentiousness
Growing up with wealth and prestige
Being accustomed to being waited upon
Having seniority
Excessive pride
Feeling unhappy and unfulfilled with one's life choices

ASSOCIATED BEHAVIORS AND ATTITUDES:
Making demands
Complaining
Not saying *Thank you*
Taking one's blessings for granted
Rudeness
A sense of entitlement from long-term hardship
Becoming frustrated with delays in correcting unsatisfactory conditions
Difficulty forgiving others
Blaming others for one's misfortunes
Grabbing something before it's offered, to avoid having to show gratitude
Impatience
Disrespect
Making threats to get what one wants
Ignoring common social niceties (not engaging with others, etc.)
Upping one's expectations
Refusing to help out
Overstaying one's welcome
Taking kindness for granted
Borrowing something and not returning it
Forgetting special occasions (anniversaries, birthdays, etc.)
Spending time and energy on others while ignoring one's inner circle
Whining
Sighing in an annoyed fashion
Speaking in a terse tone of voice
Taking more than what has been offered
Believing that someone who is well-off should share his commodities with others
Withholding compliments

ASSOCIATED THOUGHTS:

I'm not tipping her—not for that kind of service.
How ridiculous. Next time I'll call another friend who can show up on time.
Why should I thank him for doing what he's supposed to do?
I can't believe she bought this for me. Where does she shop, the Dollar Store?
Oh, now they want to help. Where were they a year ago when I was almost homeless?

ASSOCIATED EMOTIONS: agitation, frustration, impatience, pride, resentment, scorn, smugness

POSITIVE ASPECTS: Characters unburdened with a sense of gratitude can find themselves in a position of power over those who seek affirmation and appreciation. On the rare occasion that an ungrateful character does give thanks, the recipient knows that it's genuine and isn't just being offered as politeness or lip service.

NEGATIVE ASPECTS: Ungrateful characters carry a sense of entitlement that is unattractive to others. They are takers instead of givers and have unbalanced relationships filled with resentment. Characters like this are constantly dissatisfied and always find something to complain about; peripheral characters are put off by their negative attitudes and quickly become disinclined to do anything nice since their kindnesses are only going to be rebuffed.

EXAMPLE FROM FILM: Lieutenant Dan from *Forrest Gump* shows no gratitude to Forrest for rescuing him in the Vietnam War. In fact, he feels resentment and anger, not only for having to live without legs, but for not being allowed to die in battle and fulfill what he believes to be his destiny. **Other Examples from Film and Literature:** Cera (*The Land Before Time*), Nynaeve al'Meara (*The Wheel of Time*)

OVERCOMING THIS TRAIT AS A MAJOR FLAW: To overcome this lack, a character would have to be put in a situation where he or a loved one was in such peril that his well-being was dependent on the kindness or generosity of his peers. Only by facing dire consequences could the character truly understand the importance of others and feel gratitude. If he loses hope and is saved by someone else, the character can see the error of his ways and learn to appreciate the contributions of others.

TRAITS IN SUPPORTING CHARACTERS THAT MAY CAUSE CONFLICT: appreciative, controlling, generous, kind, loyal, proper, vindictive

UNINTELLIGENT

DEFINITION: showing poor judgment and flawed thinking; lacking reasoning or wit

SIMILAR FLAWS: dense, dumb, half-witted, idiotic, simple, slow, thickheaded, witless

POSSIBLE CAUSES:
Poor education
Growing up in seclusion
Mental handicaps
Genetics
Refusing to learn because it conflicts with ingrained beliefs
Growing up in a society that devalues education and independent thinking
Poor prenatal care
Poor health and nutrition

ASSOCIATED BEHAVIORS AND ATTITUDES:
Giving incorrect answers
Making excuses that others can easily see through
Lying
Embarrassment
Floundering verbally
Giving blank looks
Frequently using *ums, ahs*, and other hesitations
Having difficulty finishing tasks
Showing up to work or school unprepared
Smiling to cover one's confusion
Avoiding unfamiliar situations
Missing obvious clues that someone is untrustworthy
Blaming others for one's uncompleted tasks (not being given enough information, etc.)
Not learning lessons despite repeated attempts
Struggling to mentally keep up with a conversation or group task
Offering poor or naïve advice
Asking for time extensions
Difficulty putting events together to see the big picture
Agreeing with others in an effort to mask one's lack of knowledge
Relying upon others to help make even minor decisions
Not understanding sarcasm
Being easily manipulated
Always believing what one is told
Expressing frustration at not being able to understand or excel
Choosing a solitary or simple profession where one can succeed
Getting into trouble out of ignorance or naïveté
Panicking when something bad happens
Worrying about what others think

Trying to fit in by mimicking others' behaviors
Repeatedly making the same mistakes

ASSOCIATED THOUGHTS:
Please don't call on me!
Quick, think of something!
Maybe I can ramble my way out of this.
I'll ask Donna what he meant. She'll know.

ASSOCIATED EMOTIONS: embarrassment, fear, frustration, humiliation, shame, worry

POSITIVE ASPECTS: A character with less than average intelligence can view situations in their simplest form and not get bogged down by politics or semantics. They also are easy to talk to and aren't as judgmental as others might be.

NEGATIVE ASPECTS: Unintelligent characters often miss the nuances of social behavior and don't know when they're being made fun of. Through no fault of their own, they can easily become a target for cruel and catty associates. Characters with this flaw may grow impatient and angry at their inability to understand situations and other people, leading to trust issues, increased insecurity, and even self-loathing.

EXAMPLE FROM FILM: John Coffey (*The Green Mile*) is accused of a crime he did not commit. Because of his low IQ, he can't defend himself, is found guilty, and lands on death row. During his prison term, he is taunted for his lower intelligence by both guards and inmates. **Other Examples from Film**: Forrest Gump (*Forrest Gump*), Navin Johnson (*The Jerk*)

OVERCOMING THIS TRAIT AS A MAJOR FLAW: Training, conditioning, studying, and finding a willing mentor are all ways a character of lower intelligence can acquire knowledge. Exposure to new situations and experiences will help him understand how things work and increase his proficiency. Focusing on his strengths will also offset this weakness and create empathy in other characters who may be willing to help with situations that require savvy thinking.

TRAITS IN SUPPORTING CHARACTERS THAT MAY CAUSE CONFLICT: catty, cruel, judgmental, ignorant, impatient, intelligent, manipulative, meticulous, perfectionism, selfish

VAIN

DEFINITION: excessively proud of one's appearance and accomplishments

SIMILAR FLAWS: conceited, egotistical, narcissistic

POSSIBLE CAUSES:
Reinforcement in the formative years that one's appearance determines one's value
Growing up spoiled
Being paid for being beautiful (through modeling, etc.)
Narcissism
Having peers who are obsessed with their body image
Being surrounded by beautiful people
Fame and success

ASSOCIATED BEHAVIORS AND ATTITUDES:
Spending large amounts of money on beauty treatments and products
Comparing oneself to others
Only posting pictures that show oneself in a good light
Refusing to grow old gracefully
Obsessively working out
Strict dieting
Shallowness of character
Fussing with one's hair and clothing
Wanting expensive clothing and adornments
Not leaving the house until one's appearance is perfect
Indulging in excessive plastic surgery
Mirror gazing
Avoiding settings or scenarios that will mess up one's look (windy venues, etc.)
Following fashion and trends
Studying and mimicking idols
Talking about oneself to others
Keeping the conversation focused on oneself
Wanting the best of everything
Living at the edge of or beyond one's means
Wanting to be seen by others
Being an extrovert
Seeking to be the center of attention
Worrying about what others think while pretending not to
Choosing friends for their looks, wealth, or prestige
Cattiness; putting perceived competitors in their place
Minimizing others' achievements to feel better about oneself
Adopting popular viewpoints and beliefs
Disdainful glances
Obsessing over every imperfection and flaw

Refusing to be seen by others if one is ill, feels bloated, has rashes, or pimples
Needing constant positive reinforcement to feel worthy
Phobia-like paranoia over aging (losing one's beauty, skills, or talents, etc.)
Avoiding people who steal the limelight through greater success or beauty
Finding power, beauty, and wealth more attractive than personality

ASSOCIATED THOUGHTS:
I can't wait for everyone to see me in this dress.
Marcy will die when she sees me hanging out with the band.
A little cologne and ...looking good, Alex my man. Looking good.
Dennis is crazy. I wouldn't be caught dead shopping at Walmart.

ASSOCIATED EMOTIONS: adoration, pride, satisfaction, smugness, worry

POSITIVE ASPECTS: Vain characters are very aware of their looks, are conscious of their health, and take meticulous care of their bodies, skin, and hair. They're honest about friends' appearances and may encourage them to take the same high standard of care in their own beauty and health regimens. With their strong social skills, vain characters are a huge asset in helping others make a good first impression and maintain a pleasing physical persona.

NEGATIVE ASPECTS: Characters like this tend to make judgments about others based on how they look and act. They're often needy when it comes to affirmation, seeking compliments on their looks, talents, or strengths. Vain characters tend to be egotistical and have a hard time caring about other people's problems.

EXAMPLE FROM LITERATURE: Hilly Holbrook from *The Help* is overly concerned with her image; she's very strict about who she is seen with, what activities she pursues, and how she looks. Because she believes that her friends and associates are a reflection upon her, she is judgmental of how they behave and isn't shy about telling friends what they should do or say. Her friends, in turn, make sure that everything they do measures up to Hilly's standards out of fear of her sharp tongue and the social power she holds in Jackson, Mississippi. **Other Examples from Literature and Film**: Effie Trinkett (*The Hunger Games*), Mary Poppins (*Mary Poppins*), Tony Manero (*Saturday Night Fever*)

OVERCOMING THIS TRAIT AS A MAJOR FLAW: If a character was placed in a situation where good looks might actually be a detriment, beauty will lose its allure. As well, should the vain character wish to obtain something that outward appearance, social standing, or wealth will not influence, self-growth in this area may be achieved. Illness, a disfigurement, or the natural process of aging may also help a character overcome her vanity, but this could also lead to extreme jealousy, bitterness and/or self-loathing.

TRAITS IN SUPPORTING CHARACTERS THAT MAY CAUSE CONFLICT: arrogant, charming, flamboyant, jealous, rowdy, selfish, tactless, timid, uncouth, vindictive

VERBOSE

DEFINITION: wordy; inclined to say more than is needed

SIMILAR FLAWS: garrulous, long-winded, loquacious

POSSIBLE CAUSES:
Being highly educated
Desiring to prove oneself as an academic
Insecurity
Having a passion for certain topics
Being a natural storyteller
Having a predisposition toward melodrama; doing everything with a dramatic flair
Possessing a love of language and its history
Arrogance or vanity
Desiring to impress others
Not understanding the give-and-take of conversation
Nervousness
Having a naturally talkative nature
Bipolar disorder
Drug use

ASSOCIATED BEHAVIORS AND ATTITUDES:
Speaking at people rather than conversing with them
Going off on tangents; getting sidetracked
Cornering someone to talk at them
Beating around the bush
Not picking up on body language that indicates frustration or boredom
Pausing to consider the exact word needed to articulate a thought
Clarifying what one has said; being over-specific
Not asking questions or engaging others
Having a poor sense of how much time has passed
Muting one's body language so it won't detract from one's speech
Composing letters rather than a one-sentence email
Being uncomfortable with spontaneity or change
Interrupting the conversation to add a point one forgot to make earlier
Using big words either from enjoyment or a desire to impress
Posing a question just so one can answer it
Having strong opinions
Compulsions to educate others
Needing to cover a topic completely to do it justice
Turning a quick phone call or friendly coffee chat into a long, drawn-out event
Forgetting one's point and having to ask for a reminder: *What was the original question?*
Wanting to "have a discussion" over every little thing
A tendency to verbally work through problems

Never offering a quick, decisive opinion
Creating impatience in others
Speaking rapidly when one is stressed or anxious
Believing that one's views and ideas will help or enlighten others
Analyzing conversations afterward to see what one missed or should have better emphasized

ASSOCIATED THOUGHTS:
They're going to be impressed when they hear how much I know about this.
Oh, I should clarify what I meant.
What if she doesn't understand? I'll try it another way.
I need to get into this conversation or they will think I don't have anything to add.

ASSOCIATED EMOTIONS: conflicted, determination, doubt, insecurity, pride, worry

POSITIVE ASPECTS: A verbose character will make sure that there are no uncomfortable silences during conversation, and they never run out of things to talk about. They enjoy giving their opinions on anything and everything. These characters often have a broad range of knowledge, or at the very least, a spectrum of opinions that will get others thinking as well.

NEGATIVE ASPECTS: Verbose characters can come across as arrogant to others, as if they enjoy the sound of their own voices. They can become so focused on their own dialogue that they forget to include the people around them and end up in one-sided conversations. They have difficulty reading people and miss common cues that indicate boredom or a desire to escape. Verbose individuals tend to analyze what they've said and evaluate whether their points were clearly expressed. If they do forget a piece of pertinent information, they may be driven to relay it, even after the conversation has ended.

EXAMPLE FROM FILM: In Disney's *Shrek*, a talking donkey befriends the ogre Shrek but causes immediate friction with his inability to stop yapping. Used to the solitude of the swamp, Shrek is irritated by the endless chatter until he finally explodes. Donkey's difficulty in controlling his talkative nature almost costs him this friendship. **Other Examples from Literature**: Anne Shirley (Anne of *Green Gables*)

OVERCOMING THIS TRAIT AS A MAJOR FLAW: For a character to cull his talkative habits, he would need to practice being more succinct both through writing and speech. A desire to be more accepted, liked, or to better fit in might drive him to try harder to master conversation and the flow of give-and-take. The character would also need to place a greater importance on learning from others and listening to their opinions and thoughts.

TRAITS IN SUPPORTING CHARACTERS THAT MAY CAUSE CONFLICT: abrasive, discreet, efficient, flaky, gossipy, impatient, inflexible, rude, selfish, superficial, tactless, vain

VINDICTIVE

DEFINITION: disposed toward seeking revenge

SIMILAR FLAWS: hateful, malicious, retaliatory, ruthless, vengeful

POSSIBLE CAUSES:
Excessive ego
Desiring to be perceived as strong
Having a position or reputation that must be protected (a mafia don, a gang member, etc.)
Having been victimized in the past
Needing to be in control
Anger issues
Narcissism or antisocial personality disorder
Mental disorders (oppositional defiant disorder, intermittent explosive disorder, etc.)
Participating in deviant activities that encourage one's dark urges (watching violent pornography)

ASSOCIATED BEHAVIORS AND ATTITUDES:
An inability to forgive
Obsessing over a slight or insult
Daydreaming about ways to make the other party pay
Damaging an offending person's property
Looking for ways to discredit an enemy
Laying elaborate plans in order to exact revenge
Experiencing a sense of relief upon retaliation
Bragging about having avenged oneself
Making threats
Sending hateful letters and emails
Spreading rumors
Trying to get a person fired or ruin his relationships
Enacting vengeance on an offending party's loved ones
Criminal activity (vandalism, assault, etc.)
Avenging loved ones who have been mistreated
Stalking the other party
Turning on friends when disloyalty is suspected
Using intimidation and fear tactics to keep others in line
Becoming argumentative and confrontational with an offending party
Fits of rage
Irrational thinking
Believing that extracting vengeance is worth the consequences
Using others to get back at the other party
Impulsivity
Bitterness and resentment
Avenging oneself in such a way that innocent parties are caught in the crossfire
Anger that slowly builds and eventually explodes
Perceiving insults and slights where there are none
Taking frustration out on one's friends, family, and roommates

Reading into situations; jumping to conclusions
Feeling like one is always being attacked; remaining vigilant to avoid being hurt
Cruelty

ASSOCIATED THOUGHTS:

He's got to pay.
She's going to be so sorry she crossed me.
Jake started the rumor about me? I'll destroy him.
Mandy thinks she can waltz into this office and take over? I'll make her life a living hell.

ASSOCIATED EMOTIONS: desire, determination, eagerness, hatred, hurt, paranoia, rage

POSITIVE ASPECTS: Vindictive characters can be highly loyal to the people they trust, standing up and going to bat for them when they're wronged. Their desire for revenge also requires strong focus, which can be positively applied to other areas of life.

NEGATIVE ASPECTS: Vindictive characters are volatile; it often takes just the threat of disrespect or mistreatment to set them off. Once trust has been broken, the vindictive character's inability to forgive makes it nearly impossible for him to mend a relationship and trust that person again. His desire for revenge can quickly turn to obsession, making it difficult for him to think logically or focus on anything else. Characters with this flaw don't care if the revenge is proportionate to the original slight or if bystanders are hurt in the process; all that matters is that the other person pays.

EXAMPLE FROM LITERATURE: Prior to his unjust imprisonment for a crime he didn't commit, Edmond Dantès (*The Count of Monte Cristo*) is a kind, generous, and trusting human being. But prison changes him, making him bitter and obsessed. He eventually loses all sense of community or connection with others and makes it his life's goal to escape and avenge himself upon the men who framed him. In the end, he finds love and reclaims his humanity, but only after a decade lost to isolation and hatred. **Other Examples from Literature and Film:** President Snow (*The Hunger Games*), Keyser Söze (*The Usual Suspects*), Roger Bartlett (*The Great Escape*)

OVERCOMING THIS TRAIT AS A MAJOR FLAW: The vindictive character has been conditioned to believe that only retaliation will bring him peace, but in reality, it does nothing to assuage his bitterness and anger. In order to change, he may need to see that his actions, instead of vindicating, actually lump him in with his aggressors.

TRAITS IN SUPPORTING CHARACTERS THAT MAY CAUSE CONFLICT: devious, dishonest, disrespectful, flaky, funny, haughty, mischievous, promiscuous, proud, tactless, unethical, ungrateful, violent

VIOLENT

DEFINITION: using physical force to intimidate, abuse, or cause injury

SIMILAR FLAWS: bloodthirsty, brutal, savage

POSSIBLE CAUSES:
Growing up in an abusive environment
A genetic predisposition
Desperation caused by poverty or poor living conditions
A brain injury, particularly to the frontal area
Being abused or tortured in the past
Witnessing peer violence
Side effects from drugs, alcohol, and some medications
A lack of empathy
Antisocial personality disorder

ASSOCIATED BEHAVIORS AND ATTITUDES:
Having a quick and savage temper
Exacting revenge
Punching holes in walls
Breaking personal objects
Vandalism
Verbal abuse
Getting into fights
Being fascinated with weapons
Enjoying violence on television and in real life
Being aroused by the sight of blood
Stealing
Pushing and shoving others; inciting conflict
Using intimidation to get what one wants
Joining a gang
Playing violent video games
Profuse swearing
Using weapons to cut, shoot, stab, or bludgeon
Having tense body posture (sweating, bright and hard eyes, neck tendons standing out, etc.)
Feeling the need for release
Enjoying the feeling of pain
Desiring to destroy and cause pain
Acting without restraint or common sense
Thoughts that blank when one's rage kicks in
Allowing one's animalistic nature to take over
Focusing only on the present without thinking of future repercussions
Being unable to let go of past slights or injuries; wanting to even things up
Excessive pride
Using one's strength and power to prove one's dominance over others

ASSOCIATED THOUGHTS:

I'm going to bash his face in.
I want to hear her scream.
I'm going to rip this room apart.
Swing first, talk later.

ASSOCIATED EMOTIONS: determination, eagerness, excitement, rage

POSITIVE ASPECTS: Violent characters exude a sense of danger that causes people to give them a wide berth. As a result, many people will obey them out of fear. When grouped with other violent individuals, these characters can obtain a high level of power and influence and may even climb beyond the reach of the law.

NEGATIVE ASPECTS: Characters who are violent incite fear in others and are unable to participate in healthy relationships. Associates never know what will set them off or when they will become victims of the savage character's rage. Because violence begets violence, a character with this flaw is often in danger, as are his family and friends.

EXAMPLE FROM HISTORY: History abounds with individuals whose violent natures combined with a position of power to create a lethal result. Adolf Hitler's hatred and desire to stamp out the entire Jewish race and any others deemed inferior led to the murder of an estimated eleven million people. Had he not been defeated, his violence would have continued unchecked, and there's no telling how many additional lives would have been lost. **Other Examples from History, Literature and Film**: Attila the Hun, Nero, Voldemort (*Harry Potter* series), Captain Vidal (*Pan's Labyrinth*), Top Dollar (*The Crow*)

OVERCOMING THIS TRAIT AS A MAJOR FLAW: For a character to overcome his violent nature, he would need to experience an event that teaches how violence destroys rather than builds. Losing someone special might bring this about, or simply becoming more in tune with life and the value of it. Kindness, love, or a nurturing friendship may break through the hard layers of pain and hurt that cause the character to be violent, allowing him to find peace and the desire to move forward as a different person.

TRAITS IN SUPPORTING CHARACTERS THAT MAY CAUSE CONFLICT: confrontational, disrespectful, immoral, just, possessive, rebellious, resentful, uncooperative, vindictive, volatile

VOLATILE

DEFINITION: quick to react; having an explosive temper that may grow violent

SIMILAR FLAWS: explosive, unstable

POSSIBLE CAUSES:
Financial pressures
Insomnia or insufficient sleep
Prolonged stress
Stopping or changing medications
Alcoholism and drug abuse
Physical trauma
Paranoia
Being in close proximity to danger
Self-destructive tendencies
A feeling of powerlessness
A lengthy exposure to violence
Growing up in an abusive home
Anxiety

ASSOCIATED BEHAVIORS AND ATTITUDES:
Shouting and yelling
Going from calm to explosive in a matter of seconds
Using belittling words
Slapping someone's hand away
Shoving others
Being set off by the slightest thing
Extreme mood swings
Unpredictability
An aversion to being touched depending on one's mood
Invading others' personal space
Reacting inappropriately, and then immediately regretting it
A reddening face, a tight and focused gaze, the body going rigid
Throwing things
Asking accusatory questions that one already knows the answers to
Hurting someone without meaning to; not knowing one's own strength
Spittle flying from the mouth while one yells
An intense gaze
Abruptly leaving the room
Destructiveness; breaking things
Rudeness and insults
Irrational blame
Refusing to talk
Making unfounded accusations

Reading into things; seeing threats where none are meant

Telling others to get out

Bringing up negative moments from the past

Developing a twitch or other tell that signals a mood shift (a twitchy eyelid, engorged veins, etc.)

Frustration and shame in the aftermath of an outburst

Moodiness

Holding grudges

ASSOCIATED THOUGHTS:

Why does he have to touch everything?

That's it. I've had enough!

Who does Barry think he is?

Why does she keep testing me?

ASSOCIATED EMOTIONS: anger, frustration, guilt, rage, scorn

POSITIVE ASPECTS: Volatile characters often live their lives with great passion. They feel strongly about what they see, hear, and touch, and have intense feelings for the people they're with. While temperamental, these characters often have obvious hot buttons that friends and associates can learn to avoid, thereby preventing outbursts.

NEGATIVE ASPECTS: Characters who are emotionally reactive can cause a lot of damage— to relationships, goals or missions, and to themselves. Enemies may use this flaw against them by provoking a reaction and exposing them as weak or pushing them to act impulsively. It can be very difficult to calm a volatile character, and things said in a riled state may not be easily forgotten by others, making lasting friendships rare. Once an outburst has ended, these characters may recognize the harm they've caused and become remorseful, likely leading to a cycle of frustration, shame, and self-loathing, thus feeding more volatility. Many are unable to talk about how they feel or why without initiating another eruption, making this a difficult trait to overcome.

EXAMPLE FROM LITERATURE: The Hulk (*The Incredible Hulk*) has a very volatile nature that must constantly be restrained. While human, he is mild-mannered, reserved Dr. Bruce Banner. But once his rage is unleashed, he becomes a monster, his emotion manifesting through violence and destruction. **Other Examples from Film and Literature**: Joan Crawford (*Mommie Dearest*), Sonny Corleone (*The Godfather*), Al Capone (*The Untouchables*)

OVERCOMING THIS TRAIT AS A MAJOR FLAW: To overcome such an expressive and reactive flaw, the character must genuinely want to change. Perhaps he has a goal that can only be achieved through self-control, or he ends up crippling his life and happiness as a direct result of his volatility. Meditation, counseling, honesty, and religion are all paths this character might take in order to gain control over his emotions.

TRAITS IN SUPPORTING CHARACTERS THAT MAY CAUSE CONFLICT: abrasive, disrespectful, honest, irresponsible, judgmental, lazy, nagging, tactless, unreliable, vindictive

WEAK-WILLED

DEFINITION: gutless; easily influenced

SIMILAR FLAWS: spineless, weak

POSSIBLE CAUSES:
Having a domineering or controlling parent or partner
A lack of self-confidence
Poor self-esteem; being more comfortable following others than thinking for oneself
Social anxiety or shyness
A fear of rejection, confrontation, or letting others down
Low intelligence
Peer pressure
Naiveté
Guilt
Desiring approval, acceptance, love, admiration, or affection
A lack of education, experience, or training

ASSOCIATED BEHAVIORS AND ATTITUDES:
Nodding and agreeing with others
Asking what someone else thinks
Saying or doing something even when one knows it's wrong
Smiling to emphasize one's support or allegiance
Sticking close to an influencer
Worrying over the dress code for certain events
Giving in to the demands and desires of spoiled children
Being manipulated even though one knows what the other person is doing
Overcommitting from an inability to say *No*
Being susceptible to guilt trips
Handing over money or other hard-won resources even when one doesn't want to
Changing one's looks or personality in an effort to fit in
Seeking approval
Blindly following others
Making bad decisions
Not standing up for what's right
Not being an advocate for oneself
Letting others down because one cannot stand up to someone who is controlling them
Being duped by others or becoming a scapegoat
Hemming and hawing
Doing what one is told, even if it's something undesirable
Trying to read others before offering one's opinion on a subject
Asking for directions
Forgiving people easily—even if they don't deserve it—in an effort to keep the peace
Staying near the sidelines or at the back of the group

Not reacting until others do (displaying anger a beat after others, etc.)
Indecisiveness
Second-guessing one's decisions
Worrying about decisions that will affect others
Agreeing with others out of a fear of retribution

ASSOCIATED THOUGHTS:
I know Gwen is taking advantage, but I just can't say no to my baby girl.
Tim agreed with Beth, so I guess I should, too.
No one else seems worried, so I'm probably just being silly.
I don't want to do it, but since everyone else is in...

ASSOCIATED EMOTIONS: confusion, doubt, fear, nervousness, reluctance, terror, worry

POSITIVE ASPECTS: Weak-willed characters can almost always avoid disappointing others because of their willingness to go along with the group. They don't argue or try to force their own way, which can be an attractive asset to people with more dominant personalities. Weak-willed characters make others feel valued and needed by asking for opinions and heeding their advice. These characters do not take others for granted and often show their appreciation to the people who care for them.

NEGATIVE ASPECTS: Characters with this flaw have extreme difficulty coming to decisions on their own. They also can experience inner turmoil when their desire for acceptance conflicts with their own beliefs or morals. These dilemmas wrack them with a guilt that can't be verbalized for fear of disappointing others. They can easily be exploited by those without scruples, which can lead to deeper feelings of poor self-worth, frustration, and a loss of identity.

EXAMPLE FROM FILM: Hi McDunnough (*Raising Arizona*) is an ex-con who's served multiple prison terms for holding up convenience and grocery stores. Although he wants to stay clean, he simply can't pass a 7-11 or Piggly Wiggly without being tempted to whip out his gun and empty the register. He also has trouble standing up to his wife, who so desperately wants a baby that she convinces him to steal one from a set of quintuplets. Despite having opinions about right and wrong, Hi's will is weak, allowing him to be swayed by the arguments of others and the circumstances around him. **Other Examples from Film**: Bella Swan (*Twilight* saga)

OVERCOMING THIS TRAIT AS A MAJOR FLAW: For a character to overcome his indecisiveness, he would need to look deeply within and decide for himself who he is, what is important, and what will make him happy. He would also need to recognize that his self-worth is important and his goals and desires have value. Supportive friends could be crucial in helping to build up the character's self-esteem and enabling him to regain control of his life.

TRAITS IN SUPPORTING CHARACTERS THAT MAY CAUSE CONFLICT: controlling, cruel, decisive, fanatical, inflexible, possessive

WHINY

DEFINITION: disagreeable; inclined to complain

SIMILAR FLAWS: discontented, dissatisfied, fretful, peevish

POSSIBLE CAUSES:
A spoiled upbringing
A manipulative nature
A sense of entitlement
Never being taught responsibility
A lack of work ethic; laziness
Poor self-confidence and self-esteem

ASSOCIATED BEHAVIORS AND ATTITUDES:
Complaining
Citing boredom, aches, pains, or other conditions in hopes of getting what one wants
Using a simpering tone
Loudly letting others know how bored or inconvenienced one feels
Having high expectations of others
Not letting up; relentlessly asking for something until other people give in
Making comparisons: *Jimmy's dad always drives him to the bus stop!*
Insulting those in charge in an attempt to erode their power and gain control
Speaking loudly to draw attention
A reluctance to make sacrifices
Being judgmental of others
Agreeing to future promises as a way of avoiding current commitments
Letting out heavy, disagreeable sighs
Acting annoying just to get on someone's nerves
Lying or exaggerating the truth
Passive-aggressiveness
Using whatever means necessary to get one's way
Making empty threats
Accusing others of favoritism
Not being able to let go of one's negative feelings
Petulance
Putting up a fight at every suggestion
Saying *No* to everything
Melodrama
Throwing past mistakes in someone's face to make them feel worse about a present situation
Dragging one's feet, figuratively or literally
Moaning and groaning
Voicing how unfair everything is
Exaggerating each movement, hoping slowness will cause frustration and lead to change
Speaking in a voice that grows higher and drags out one's words: *But Mommmm...*
Pouting

ASSOCIATED THOUGHTS:
I can't believe I have to sit through the opera. What a snooze.
Hauling this wood to the house is totally wrecking my nails.
Mr. James gives way too much homework. I wish he'd eat poison and die!
Aunt Dena's farm sucks. It's too hot, the animals stink, and I'm dirty all the time.

ASSOCIATED EMOTIONS: agitation, annoyance, contempt, fear, frustration, insecurity, resentment

POSITIVE ASPECTS: Whiny characters are experts at getting out of undesirable situations. They aren't concerned with keeping up appearances and say what they need to say to achieve the desired result.

NEGATIVE ASPECTS: Whiny characters are both annoying and emotionally draining to be around. Their incessant complaining about everything—including events beyond their control—brings down morale. Their attempts to escape their fair share of work can cause resentment in others, making associates disinclined to work with them.

EXAMPLE FROM FILM: Private Hudson (*Aliens*) is only seventeen days from release of his term of service with the Colonial Marines when his unit is cut down by aliens. Death seems inevitable, and Hudson voices his displeasure at every opportunity, usually at the top of his lungs in a high, whining tone. In an already volatile situation, his verbal tirades keep the other survivors on edge, and he constantly has to be told to calm down. His whininess makes one wonder how he ever made it as a marine. **Other Examples from TV, Film, and Literature**: Ross Geller (*Friends*), C3PO (*Star Wars*), Willie Scott (*Indiana Jones and the Temple of Doom*), Wilbur (*Charlotte's Web*)

OVERCOMING THIS TRAIT AS A MAJOR FLAW: Forcing the whiny character to be responsible and not let up until a specific goal is met will build confidence and self-esteem, showing him that he is indeed capable of achieving things he previously thought were beyond him.

TRAITS IN SUPPORTING CHARACTERS THAT MAY CAUSE CONFLICT: appreciative, callous, cruel, cynical, impatient, inflexible, optimistic, patient, temperamental

WITHDRAWN

DEFINITION: detached from others, having retreated inside oneself

SIMILAR FLAWS: aloof, detached, standoffish, unsociable

POSSIBLE CAUSES:
Being a highly private person
A mental disorder (bulimia, depression, social anxiety disorders, phobias, etc.)
Low self-esteem
Shyness
Past or present abuse
Autism
High intelligence
Alcoholism or drug addiction
Chronic pain or a long-term illness
The inability to move past a traumatic event (a death, divorce, etc.)
Trust issues
Guilt or shame
A fear of being hurt or rejected by others

ASSOCIATED BEHAVIORS AND ATTITUDES:
Avoiding people and social activities
Needing few friends; being highly independent
Living on the fringes (not joining clubs at school, not having people over for dinner, etc.)
Focusing on work or projects
Entering into new relationships with hesitancy and trepidation
Having a string of short-term jobs
Taking solitary jobs that don't require face-to-face interaction with others
Blending in; not calling attention to oneself
Making decisions for oneself instead of seeking the advice of others
Introspection
Not paying attention
Difficulty focusing on or participating in conversations
Preferring to be alone
Feeling misunderstood
Going for walks alone, reading, gaming, retreating online where one feels safe
Thoughts of self-harm or suicide (if depression is a factor)
Finding safety and comfort in routine
Making choices that support a solitary lifestyle (shopping online, having groceries delivered, etc.)
Exhaustion
Feeling alone, even with others
Confusing inquiries of concern with meddling
Tuning out the outside world

Avoiding personal questions

Difficulty maintaining eye contact

Drinking or taking drugs and medications to cope

Frequently retreating to one's room or home

Avoiding one's neighbors or living somewhere where one has none

Thinking too much

ASSOCIATED THOUGHTS:

I'm so tired. I wish I could sleep. Why can't I stop thinking about everything?

I better go to the dinner or my sister will just show up here to find out why I didn't come.

I need a way to work from home. Not dealing with people sounds like bliss.

These people are driving me crazy. I can't wait to get home.

ASSOCIATED EMOTIONS: anxiety, depression, disappointment, guilt, overwhelmed, sadness

POSITIVE ASPECTS: Withdrawn characters can easily tune out everyone else's noise and avoid unnecessary drama. Preferring one's own company to others, a character with this flaw often has deep insight into who they are, far beyond what most people will ever discover about themselves.

NEGATIVE ASPECTS: Withdrawn characters take isolation and introversion to a point of dysfunction, allowing social fears and phobias to form. When they find themselves unable to cope with the outside world, it potentially puts them in danger; should they ever need help, they may not be able to reach beyond their self-imposed walls to get it.

EXAMPLE FROM FILM: Lisbeth Salander from *The Girl with the Dragon Tattoo* is a very troubled yet talented computer hacker. Her abusive past leaves her with strong trust issues and she generally avoids people. Abrasive in nature, Lisbeth is impatient whenever she has to deal with people and her inability to open up to others means she has few close relationships. **Other Examples from Film:** Cole Sear (*The Sixth Sense*), Ryan Bingham (*Up in the Air*)

OVERCOMING THIS TRAIT AS A MAJOR FLAW: For a character to come out of her shell, she would need to feel that it was safe to do so. Learning to trust someone who truly values her would help her open up and develop a stronger feeling of self-worth. Being accepted for who she is may cause a character to want to stay connected with others and balance her need for sanctuary with a desire for enrichment through relationships and experiences.

TRAITS IN SUPPORTING CHARACTERS THAT MAY CAUSE CONFLICT: extroverted, friendly, pushy, needy, nosy, melodramatic, reckless, uninhibited, verbose

WORKAHOLIC

DEFINITION: someone who works compulsively, sacrificing other interests and responsibilities

POSSIBLE CAUSES:
Desiring to avoid problems at home
Believing that one's value is based on productivity or success
Needing to be the best; wanting to prove oneself
Being raised by caregivers with unrealistic expectations
Desiring status, recognition, success, or wealth
Unresolved conflict from one's past; working to avoid dealing with negative memories
The need to control
Being forced at an early age into a caregiver's role

ASSOCIATED BEHAVIORS AND ATTITUDES:
Valuing work over other pursuits in one's life
Thinking excessively about work
Experiencing short-lived satisfaction at reaching milestones
Feeling like there's always more to do, that one can never catch up
Easily becoming restless or bored
Difficulty relaxing
Having broken or strained relationships due to one's obsession with work
Constant multi-tasking
Competitiveness
Perfectionism
Doing everything quickly (walking, talking, eating, etc.)
Micromanaging others; having difficulty delegating
Difficulty saying *No*
Expressing annoyance when one's work is interrupted
Demanding that others live up to one's high work standards
Becoming defensive when one is accused of working too much
Working at home, during meals, and on vacations
Skipping social or family functions to work
Working late into the night
Overestimating one's capabilities
Looking ahead; planning for (or worrying about) the future
Emotional volatility (being quick to anger, venting on people, etc.)
Feeling overburdened with responsibility
Wishing that family could be more understanding about the pressures of one's job
Being intensely loyal to one's employer or employees
An inability to stop working until a certain project is finished or daily goals have been met
Egotism
Insecurity
Repressing one's emotions
Ignoring one's health (being too busy to see the doctor, going to work sick, etc.)
Missing deadlines due to overcommitment

ASSOCIATED THOUGHTS:

I don't have time for this, but I'm the only one who can do it right.
I have to finish this or Don will think I'm not a team player and I won't get the promotion.
What's her problem? You'd think she'd be grateful that I'm providing for her and the kids.
No way am I going to finish this today. I'll have to skip the kids' soccer game tomorrow.

ASSOCIATED EMOTIONS: annoyance, anxiety, denial, desire, desperation, elation, frustration, insecurity, irritation, overwhelmed, satisfaction, worry

POSITIVE ASPECTS: Workaholics are go-getters. Driven by a strong work ethic, they give 110% to any job they're given. Some are born leaders while others make excellent worker bees. Many workaholics are driven to be the best and won't declare a job finished until it's as perfect as possible.

NEGATIVE ASPECTS: Workaholics are more than just hard workers; for these characters, work is a compulsion that can't be ignored. It's the most important part of their life, leaving family and friends to feel marginalized and second-best. While workaholics may start out with good intentions, their compulsive need drives them to work more and more over time. As a result, the quality of their work suffers, their credibility takes a hit when they can't be counted on by family and friends, and the stress begins to negatively impact their health. In spite of all of these drawbacks, workaholics may have difficulty cutting back to a normal workload.

EXAMPLES FROM FILM: Ryan Bingham's (*Up in the Air*) job as a corporate downsizer requires him to travel up to 270 days a year, and he is happy to do so. He has no friends outside of work, little connection to his family, and claims to enjoy a life unburdened by relationships. In truth, work allows him to escape an unfulfilled personal life, and travel keeps him from having to face a sterile and empty apartment. When his firm considers adopting new technology that will enable Ryan to fire people via conference call from the comfort of his hometown, Ryan is incensed and fights tooth and nail to maintain the extreme work and travel hours so he can continue to live a disconnected existence. **Other Examples from Literature, TV, and Film:** Peter Banning (*Hook*), Fox Mulder (*The X Files*), Aaron Hotchner (*Criminal Minds*)

OVERCOMING THIS TRAIT AS A MAJOR FLAW: Many workaholics would deny that work comes before family, but it's clear to everyone else that work is the number one priority. It often takes losing an important person in the workaholic's life for him to realize what's happening. To overcome his compulsion, it's imperative to identify the reason behind it and resolve that issue. In addition, the workaholic can take steps toward changing his ways by setting boundaries, taking up hobbies that don't revolve around work, and deciding what should take first priority in his life, then acting accordingly.

TRAITS IN SUPPORTING CHARACTERS THAT MAY CAUSE CONFLICT: controlling, lazy, needy, perfectionist, self-indulgent, selfish, ungrateful, whimsical

WORRYWART

DEFINITION: inclined to excessive worrying

POSSIBLE CAUSES:
Anxiety (panic disorders, phobias, post-traumatic stress disorder, etc.)
Overprotective parents
Being raised by a caregiver who worried unnecessarily
Not being protected and nurtured as a child
A lack of trust
A past failure or emotional hurt one cannot forget or move past

ASSOCIATED BEHAVIORS AND ATTITUDES:
Knowing that one's worries are silly but being unable to stop
Being plagued by obsessive thoughts
Health issues (irritable bowel syndrome, migraines, nausea, etc.)
Keen observation skills
Fatigue
Depression
Fearing that a loved one will be hurt
Worry that a past traumatic event will happen to one's child (a car wreck, almost drowning, etc.)
Being unable to turn off one's thoughts
Frequently visiting the doctor due to imagined ailments or those caused by chronic worrying
Worrying about things beyond one's control: *What if I get cancer?*
Assuming the worst about any deviation in schedule: *Ann's late. What if her car broke down?*
Avoiding situations that make one uncomfortable
Pessimism
Resisting change
Being overprotective of one's children
Obsessing about cleanliness and germs
Not letting others (sitters, family members, etc.) watch one's children
Obsessing over a new ache or pain, assuming it's something serious
Suspicion and paranoia
Jumping to conclusions
Difficulty relaxing
Careful planning
Thoroughly thinking things through before making a decision
Insomnia
Loss of appetite
Difficulty focusing on work or school
Becoming fixated on death or loss
Being addicted to the news; needing to stay current on all threats and dangers
Requesting that people call when they arrive at their destination safely
Visiting in person to make sure a loved one is doing well
Investing in protective measures (miracle vitamins, organic foods, etc.)

ASSOCIATED THOUGHTS:

My throat's sore. What if it's strep?
Is that guy looking at me? He looks creepy. Where's my pepper spray?
What will I do if John has a heart attack and dies?
Did Joe lock the back door? Someone could snatch the baby from his crib and we'd never know.
Is Karen crazy? If we put in a pool, one of the kids could fall in and drown.

ASSOCIATED EMOTIONS: anxiety, depression, dread, fear, suspicion, uncertainty, wariness, worry

POSITIVE ASPECTS: Worrywarts fret about everything, so it's hard to take them unawares. Hyper-vigilant and intensely aware of their surroundings, they notice details that many other characters would miss. Because they're always alert for danger, worrywarts usually are prepared and can be of assistance to the hero in a time of crisis.

NEGATIVE ASPECTS: Worrywarts take worrying to an unhealthy limit and find it almost impossible to relax. They can be overprotective or "mother" people in an attempt to make sure everyone is safe. Their need to assuage their worries may have them calling the sitter several times a night to check in, or send them backtracking to their house to make sure the stove wasn't left on. This amount of worrying can leave family members feeling constrained by the worrier, especially children or teenagers.

EXAMPLE FROM FILM: Gil Buckman (*Parenthood*) has a seemingly blessed life: a supportive family, a beautiful house, a productive job. But he worries over everything, from the mental well-being of his children to the possibility of his turning into a workaholic like his own father. When Gil's wife announces that she's pregnant, he fears that he will be mentally, financially, and emotionally unable to raise a fourth child. Gil has a lot to be thankful for, but his chronic worrying makes it difficult for him to relax and enjoy the ride. **Other Examples from Film and TV**: Marlon (*Finding Nemo*), Sheldon Cooper (*The Big Bang Theory*)

OVERCOMING THIS TRAIT AS A MAJOR FLAW: If a specific neurosis is the cause, medication may be needed to provide the necessary chemical balance. Otherwise, it might benefit the worrywart to see how chronic worry is cheating him. Like Gil, he may have a life that other people envy, but his worry is robbing him of peace, joy, and fulfillment. Once a worrier sees that his constant hand-wringing is both ineffective and intrinsically harmful, he may be motivated to seek help and change his way of thinking.

TRAITS IN SUPPORTING CHARACTERS THAT MAY CAUSE CONFLICT: bold, cruel, easygoing, happy, independent, nervous, optimistic, rebellious, rowdy, sensible, sleazy, trusting

FURTHER READING ON CHARACTERS AND DEVELOPMENT

Breathing Life into Your Characters: How to Give Your Characters Emotional & Psychological Depth ~ Rachel Ballon, PH.D.

Bullies, Bastards, and Bitches: How to Write the Bad Guys of Fiction ~ Jessica Morrell

Save The Cat ~ Blake Snyder

The Writer's Guide To Character Traits ~ Dr. Linda Edelstein

The Writer's Guide To Psychology: How to Write Accurately About Psychological Disorders, Clinical Treatments and Human Behavior ~ Carolyn Kaufman, Psy.D.

Writing Screenplays That Sell ~ Michael Hauge

The Hero's 2 Journeys (CD/DVD) ~ Michael Hauge and Christopher Vogler

JOIN US AT WRITERS HELPING WRITERS!

If you enjoyed this resource, we hope you'll visit us at our home site, *Writers Helping Writers* (http://writershelpingwriters.net). There you'll find our description hub, *The Bookshelf Muse* blog, as well as other descriptive thesaurus collections and tools available free to writers. To stay up to date on forthcoming books, discover unique writing resources, and enjoy writing tips to help you improve your craft, you can sign up for our newsletter as well.

If you have time, we would love for you to review our book! Reviews on Amazon, Barnes & Noble and Goodreads really help a book to become more visible. And if you've told someone about this resource, thank you! Referrals are also very much appreciated.

APPENDIX A

NEEDS AND LIES

A character's needs fall into five basic groups: physiological, safety and security, love and belonging, esteem and recognition, and self-actualization. This appendix contains a list of needs and associated lies, broken down by category.

Please note that needs may fit into multiple categories depending upon the character's motivation. For example, the need to acquire an education could be based on a need for security (if the character's purpose is to escape a dangerous neighborhood), esteem (if the goal is being pursued out of a desire to prove oneself to others), or self-actualization (if the character is seeking knowledge as a way to become more self-aware).

PHYSIOLOGICAL: the need to secure one's biological and physiological needs

Associated Needs:
Obtaining or securing food, water, shelter, warmth, or sleep
Avoiding pain
Having sex
Procreation

Associated Lies:
I don't deserve to be safe.
I haven't earned the right to be comfortable and secure.
I've brought this pain on myself.
No one would want to have sex with me.
I would be a terrible parent.

SAFETY AND SECURITY: the need to keep oneself and one's loved ones safe

Associated Needs:
Living a life categorized by order
Upholding laws, rules, or limits
Seeking stability
Valuing structure
Pursuing security
Securing health care for oneself or one's family
Securing or keeping a job
Protecting one's home, land, or resources
Protecting one's source of livelihood
Protecting one's family from mistreatment, persecution, or attack
Getting out of a bad neighborhood
Escaping prison
Regaining or holding onto one's sanity
Cleaning up one's environment
Rescuing someone from danger

Escaping an abusive relationship
Pursuing education in an effort to escape a bad living situation
Becoming free
Gaining the protection of an influential person
Surviving a life-or-death ordeal
Protecting oneself from the elements
Improving one's health
Avoiding or ending a war or life-threatening conflict

Associated Lies:
I'm above the law.
Structure is confining and stifling. I can't live that way.
The rules don't apply to me.
Rules were made to be broken.
I'm not qualified.
I'm not worthy of anyone's protection.
I'm not strong enough to keep others from taking what I have.
I can't protect myself, much less anyone else.
I'm stuck here.
This is all I'm good for.
I can't keep him/her safe.
I deserve this treatment.
I wouldn't know how to provide for myself.
Nothing is going to change; it's going to be like this for the rest of my life.
Sometimes you have to just accept the way things are.
I couldn't keep my spouse/child/friend safe, so I can't be trusted to safeguard others.
If I work hard enough, I can forget what happened to me.

LOVE AND BELONGING: the need to connect with others

Associated Needs:
Gaining someone's affection
Being accepted by others
Finding a spouse
Obtaining a date to the prom
Having children
Building deep relationships with others
Experiencing sexual intimacy
Belonging to or fitting in with a group (a school club, the marines, a church, gang, etc.)
Connecting with one's children
Healing a broken relationship
Expressing one's feelings

Associated Lies:
No one will be interested in someone as screwed up as me.
I refuse to bring a child into such a messed up world.
I'm too selfish to be of any use to anyone.
I don't need others in order to be fulfilled.

I don't want any attachments.

I'd rather be alone.

My kids don't need me.

I don't deserve anyone's affection.

They're never going to accept me.

I don't want or need their acceptance.

Emotions make you weak.

If I make myself vulnerable, I'm going to get hurt.

If I show them who I really am, they'll reject me.

I only know how to pick losers.

I have to push others away before they have a chance to hurt me.

If I let others in, I'll only end up letting them down.

I don't know how to love.

If I do whatever he says, he'll eventually forgive me.

If I follow in my father's/mother's/idol's footsteps, then he/she will have to accept me.

If I tell the truth about my past, everyone will hate me.

I'd rather be in a bad relationship than in no relationship at all.

ESTEEM AND RECOGNITION: the need to increase one's sense of esteem

Associated Needs:

Increasing one's confidence

Increasing one's self-esteem

Increasing one's sense of perceived value or worth

Increasing one's wealth

Experiencing achievement

Gaining the respect of others

Distinguishing oneself

Gaining independence

Gaining status or prestige

Overcoming a stereotype

Overcoming addiction

Accomplishing something that no one has ever accomplished before

Obtaining a certain job or position

Joining a prestigious group

Winning an award

Improving one's social status

Improving one's physical appearance

Winning a court case

Winning a game or contest

Proving someone wrong

Seeking retribution or exacting vengeance

Dominating or controlling others

Associated Lies:

I can't do anything.

I'm not worth the trouble.

I'll never be successful.

I'm going to end up just like my dad, mom, brothers, ancestors, etc.

They'll always see me as second-rate.

I'm not strong enough to do this on my own.

What they say/think about me is true.

I'm not good enough for that person, that high-level job, that club, etc.

I'm ugly.

I'm dumb.

I can't compete at that level.

I don't care what they think.

I have to be perfect for others to like me.

If I avenge my loved ones, I'll finally be at peace.

I can't trust others to do things right so I'll have to do it myself.

If I can achieve ___, then they'll have to admit how good I am.

If I let someone else be in control, they're going to take advantage of me.

They can't survive with me.

I can't survive without him.

I'm not strong/smart/important enough to right this wrong.

I have nothing to offer.

I can't overcome this addiction.

I'm better than them.

I can't take another disappointment.

Their divorce/Her death/The accident is all my fault.

If I try to compete with him, I'll lose.

If I try again, I'm going to fail like last time.

SELF-ACTUALIZATION: the need to realize one's full potential

Associated Needs:

Becoming a better mother, student, employee, friend, etc.

Challenging oneself

Obtaining a higher appreciation for art, nature, literature, music, etc.

Achieving personal growth

Growing spiritually

Being true to oneself

Doing what's right

Edifying others

Achieving enlightenment

Associated Lies:

This is who I am. I can do no better.

There is no true enlightenment.

If I can achieve perfection, then I'll be happy.

I'll never be as good a mother/student/employee/friend as _____.

You can't change who you really are.

I'll never be able to be my true self.

APPENDIX B

Filling in this **Reverse Backstory Tool** for your characters will help you understand the big picture: what they want and need, what motivates them, what their backstories might be. Planning out their wounds and the lies they tell themselves will also help you choose what traits might help them succeed and which will get in the way.

Reverse Backstory Tool

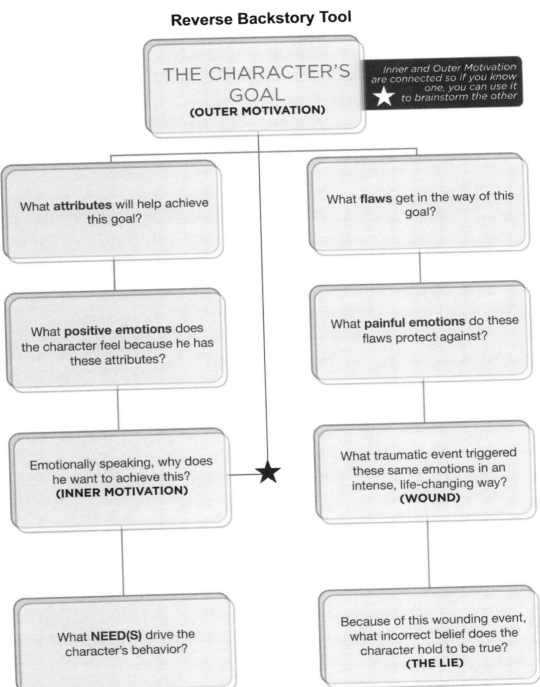

THE CHARACTER'S GOAL
(OUTER MOTIVATION)

Inner and Outer Motivation are connected so if you know one, you can use it to brainstorm the other

What **attributes** will help achieve this goal?

What **flaws** get in the way of this goal?

What **positive emotions** does the character feel because he has these attributes?

What **painful emotions** do these flaws protect against?

Emotionally speaking, why does he want to achieve this?
(INNER MOTIVATION)

What traumatic event triggered these same emotions in an intense, life-changing way?
(WOUND)

What **NEED(S)** drive the character's behavior?

Because of this wounding event, what incorrect belief does the character hold to be true?
(THE LIE)

To help illustrate how this works, we've used the Reverse Backstory Tool on Columbus, the highly neurotic protagonist from the film, *Zombieland*:

Zombieland Example

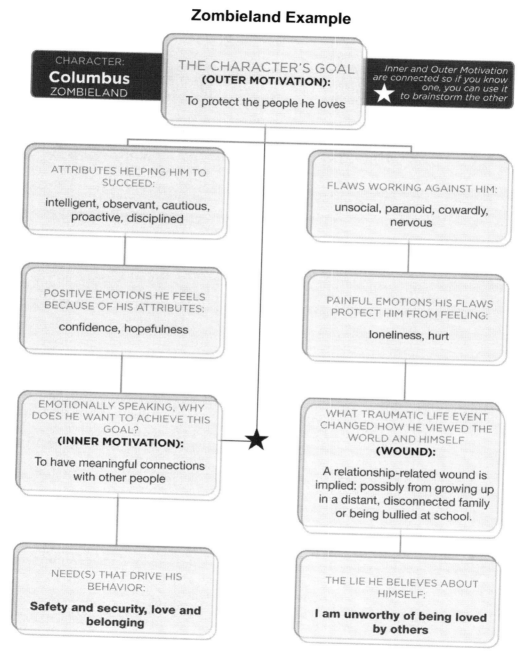

Even if the movie *Zombieland* is unfamiliar to you, this example illustrates Columbus' important character arc elements, reveals what he strives for and why, and shows the weaknesses that he must overcome to become a happier, more complete individual. Plotting this information in the brainstorming stage (or even as you revise, to add depth to your character) will help you determine what sensitive areas to target, creating challenges for your hero.

Would you like to try plotting your character's backstory? Please visit *Writers Helping Writers* for a printable blank version of the Reverse Backstory Tool: http://writershelpingwriters.net/writing-tools

APPENDIX C

This handy **Character Pyramid** can help you organize your character's flaws, allowing you to sort which flaws are the driving force in your character's personality from the ones that are secondary and less noticeable. It's also useful in planning out the thoughts, behaviors, and actions that your character will exhibit. We've used the main character from Young Adult Author Janet Gurtler's *Who I Kissed* as an example below:

Would you like to use the Character Pyramid to brainstorm your characters flaws? Please visit *Writers Helping Writers* for a printable blank version of this tool:
http://writershelpingwriters.net/writing-tools

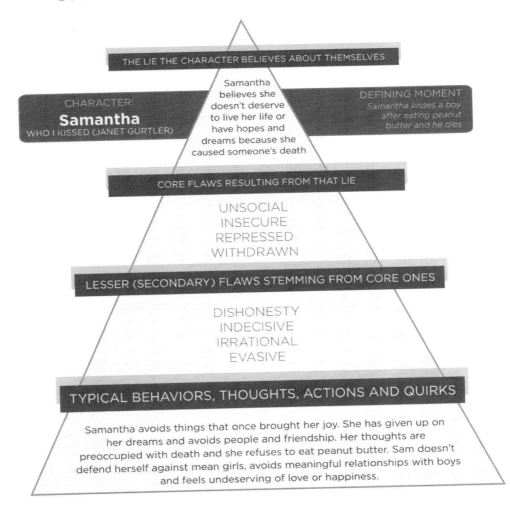

CHARACTER PYRAMID EXAMPLE

THE LIE THE CHARACTER BELIEVES ABOUT THEMSELVES

CHARACTER:
Samantha
WHO I KISSED (JANET GURTLER)

Samantha believes she doesn't deserve to live her life or have hopes and dreams because she caused someone's death

DEFINING MOMENT
Samantha kisses a boy after eating peanut butter and he dies

CORE FLAWS RESULTING FROM THAT LIE

UNSOCIAL
INSECURE
REPRESSED
WITHDRAWN

LESSER (SECONDARY) FLAWS STEMMING FROM CORE ONES

DISHONESTY
INDECISIVE
IRRATIONAL
EVASIVE

TYPICAL BEHAVIORS, THOUGHTS, ACTIONS AND QUIRKS

Samantha avoids things that once brought her joy. She has given up on her dreams and avoids people and friendship. Her thoughts are preoccupied with death and she refuses to eat peanut butter. Sam doesn't defend herself against mean girls, avoids meaningful relationships with boys and feels undeserving of love or happiness.

INDEX

This index includes all of the attributes and similar traits listed in this thesaurus. Keep in mind that, due to size limitations and our desire to include as many different attributes as possible, not every trait here has its own entry. But by consulting the associated entry for each trait below, you should find ample information on each attribute.

27761696R00150

Printed in Poland
by Amazon Fulfillment
Poland Sp. z o.o., Wrocław